THE KIDDS OF BRAZIL

Wilma Alice Kidd   *Jesse L. Kidd*

THE KIDDS OF BRAZIL

AUTOBIOGRAPHIES
OF
JESSE L. AND WILMA ALICE KIDD

Library of Congress Catalog Card Number: 99-72089
ISBN: 0-7392-0376-2

Cover Photo by Edgar R. Talley
Where the Amazon and Rio Preto come together,
flowing toward the Atlantic Ocean

Printed in the USA by

MP
MORRIS PUBLISHING
3212 East Highway 30 • Kearney, NE 68847 • 1-800-650-7888

TO THE DESCENDANTS

OF

John and Ida Kidd   Robert and Ellen Gemmell

Our parents who upheld the Bible and reflected its teachings
in their hearts and lives.

FOREWORD

As you begin reading THE KIDDS OF BRAZIL, prepare yourself for an interesting journey. Jesse and Wilma Kidd share with you their story "as a gift." It is a gift of love, faith, perseverance, deep commitment to the Lord, to each other and to the people their lives touched. It is also a gift of insight, of delight, of fun, of victories, as well as difficulties, struggles and loneliness. Above all, it is a gift of joy in finding their place in God's will and in knowing His guidance, mercy and grace at each step.

If you do not know the Kidds, you will be surprised at the diversity in their backgrounds, talents and responsibilities. You will be interested in the way the Lord led in their lives from early childhood to fruitful joint-ministry. You will be amazed at the scope of their influence. And if you will read between the lines, you will also sense the wonder of their courage in faithful service.

If you know the Kidds, as we do, you will have a grand journey back into their lives! What fun to recall some of the experiences we had with them! What gratitude comes to our hearts as we remember how they shared their lives with our family, influenced our children and let us become part of their circle of friends! You will also read new information about Jesse and Wilma that will throw more light on how our Heavenly Father directs our lives and holds us in the palm of His hand.

Thank you, Jesse and Wilma, for sharing your lives with us in this written account. We admire you and congratulate you for this accomplishment. As we read it, two passages of scripture come to our minds:

"And let the beauty of the Lord our God be upon us:
and establish thou the work of our hands upon us;
yea, the work of our hands establish thou it."
Psalms 90:17

"And Jesus answered and said, Verily I say unto you,
There is no man that hath left house, or brethren, or
sisters, or father, or mother, or wife, or children,
or lands, for my sake, and the gospel's, But he shall
receive an hundred-fold now in this time, houses,
and brethren, and sisters, and mothers, and children,
and lands, with persecutions; and in the world to
come eternal life."
Mark 10:29 & 30

Joan and Boyd Sutton

FOREWORD (Continued)

Please seat yourself in a comfortable chair in a quiet
place. You may need to circle a day on your calendar, not
allowing for interruptions. You're about to begin a reading
journey taking you non-stop from the first page of this book
to the bibliography at the end.

The missionary stories of Jesse and Wilma Gemmell Kidd read
like some of the stories from the New Testament. You'll turn
every page with thanksgiving to the Lord for His "wonderful
ways to the children of men."

God used the tough, pioneer Nebraska plains for the shaping of Wilma's early life.

Jesse's younger years had a two-state, three-geographical
area, dimension. The Kidd family moved from rural South Arkansas (near El Dorado) to a rugged wasteland in South Texas
near San Diego! The spiritual and financial struggles of the
family during that epoch merit serious perusal. Depression
years caused the family to move to the Ozark mountains in North
Arkansas, and a few years later they settled again in the old
home place in South Arkansas.

From the human viewpoint Jesse and Wilma would never meet.
And yet, as William Cowper wrote in "Light Shining Out of
Darkness,"

"God moves in a mysterious way, His wonders to perform;
He plants His footsteps in the sea, and rides upon
the storm."

You'll read with awe and wonder some of Jesse's experiences
in World War II. God miraculously preserved his life in China,
India, and on the Burma Road. The accounts of Jesse's and
Wilma's preparation at Howard Payne College, Ouachita Baptist
College, and Southwestern Seminary add another aura of glory
to their story.

God often prepares His people for greater tasks through the
crucible of trials and suffering. Even the common duties of
life may turn into the "fiery furnace." Wilma taught country
school, was Assistant to the Dean of Women at Howard Payne,
and served in First Baptist Church, Stephenville, Texas. She
continued working while studying for the Master of Religious
Education at Fort Worth (the M.R.E. degree; the Mrs. would
wait for a long time).

VIII

FOREWORD (Continued)

Jesse served in student pastorates while in college and seminary, then as full-time pastor of Ebenezer Church at El Dorado, all of which enriched his life and honed him for later years of missionary service in Brazil.

The journal of the exciting, exhausting, and long years of ministry in Brazil encompasses the major part of the writing. Jesse's nine years' service in Central Baptist Church and its school in Volta Redonda merits book-length treatment. His post-Volta Redonda appointment as a missionary of the Foreign Mission Board, Southern Baptist Convention; the couple's courtship, and their fruitful ministry together in Brazil, leave the reader with the assurance of God's hand upon these two.

You'll be moved to laughter, tears, joy, sadness, praise and wonder as you walk with Jesse and Wilma.

You'll read these pages with unending spiritual benefits. You'll soon be telling a dozen friends about this journal that will also put them on "The Missionary Trail." If your own heart and soul are ignited with missionary passion because of this reading, then the writing effort of the Kidds will have been worth their "travail of soul."

A Friend of the Missionaries,
Preston A. Taylor

CONTENTS

CONTENTS (Continued)

ACKNOWLEDGMENTS

There are many who gave encouragement, love and interest in the writing; there are so many that their names would fill pages and pages. We can only cite a few people here.

Willie Mae Mathews and her late husband Rex always cherished "family" and were a part of her brother Jesse's ministry. They saved Jesse's letters, even through the destruction of a devastating tornado. And these letters became the backbone of our writing. There was always a word and a hug of encouragement, and immeasurable love.

Elizabeth Norris and her late husband Charles kept everything that came to their house from her sister Wilma and the correspondence became the history and body of our writing. While Wilma was a single missionary and then when the Kidds were in Brazil the Norrises were business manager and counselor. There was always love; there were always prayers.

Joe and Leona Tarry's cabin near Las Vegas, New Mexico became our Shangri-La, ideal for writing. These, our Brazil colleagues with whom we served many years, are authors themselves and this inspired us.

LeRoy and Stella Bearce read the first rough draft, and helped us to continue with the writing.

In First Church San Angelo, the Ona Jones Women's Sunday School Class of Department 6 patiently carried on while Wilma the teacher was gone to New Mexico.

In Immanuel Church San Angelo, the Men's class and Women's Sunshine Class in Senior Adult I were supportive and lovingly interested even though their teachers were away for periods. Of this department, Vernon and Alta Brook proofread the manuscript and were caring advisors; Betty Gifford quietly accompanied the writing, giving special encouragement.

Leigh Stipe gave us the Smith-Corona word processor on which we wrote the story.

Phillis Mitchell skillfully made the computer designs.

We simply say, "Thank you."

PREFACE

October 1988 we came away from Brazil for thireen months' furlough after which we retired December 1, 1989. In Brazil we were caught up in a rapidly developing work where God was blessing, and we felt our lives were being multiplied in service. So when we came to the States, it seemed we couldn't leave Brazil behind nor could we be at home in our native country and language.

We don't know when the impulse to write first came to us, but we simply felt that we had something to say and that writing would be the best expression of it. We knew we had a message.

We needed to write; to re-discover ourselves. During our six years in Lajes, Santa Catarina we drove over seven hours to the nearest missionary colleagues. We were six hours by auto from American colleagues when we were in Montes Claros for over ten years. So when we actually retired we realized we had been so engrossd in our work that we needed to reaffirm our identities; we needed to record our memories and to evaluate our lives.

Leona and Joe Tarry invited us to their cabin twenty-six miles out from Las Vegas, New Mexico and we spent several days with the family. When the cabin was offered to us the summers of 1993, '94, and '96 we returned. The majestic trees, Sangre de Cristo Mountains, the wild flowers and solitude - encouraged our task. We were engrossed in the history of the valley where the cabin was; the fauna, and distant neighbors.

The summer of 1995 we house-sat in Las Vegas, N.M. for LeRoy and Stella Bearce while they served a church in Naples, Italy. We set up our word processor in their living room.

Most of Jesse's family things were destroyed when a tornado struck his sister's home near Hemphill, Texas the spring of 1974. Wilma had received some family items; among them the solid oak trunk made from her grandparents Tharp's dining table. We kept the trunk containing our keepsakes in the storeroom of Ebenezer Baptist Church, El Dorado, Arkansas until our last furlough.

We started by reviewing our correspondence which the Norrises and Mathews had saved.

XIII

It took weeks to arrange, sort, and recall what we had
written in all the letters. Then with temerity we took pen-
cils and yellow pads in hand and began. We laughed and we
cried; we talked and cherished the silences; we disagreed
and compromised. Amazingly, one thought would trigger another
and memories sprang to life that we had thought were buried.
We scrambled to record those precious impressions on paper.

The initials JLK or WAK are on the left of the page to
identify the writer of that part. Actually, it should read
JLK/WAK or WAK/JLK for we wrote and re-wrote together - discussing, planning, deleting and adding.

The writing was therapeutic, giving us a clear picture of
ourselves. We looked at our failures and gave them all to
God. Then we looked at what God had done, and we were grati-
fied by what we saw.

These pages are filled with the people who came into our
lives. We desire that you will hear their voices, see their
faces and let them speak to you: the humble; leaders and
teachers; co-workers. The silent ones and those who communi-
cated vocally; the agreeable and disagreeable. They all wove
the warp and woof of our lives.

The word "Missions" conveys growth and an expanding hori-
zon. Since the actual writing, the name "International Mission Board" has supplanted "The Foreign Mission Board," Southern Baptist Convention. There are other terminology changes.

Wilma met the Tarry's baby daughter Charlotte in Brazil
in 1965. She called us Uncle and Aunt when we worked alongside her parents in Minas Gerais state and we accompanied her
stateside through college and seminary.

Charlotte has grown to a beautiful, wonderful woman. We
were in Richmond, Virginia July 21, 1998 when she and her husband James Whitley were appointed missionaries to Romania.
We saw Sherman James when he was born September 16, 1998.
And we were with the twins Janis and Charis, to be four years
old that November 2.

All of this leads us to submit to you our story in praise
to Jesus Christ.

I.

URBANA, ARKANSAS

I was born September 20, 1923, son of John and Ida Kidd.
My father came from Illinois; my mother was from Union County,
Arkansas. I was the middle child; Willie Mae was six at my
birth and George was born when I was three. Dad had built
our farm home where I was born - about one mile from the south
Arkansas town, Urbana. It stood on the hill which today is
known as Kidd Hill. Mom and Dad grew the typical crops of
that area; there was a ten-acre peach orchard on the hill
sloping north; and there were several pecan trees.

Dad built and operated his own sawmill, producing lumber
from his trees. My parents were active in their community
and were members of the Urbana Baptist Church. When Willie
Mae was nine, she was seriously ill with a lung problem, so
to save her health we moved to south Texas, leaving the Urbana
home December, 1926.

My parents bought land in a newly established community in
the center of Duval county. We lived thirty miles (by a winding country road) from San Diego, the county seat. There were
only about a dozen families in the community and the one-room
schoolhouse served as the center of all important events.
During the week it was our school; Saturday night, a dance
hall; Sunday it was our church, providing there was someone
to preach.

My childhood memories start when we moved to Texas, when
I was just over three. Perhaps the first thing I remember is
when Dad hitched his two big, white horses to the wagon and
went to San Diego to buy lumber to build a windmill. It
seemed to take a long, long time for him to return. He had
to go in the wagon because the length could be adjusted to
accommodate the long timbers he bought. There were monthly
trips to San Diego to buy supplies and pick up the mail.

The Angel Of The Lord
How I Learned About The Activity Of The Lord in The Lives
Of His People

**The angel of the Lord encamps all around those who fear
Him, And delivers them.   Psalm 34:7 NKJ**

That first winter in our new home, Dad went back to Arkansas to close out some business. He thought he had made adequate preparation for us, since winters in south Texas are
usually mild, but this year was different. A misty rain turned
to ice. As I was about four years old, I stood at the dining
room window, fascinated that the clothesline grew until it
collapsed under the weight of ice.

George was just over one year old and became dreadfully
ill with pneumonia. The house was cold and there was no more
firewood. There was no way that Mom could get the sick baby
to the doctor thirty miles away. She dressed us children in

JLK

layer upon layer of clothes. The night the sickness was draw-
ing to a crisis, Mom placed a chair on both sides of her rocker.
She wrapped George in a warm blanket and held him to herself.
She said to Willie Mae and me,
    "Sit here by me and pray."
We could hardly stay awake. She called to us once in a while,
    "Stay awake, children, and pray."
About midnight she called us again, saying,
    "You may go to bed now. Everything is going to be all right.
    The angel of the Lord is here."

                    ****

    Most of our clothing was made on Mom's pedal sewing machine.
She ordered cloth from the catalogues - Sears & Roebuck or
Montgomery Ward. She sewed and sang hymns:

    Onward, Christian Soldiers   What A Friend
    When They Ring the Golden Bells   Sweeping Through The Gate
    Beulah Land   Never Alone

Food Supply

For the Lord God is a sun and shield;
    The Lord will give grace and glory;
        No good thing will He withhold
            From those who walk uprightly.   Psalm 84:11 NKJ

    Feeding a growing family in the isolation of Duval County
was a challenge. In Arkansas there were fruits and vegetables
in abundance to can for the winter months. But in south Texas
Mom and Dad planted a garden every year, hoping for the blessed
rainfall to produce the harvest and there was usually nothing
but disappointment.

    Mom asked a Mexican woman to walk with her through the bushes
and mesquite, pointing out edible plants that grew wild. She
couldn't store food because she didn't have refrigeration. Dad
built a trap to catch quail, and he hunted dove, deer, and
rabbit. He never slaughtered a steer because that much meat
would only spoil. He bought dried fruit in large, wooden crates
- prunes, raisins, apples, and apricots.

    In all their struggles to provide a good variety of food,
we children were never made to feel that the situation was
critical. Once the food served for a meal was almost totally
from the woods, that is, gathered wherever it grew, and Dad
said,
    "Look what God has provided!"
Sometimes there were greens and berries. Mom was an artist
at stretching a can of salmon to feed her hungry family.
There were lots of fried potato cakes and hoe cakes (this was
a batter made of corn meal and fried like a pancake).

Babes In The Woods

One of my early memories of Dad was when he sang a very sad song to us, about two little children lost in the wood. I see now that his reason was clear and his method most effective! It would have been very dangerous for us to wander far from adult watchfulness as the rattlesnakes in the mesquite thickets were the greatest peril. Also there were wildcats, javelina pigs, and an occasional rumor of panthers brought dread and fear to us children. So Dad's song was just right to discourage us from wandering away on our own. Willie Mae sings "Babes In The Woods" and my niece Alice Neal found the poem.

MY EXPANDING WORLD

"He found him in a desert land And in the wasteland,
   a howling wilderness;
He encircled him, He instructed him,
   He kept him as the apple of His eye.
As an eagle stirs up its nest, Hovers over its young,
   Spreading out its wings, taking them up,
   Carrying them on its wings,
So the Lord alone led him,
   And there was no foreign god with him.   Deut. 32:10-12   NKJ

I started to school in the one-room school building at the place named The Cross Roads. There was no town, nor post office, nor electric lights, nor free lunches. There was just a building with four walls, a few desks, a picture each of Washington and Lincoln on the wall; no playground equipment. When we were thirsty, we children pumped water from the pump outside. We were children of the sparsely settled countryside, ranging from the first to the eighth grade. Those wanting to go to high school had to go away to a boarding school.

A Birthday Party At School

In 1974 I was back in this same area - in the town of Freer (the name given to that small municipality which sprang up there). I stopped at the gas station and got to talking with the owner. We introduced ourselves, and when he realized who I was, he began reminiscing about "that wonderful birthday dinner at the school."

"That wonderful birthday dinner" was served over forty years before our chance encounter. Willie Mae and George both had the same birthday - November 15, but nine years apart. Mom decided to make a birthday dinner and share it with all the school children. Since the teacher boarded at our home they planned it together. This was before the oil boom and there were fewer than thirty pupils. Mom planned to take George with her so he could be honored, although he wasn't in school yet.

JLK

Mom harnessed the two mules to the wagon, since Dad was
away. She carried the birthday dinner to the school one mile
away, and served it to us children - chicken and dressing
and all the accompanying goodies.

Oil!

Around 1928 oil was discovered in our remote community,
and nothing would be the same again. People came from everywhere and lived in tents, tarpaper shacks and under tin shelters. Since Dad was a skilled carpenter, he was kept busy
building what were called "shotgun houses," made of rooms
built one behind the other, in a straight line.

A town grew up and it needed a name, so names of the first
settlers were written on slips of paper and placed in a hat
for the drawing. "Freer" was drawn hence the town was named
and incorporated. It was a mile from the school. The influx
of families reflected, of course, in the school.

When I started the third grade the fall of 1931 they needed
to divide the large, one room; we now had two teachers instead
of one. Dad devised a movable partition so the entire space
could be used for larger gatherings. That original school
building where I started out as a first grader, now serves
as the library of Freer.

Where there had been a quiet, one-room country school with
a handful of children; where the teacher had been a young lady
still doing her college work - there was now a madhouse.
There were many disorderly children. The community leaders
built a room on each end of the original school. Teachers
were quickly gathered from wherever they could be found.
There were not enough books to go around; even chalk was scarce.

Mrs. McCullough's Maypole

The new principal, Mrs. McCullough, was middle-aged, being
skilled in producing dramas and pageants. Not only that,
she was skilled in using whatever was available for the pro-
ductions. She solicited the aid of oil field workers and their
equipment. Since there was not even a movie theater in the
booming town, this new activity went over big.

We boys looked askance at the preparation for THE event of
the year - the Maypole celebration. Mothers busily made costumes from colored, frilled crepe paper. The drilling and
practicing were endless - as we were willingly, or unwillingly
trained in dancing around the Maypole, weaving in and out,
hopefully bearing the right streamer. To us boys who had
grown up in the rough-and-tumble ranch country, it all seemed
ridiculous. None of us hankered being dressed like daisies,
poppies, or sunflowers, and dancing around that consternating
Maypole. Actually, we were embarrassed.

6.

JLK　　　　　　　　　**To The Fourth Grade**

Mom and Dad looked on the curriculum with dismay, since their philosophy of education was: Readin', 'Ritin', and 'Rithmetic. A thought in retrospect: What more could the teachers have done for maintaining a growing school system, with few books and little equipment?

Now the population really exploded as people came from everywhere - and there was pandemonium. The dictionary describes it:
"Any place or gathering remarkable for disorder
    and uproar."
There was not enough of anything but violence and vice. Along with those skilled in discovering and producing oil, came the skillful in lawlessness.

A fine brick school was built in town, then the town kids didn't have to walk a mile to school. A bus was bought to pick up us kids living in the country, but this required a mile's walk to catch the bus. In just two years we moved from a one-room, eight-grade school in the country to a full-fledged high school with a football team! Again there had to be expansion, so a second permanent building, larger than the first, was built.

For myself, I have some vague memories. When I was a fourth grader, my class met in what was intended to be the garage for the school bus. Since the fifth grade was there in the afternoon, we only had a half day of class. I got sick with dust pneumonia; nevertheless I went on to school and that day I fainted. That was the end of school in Freer for me.

A Boy And His Pets

As a child living in the isolation of south Texas, life could have been lonely, but I had some wonderful pets. We had our own white spitz dog, and we raised two fawns until they were old enough to return to the wilds. I had four coyote puppies, but since our chickens were more precious to us than my pet coyotes I gave them away. We even had three javelina pigs for a while but they never became gentle - they just became tiresome. I kept a hawk in a cage for a while. When we got ready to move to Arkansas I opened the cage door and watched it fly away.

Andrew Haden was crippled, walking with steel braces on his legs. He drove a rickety, little Ford truck. Occasionally he came to our community with his truck loaded with fresh vegetables - welcome produce. Mr. Haden liked to spend the night in our home where he was always welcome. I was about seven years old when he asked me if I would like to have some Bantam chickens. I didn't know what they were so I asked him. His explanation was more than adequate to help me decide "Yes!"

JLK

It was hard to wait for Mr. Haden's next visit. True to
his word, he brought a crate with a Bantam rooster and two
hens on top of his load. No chickens ever received so much
attention! One of the chicks became quite a pet. She would
sing her heart out for a handout. She was always ready for
a handout and a song.

The Depression

There was a time before the oil boom when we felt the depression severely. I helped to make ends meet at a very early age. (I still find satisfaction in recalling that at such a young age I contributed to our family income in those difficult times.) My job was to milk the three cows that furnished milk for the family. There was a small community about a half mile from our house, where the people operated a booster station on an oil pipeline for Magnolia Petrolium Company.

Some of them wanted to buy milk from us. I would milk the cows, then Mom filled quart jars. I walked to the station carrying four quarts in my arms, delivered to separate houses, and collected empty jars. Then I walked the half mile home. It was another mile to school, so I had to hurry to be on time for the nine o'clock bell. The school bell was brass, with a wooden handle.

Another project to make money was growing ducks to sell. They were large, white creatures with bright red heads. I fed, watered, and gathered them into their pen at night. Mom dressed them and I carried them to the customers who arranged an exchange of goods for the ducks.

One of my customers was a Russian Jew, Harry Altoman, and his sister. I liked to hear him tell of his younger days in Russia. He operated a clothing store - the first one in our area, and something new in our remote community. Most of my school clothes came from his store (my first store-bought ones). The oil boom attracted merchants and other businessmen.

They Yearned For A Church

Mom and Dad keenly felt the loss of their church back in Arkansas. They tried hard to maintain a Sunday worship service in the schoolhouse. Dad was a very quiet man. He would never have tried to conduct a service himself, but he gave full support to anyone who would. He encouraged Mr. Johnson, a Primitive Baptist, to preach. He had a singsong delivery and it didn't work, so Dad sought another preacher. He preached a few times, but since he was an alcoholic this too was a disaster.

Finally, no doubt after much prayer, a retired preacher, John Jackson from Sandia was engaged. When he and his wife Jeanie came once a month they stayed in our home. She had a folding organ which she played in church, and we really enjoyed her music.

JLK

Once a year the Jacksons came for what was called a "protracted revival meeting" which lasted for several nights.
Brother Jackson usually preached an hour, and it was hard for
little boys to stay awake that long. One night when the preacher was in his best form, I fell asleep on top of a desk. Something happened so my weight shifted and I fell off, making
what seemed a thunderous "boom" on the noisy wood floor. I
was so embarrassed! I felt that all eyes were upon me.

I was truthfully convinced that there was something special
about these "protracted meetings." They always sang"Amazing
Grace"and at the close of the services the pastor said,

"Now we are going to open the doors of the church."

Many times I looked back to observe that they were already
open. Someone finally explained to me that it was an invitation to people who wanted to join the church. Willie Mae
was among the first ones to make such a decision. She was
about twelve years old when she "entered the doors of the
church." She and some others were baptized in a cement tank
in the corral on our farm.

A Food Crisis And The Pastor's Visit

Once when Brother and Mrs. Jackson came on their monthly
visit, there was a very heavy rainfall. Since the roads were
washed out in low places, our guests were stranded with us.
Mom was beginning to worry because our food supply brought
from San Diego was running low.

Sensing Mom's concern, the pastor asked if she had any corn
in the barn, and she sent us children to bring some. He carefully shelled it and requested Mom's pressure cooker. When
the corn had been washed he put it in the pot with water, then
he asked for some lye. (Mom made our soap so she usually had
lye on hand.) She could only reply that she was out - that
lye was on the shopping list.

The next item needed was a small, cloth sack. Almost everything was bought in cloth sacks: from Bull Durham tobacco to
salt, sugar, flour and meal. This was before the days of plastic packaging. Next, Mr. Jackson scooped ashes from below the
firebox of the kitchen stove and tied them in the sack. (Dear
Reader: ashes contain lye.) He dropped the sack into the
pot, fastened the lid, cooked the corn, and removed the ashes.
Now that the husks and germ were loosened he washed the corn
thoroughly until all residue was gone.

JLK

Next Brother Jackson put the corn into the clean cooker with fresh water. It was to cook until the grain swelled to several times its normal size. This was a slow process on a wood burning stove. When night came he suggested we all go to bed and let him care for the hominy. He filled the fire-box and pulled the oven door open so he could sit and rest his feet on it. All the warmth and relaxation must have made him fall asleep. Later, when it was quiet and we were all asleep, the sound of an explosion woke us.

"Whoooooomp!"

The cover had blown off the pressure cooker. When we rushed to the kitchen there was Brother Jackson dancing brisk-ly, with his feet scalded! Now what to do for his feet? The contents of our medicine cabinet were limited: castor oil, epsom salts, liniment, turpentine, and mustard for making plasters and poultices. We decided the feet should be swabbed with bluing (used for whitening clothes in the wash) and then coated with cow's butter.

The hominy was saved, and the Jacksons stayed with us until his feet were well enough so he could drive their Model A home.

not forsaking the assembling of ourselves together,
   as is the manner of some,
but exhorting one another,
   and so much the more as you see the Day approaching.
      Hebrews 10:25 NKJ

Baptists, Methodists, and others came with the population
growth. Mom and Dad were two of the thirteen charter members
of the Freer Baptist Church organized January 25, 1933. When
Dad and three other men were ordained as deacons, I tried to
see the "laying on of hands." I stood on my tiptoes trying
to see over the heads of the grownups, to watch those important
men place their hands on my Dad's head.

The church met in the schoolhouse; then in the simple wood
building constructed under my Dad's direction. Later they
enlarged it and added a baptistry.

On a Sunday night when I was about ten years old, I made
my decision to trust Jesus as my Savior. Soon I was baptized
along with several others in a pond on Mr. Burch's property.
The pastor who baptized us was D.E. Moore, a truly dedicated
man. Unhappily for the church he soon moved away.

The oil boom was going full blast. The responsible people
with leadership ability were having to give full attention to
the newly incorporated town of Freer. Thus the children of
the church got very little attention. We didn't even have
Sunday School classrooms; and there was minimum training for
young Christians.

Planting Missions In The Heart

However, someone gathered us small children every week to
study and pray about Missions, and to sing about Jesus who
loves the little children of the world - red and yellow, black
and white. We called it Sunbeam Band, Missions education for
young children.

In the Freer church I was first impressed that people went
to other nations to preach the Gospel. A Black couple who
came to tell about their work in Africa had a little girl
with them who sang choruses in an African language.

JLK

Trouble In The Church
Trouble On The Land (1937, 1938)

My parents John and Ida Kidd had done well in spite of the hardships of moving to Texas and building a new home in an isolated community. Their 160-acre farm had grown to 2,000 acres with another 500 under lease. They were contributors to their community. They were devoted to the school and to their church. Teachers were boarders in our home, and pastors were always welcome there.

Then a noticeable change came over my parents when I was about thirteen. They never discussed the problems in the church with us children, but I realized that our new pastor never came to visit. When Mom was in the hospital, her Sunday School class was very attentive, but the pastor never visited. When Dad was sick the deacons gave constant attention, but the pastor never came to see him.

Next, the pastor's wife left and took their little boy. The church gave him full support through it all. Dad overlooked the absence of visitation, but the breakup of the pastor's family was too much for him. Dad said nothing to anyone, but he never returned to that church.

This was a costly decision. His faithful stewardship ended; he no longer supported that church financially. He would never see his youngest son, George, trust the Lord and be baptized. Taken out of the church, George went a different direction.

LOOKING BEYOND FREER

Our community in the middle of Duval County was pretty barren. That is probably why some trips stand out in my mind.

Corpus Christi

The surging waves of the Gulf of Mexico were awesome. Never had I imagined that there was so much water. When we parked in front of a hotel there stood a man in a dark blue suit; he had bright red stripes on his coat sleeves and trouser legs. Several buttons on his chest flashed in the sunlight. I loudly exclaimed,
   "Oh Mom, there is the richest man in Texas!"
   "Oh hush. He is just a bellhop."
I think of that man and his wonderful suit when I read,

   For a day in Your courts is better than a thousand.
   I would rather be a doorkeeper in the house of my God
   Than dwell in the tents of wickedness.
   Psalm 84:10 NKJ

13.

JLK

We went to a department store and I was captivated by the strange behavior of the people. Some would go through an open door and it would close. Then the room would go up. After an interval it would come back down. The door would open and other people would come out. I ran to tell Mom about this as I thought she needed to know. She explained that it was an elevator.

A little later a man walked out of the elevator wearing a long, black robe. Again, I ran to Mom and explained loudly that a man had just come out of the elevator wearing a long, black dress. Mom said to be quiet - the man was a priest. I had trouble with that for some time. Whatever he was, it seemed to me that he should have worn trousers. Well, why not?

Mexico

A trip to Mexico introduced me to a world vastly different from what I had known. (We had Mexicans working on the farm, and the children attended our school.) It was all very different as they had their own money and their own police. In Mexico, I understood that I was a guest. I came away with a new respect for the Mexican people in my own community and school. Perhaps even then I was given an impression of what was in store for me in years to come.

"You shall not oppress a hired servant who is poor and needy, whether one of your brethren or one of the aliens who is in your land within your gates. Deut. 24:14 NKJ

1935: A Visit to Arkansas

Dad sold some royalty to an oil company, and with part of the money he bought a new Ford V8; so we traveled to Arkansas. This was the first time that our family (Dad, Mom, Willie Mae, George and I) had gone back to Arkansas since we moved away in 1926. I had no memory of grandparents, uncles, aunts, and all the cousins. Nor did I remember the tall trees. It was all very strange and I took days to absorb it. I walked for hours through the tall pines; their fragrance was amazing. I went with my cousins to the blackberry patches where we feasted on the fruit, delightedly staining mouth, hands, and clothes.

Another thing that caused wonder was that occasionally on our walks we came to cool, fresh water gushing from the ground. Our dry countryside in south Texas had none of this. There, Dad drilled three wells and built windmills to furnish water for the cattle and our home. But always the water was far too salty for home use although it was fine for the cattle. For us, Dad provided cisterns to capture the rain water falling on the roofs of the house and barns. We used this with care, to last from one rainy season to the next.

14.

JLK
The cistern by the barn had been dug deeply in the ground, then plastered. The one by the house had been built hastily above the ground. It was fine when it had water, meaning that we didn't have to carry water so far. Being above ground, it was amazing how quickly the water evaporated in the relentless heat of the sun. Like the broken cistern in Jeremiah 2:13, it held no water.

DROUGHT

When we returned to our home from Arkansas a drought had started. In the dreadful days that followed, I remembered those springs of refreshing water back in Arkansas many, many times. It was the end of July and very hot. There was no wind to turn the three windmills located strategically for the cattle. (Dad had already understood that the area was not for farming so he turned to cattle. Our land never produced oil.)

The men who were left in charge while we were gone, were trying hard to haul water, but it was hopeless for several hundred head of cattle. Dad quickly located some used gasoline engines in the oil field. With them he devised a way to pump water, having disconnected the motionless windmills from the rods going down into the well.

Soon water was flowing into the tanks but those engines needed attention day and night. As the drought continued, a good water supply was not enough. Pastures dried up. Dad used flame throwers to burn the thorns off the cactus, but cactus alone did not provide the nutrition the cattle needed to survive.

Finally the hot, dry summer of 1935 came to an end, and 1936 was a good year. The rains were adequate to produce an abundant harvest and enough grazing for the cattle. It couldn't have been better. Then drought struck back with implacable vengeance.

Normally a cool breeze blows in from the Gulf of Mexico, but during much of the time in those long months it was still. There was not enough wind to turn the windmills; water tanks stood dry. Dust hung in the air and there was no escape from it. Occasionally a wind blew but it was hot and dry, and it seared like a blast from a furnace. There was no relief.

The resultant dust pneumonia brought down Mom and she was hospitalized in the small local hospital. Both Dad and I were sick at home. Willie Mae's husband Rex had to be flown to a hospital in San Antonio.

Large numbers of cattle died. Dad was crushed. The doctor who cared for him, realizing the seriousness of his condition, suggested that he move to the Ozark mountains where he, himself, had grown up.

15.

The Valley Of South Texas

While Dad was making a decision about this suggestion, we took a trip to see the orange groves of Falfurrias where a citrus farm was for sale. Dad wanted to see it as he still hoped to remain in south Texas. We liked it. The endless rows of trees loaded with oranges, grapefruit, etc. were beautiful.

After a second trip to visit the farm at Falfurrias, Dad decided he should heed his doctor's advice and visit the Ozarks. The Ozarks won and we were to spend the next four years in north Arkansas. There Dad would regain a measure of health and I would receive the challenge to pursue my education. God was very much at work in my life even though I was not aware of it.

WE MOVE TO THE OZARKS

The move to Marian County in north Arkansas, spring of 1938, was intended to be permanent. The cattle surviving the many years of drouth had to be sold. Dad hired Mexican cowboys to gather them out of the mesquite thickets and herd them into a holding pen. They were held until they were sold, bringing $15.00 per head.

Dad bought a Chevrolet pickup and we drove to the town of Cotter on the White River in the Ozarks. Our route was by way of Houston, Nacogdoches, Texarkana, Little Rock, and on to Cotter - much over unpaved roads.

An Important Choice

Dad had gotten a realtor's Cotter address from the magazine "The Farm and Ranch" so that is where we went. Dad was in that office several hours, studying the listings that were for sale. Finally he asked for directions to a 140-acre farm on the White River about twenty miles from Cotter.

We passed through the town of Flippen, which would be our post office. Our destination was ten miles beyond Flippen. The first six miles were graded, being maintained by the state or county since this was the mail route. The last four miles were maintained by the people living along the road.

We were going to the end of the road. Dad liked the place and we spent several days there while he purchased the farm, two horses, a Jersey cow, farm equipment, and some household furniture. The house was small, compared to our Texas home.

The Bantam Chickens Go, Too

We returned to Texas to close out there, then the actual moving to the Ozarks could start. We loaded household goods on the pickup. I caught a Bantam rooster with two hens and put them in a bushel basket. When we pulled out early the next morning my basket of chickens was securely tied on top of the load.

Two impressions were indelibly written in my memory. First, Mom was very quiet. I think she realized that she was leaving her only daughter and two grandchildren behind.* Second, Dad sang all the time. I had rarely heard him sing spontaneously and now, over and over he sang, "I Must Tell Jesus" and "Take Your Burdens To The Lord."

After a long day on the road we pulled into a tourist court to spend the night. Off the pickup came my basket of chickens. Mom asked,
"What are you going to do with them?"
"Well, if I leave them on the truck someone will take them." It didn't worry me that someone might take something of far more value. I put the Bantams in our room (where all four of us were) and it went well until a little after midnight. Mr. Rooster started to crow, and he didn't stop. Mom and Dad were pretty unhappy with me!

Those chickens and their descendants became a very busy part of our Ozark farmyard. Our neighbors had little interest in what they considered very scrawny, useless chickens. (When we moved to Urbana later all our "real" chickens were sold and we left the Bantams. Perhaps there are still Bantam roosters crowing from the tops of the tall oak trees on the shore of Lake Bull Shoals.

Life In The Ozarks

The land in Texas had been bought over several years, small acreages being purchased from different owners. The buyer was very exacting in his requirements concerning the titles. It took several months to negotiate for clear titles, and it was very expensive. It now was a relief to have it all behind us. The money from the sale of the Texas place enabled Dad to buy additional farm animals and equipment.

Life in the Ozarks was a big adjustment. We were back in a community with a one-room school and no church. But it seemed to be what Dad needed to find some measure of recovery from the crushing blows he had experienced. We had come from the mild climate of south Texas - at fifteen, I had never seen snow.

* Willie Mae was married to Rex Mathews October 26, 1934. They had two girls - Alice and Rexene. Later they had a boy and a girl - Johnny and Curtis Ann.

JLK

Our house was standard for its time and place, but Mom
realized we would suffer from the cold. Since there were not
a lot of insulating materials on the market, we gathered up
cardboard boxes each time we went to Flippen. We tacked layer
upon layer of cardboard on the walls until the insulation was
about one inch thick. Then we papered over the cardboard.
When winter came and temperatures fell below zero, we were
snug and warm.

The Newton Flat school was 1 3/4 miles from our house.
Often we walked there in the snow. Drinking water for the
school came from a spring several hundred yards away. The
teacher assigned two boys each day to carry water; everyone
used the same dipper.

After school was let out each day we walked to the mail route
which was beyond the school. We were always anxious to have
letters from the outside world. This walk took us 1 1/2 miles
in the opposite direction from home. When we got to the mailbox we were 3 1/4 miles from home!

Miss Mary Link: Educator

Miss Mary Link, the teacher, was a gifted educator even
though she was not a college graduate. This school was for
first to eighth grades; I started with the two seventh graders.
In just a few days Miss Link determined that I was not ready
for the seventh grade - not in her school. We had a talk
and she kindly but firmly said that I should join her three
fifth graders.

The school year was divided. After three months we broke
to harvest the crops. Then there was a five-month session,
giving only an eight-month school year.

I completed the fifth grade to Miss Link's satisfaction,
in the three-month session. I did the sixth grade in the
five-month session. This placed me in the seventh grade. I
owe a great debt of gratitude to Miss Mary Link, now Mrs. Coy
Martin of Flippen.

I became a student under her tutelage. She loaned me her
books, and I read constantly. Beyond regular assignments I
read Greek mythology, history, and biographies. All during
our four years in north Arkansas, I lived under the shadow
that there was no possibility to leave home to go to high
school.

18.

Rich And Productive Land

The farm was a good one. The land was rich and productive.
We grew corn for the horses and pigs and hay to feed the cattle
during winter months. There was hardwood timber as well as
cedar to harvest. In this climate we produced fresh vegetables
and fruit, and Mom canned several hundred quarts each year.

I was too busy learning to operate the farm to have numerous pets as I had in Texas. Running a farm on White River
was vastly different from ranching. Dad wasn't well enough
yet to do much more than to instruct us two teenagers. Actually, George was only twelve years old, so I did most of the
plowing and mowing. Besides, farming was just not George's
bent.

An English shepherd dog was my only pet. She was instinct-
ively a stock dog; she kept the goats out of the orchard.
When she saw me with my bucket at milking time she would go
to the pasture and bring the cow.

Swimming And Fishing

The river constantly invited us to fish and swim. After
living in an arid climate for so long, the lure of the river
was often overwhelming. We took frequent breaks from plowing and mowing to dive nude into the cold, refreshing waters
of the White River.

Learning the names and merits of the trees was very important. We gathered nuts from the black walnut, butternut
and hickory trees. There was an abundance of berries and we
gathered many for Mom to can. We boys spent some time exploring a cave near the school. It is now a tourist attraction
with several log cabins around it. It is called "Ozark Village" and none of the stories they tell about it are true.

During the four years we lived in the Ozarks my Dad was
restored to better health, although he would always have a
heart condition. Those four years for me had unmeasured value -
mainly because I was set on a course toward education. This
quest eventually lead me to a deep and lasting faith in God.
On this course I would find the will and purpose of the Lord
for my life.

**And you will seek Me and find Me, when you search
for Me with all your heart. Jer. 29:13 NKJ**

The Bull Shoals Dam was built on the White River, a little
less than a mile below our farm. We knew our farm land would
be flooded so we planned to move back to Urbana - from where
we left sixteen years ago. After we had moved away and the
waters began to rise, our house, so well insulated with cardboard - was intentionally torched. It must have made a ter-
rific fire.

19.

JLK   **A DOOR TO MORE EDUCATION**

In the summer of 1942 we moved back to the farm at Urbana,
Arkansas - to the same house where I was born in 1923. Wisely,
Dad had retained this holding through the years. Now George
and I shared the very same bedroom where we were born. When
Mom and Dad settled in, they returned to the church they left
when they moved to Texas. The Urbana Baptist Church gave them
sorely needed support when they saw their two sons go away to
the army.

Now I could continue my education since I had completed
the eighth grade. I was small in stature, and only the school
principal at Urbana knew that I was nineteen years old when I
enrolled in the ninth grade.

This was a small, class C high school. The ninth and tenth
grades met together in one room and the eleventh and twelfth
in another. Two young men were our teachers in their first
year of teaching; they were both Baptist pastors. In my sophomore year we had different teachers - a middle-aged lady
for the ninth and tenth grades and a man of some years' experience taught the eleventh and twelfth grades.

Basketball And Drama

Although the high school was small we had a basketball
team, and I played on it. Our drama group of students and
teachers presented plays in Urbana and neighboring communities.
It was a very worthwhile part of high school, since I had
spent most of my life in a rural setting. I needed this experience of working in a group.

We had to buy our own textbooks. I worked in the Urbana
grocery store owned by Mr. Hubert Garner, to pay my expenses
and support myself. For two years, I opened the store early
every morning and worked until school started. I also put in
long hours after classes were dismissed, and on Saturday.

The Army Calls

During the winter of 1943 I suffered from chronic tonsil-
litis and much of the time I took only a liquid diet. My determination to go to school kept me in classes and on my job
at the grocery store. World War II was raging in Europe and
the Pacific and I was called to report for my physical. There
was no way I could pass that exam as I was small in stature
and very run-down. I was classified 4F which was a terrible
blow to my ego.

Mrs. Ruby Knighten

I thought I should take a job to be useful, for I was twenty. I was considering leaving school when Mrs. Ruby Knighten sent for me to come to her classroom. With kindness and wisdom she talked to me.

> "Jesse Kidd, your problem is boredom. You aren't being challenged properly. If you will stay in school I will set up a schedule for you to do extra work and gain additional credit."

I agreed and she added American History and Civics to my study load. At the end of the 1944 school year I was called up again. This time I passed the physical and was inducted into the army at Little Rock, Arkansas May 10, 1944.

Scene

of

the

BURMA

ROAD

Near here the Mars Task Force buried its last
casualties of the bloody battle to reopen the
Burma Road, lifeline to China. We reached this
place after one of the longest, most difficult
marches of World War II.

CHINA - BURMA - INDIA

**You hem me in - behind and before;
you have laid your hand upon me.
Such knowledge is too wonderful for me,
too lofty for me to attain.**

**Where can I go from your Spirit?
Where can I flee from your presence?
Psalm 139: 5-7 NIV**

After finishing six-month basic training at Ft. Riley, Kansas, my company along with others shipped out to Ft. Ord, California. We prepared for overseas. We sailed to Bombay, India via Melbourne, Australia, taking thirty-three days. At Bombay we boarded a troop train and crossed India to Lido on the border of Burma. Every mile, we saw the tragedy of famine and unbelievable poverty. The dead were loaded onto trucks to be hauled out of the cities and burned.

At Lido we boarded a convoy of army trucks bound for Myitkina in Burma. We ate Christmas dinner 1944 in Myitkina, standing at tables made of bamboo strips, under a thatched shelter. Myitkina was the scene of terrible fighting. Hollywood made a film based on the conflict called "The Walking Dead." Myitkina had once been an important city of Burma but it was destroyed.

The Burma Road

We moved deeper into the jungle to begin an offensive that would re-open the Burma Road to China. Japan had captured all of China's port cities until her only supply line was the Burma Road. Having taken the Road, Japan was slowly squeezing the life out of China.

The United States had sent a force of specially trained troops from the Pacific under Brigadier General Frank D. Merrill, known as Merrill's Marauders. It was to set the stage to liberate Burma and recapture the Burma Road.

When we arrived at the point in the jungle where we were to begin our long march, we encountered a pretty grim picture. At this point we were known as the Mars Task Force under General Joe Stilwell. This included the 475th Infantry, the 124th Cavalry, and Chinese fighting forces. These Chinese troops had been pushed out of China. In India they had received special training in jungle warfare. They would play a vital role in the offensive.

We were ordered to get rid of everything we did not want to carry for the next several hundred miles through the jungles. I had discarded a number of things and was standing with a little New Testament in hand. Upon boarding ship in California each soldier was given one by an army chaplain. Now, I had grown cold and indifferent to the Gospel. As I was about to cast the New Testament aside a Chinese soldier rushed up and spoke in perfect English,

"Soldier, don't throw that away. You are going to need it."

Completely surprised, I replied,

"How do you happen to speak English - and what do you know about this New Testament?"

"I attended a high school in Chungking run by Baptist missionaries from your country. I know about that book; keep it."

I put it in my pocket. He was right. I found out I did need it.

We spent the next several months moving through the trailless jungles. Food and supplies, when there were any, were dropped by parachute. We slept on the ground and in foxholes. Captured Japanese soldiers said that we never made that march - that we were paratroopers. "The Bastards of Burma," Page 21:

"Jan. 19, '45: The battle still rages. I can now look down on the Burma Road. Since my last entry, we have made one of the roughest marches any outfit has made in this war yet - 36 hours on the trail without sleep, over mountain trails almost impassable in daylight, and we made them at night."

Water Buffalo Steak

For several days it was so cloudy the Air Force couldn't make the air drops of food and ammunition. A water buffalo had the misfortune of wandering by our outpost, so of course the Sergeant shot it. We made a big fire and roasted the meat. We ate it without salt because there wasn't any salt.

The animal's owner went to our commanding officer and through an interpreter made a complaint, so he was paid. When we returned from our patrol duty the entire squad was called before the Captain. He gave us a thorough military chewing out, and coming into fine form he bellowed,

"I have a mind to throw you all in the brig!"

We simply couldn't restrain ourselves any longer, and howled with laughter. The Captain turned and walked away. Where would he find a brig in all the jungles of Burma? Laughter was a rare sound in those days.

JLK
   Our final thrust to open the road cost many lives. A fellow soldier next to me was mortally wounded and my clothing
was stained with his blood. After days of tense fighting there
came a lull, and I decided to slip away to a nearby stream.
Maybe I could bathe and wash the blood out of my clothes. But
I met a soldier standing squarely in my path - a chaplain.

   "Where are you going?"

I told him my intentions and he said to return to my platoon
(he didn't make it sound like an order). I started past him
and he drew his gun and without pointing it at me, he ordered
me to follow him. He led me to a burial detail at work. There
I went to work helping to bury the bodies of fellow soldiers.
We wrapped them in their G.I.blankets and buried them near the
Burma Road. As we worked, enemy shells rained along the stream
where I had hoped to bathe.

   I have been questioned about a chaplain bearing arms, but
this was jungle warfare. We were engaged in a battle with an
enemy who knew little or nothing of the meaning of the small
cross stamped on the chaplain's helmet or worn on his collar.
He was just another American soldier to be treated like any
other enemy. Without the chaplain's show of force I doubt
he would have persuaded me to change directions. I am thankful for God's providential care.

   Once the Road was opened we were sent on to China. We were
flown over the "hump" to the Chinese city of Kunming. We were
there for only a few weeks, and the 475th Infantry was broken
up into training detachments. The Chinese government had de-
creed that foreign troops would not fight on China's soil in
her defense. We were assigned to different Chinese regiments
to train the Chinese in using American equipment. My group
went to Chihking, about five hundred miles south of Chunking.

God's Angel

**The angel of the Lord encamps around those who fear him,
   and he delivers them. Psalm 34:7 NIV**

   Now we were in the heart of China. The enemy whether spiritual or military goes for the heart. Japan was determined
to have China's heart and made an all-out attack. We were too
far from our main source of supplies. (The lesson here is never
to distance yourself from your source of supplies whether human
or divine.) We had to evacuate! Our officers told us that
there would be a long march with no stops. If anyone dropped
by the wayside they would be left, and if they fell into enemy
hands they would be tortured and executed without mercy.

JLK

The day was mercilessly hot and humid. About mid-afternoon
I came down with dysentery so severe that I could not go on.
I crept into some thick bushes in an effort to hide and I must
have passed out. Later someone awakened me, and I realized it
was a very old Chinese man. I couldn't understand him, but
he motioned for me to get up and follow him. He had a severe
curvature of the spine and walked with a long, wooden staff.

I couldn't manage alone so he took me by the hand and pulled
me up. He had me take hold of his staff with him and as he
picked up my heavy pack, slowly we started out. It was growing dark when we finally reached the old, ancestral temple
where my companions were camped.

I offered to pay my rescuer for his kindness but he would
not receive the money I held out to him. Remembering some
hard chocolate bars that were part of my food ration, I opened
my pack to give them to him. When I turned back to my rescuer,
he was gone. I remember him now when I read Psalm 34:7.

When we think of angels we envision blinding light, heavenly
beings and unearthly creatures. This time the angel of the
Lord was an old, Chinese man with a curvature of the spine,
walking with a long wood staff.

"All the Way My Savior Leads Me"

All the way my Savior leads me; What have I to ask beside?
   Can I doubt His tender mercy,
   Who thro' life has been my guide?
Heav'nly peace, divinest comfort,
   Here by faith in Him to dwell!
For I know whate'er befall me, Jesus doeth all things well;
For I know whate'er befall me, Jesus doeth all things well.

I received the honorable discharge April 14, 1946, almost
two years after entering military service. Now, my burning
goal was to continue my education. The pastor of the Urbana
Church was interested in my plans. I explained that I wanted
to continue my education and since I had only two years of
high school I was thinking of enrolling in the large high
school in nearby El Dorado.

He was recently out of the army and knew the adjustment
problems I would face. How wise and helpful he was! He counseled me to enroll in Ouachita Baptist College (now University)
at Arkadelphia, Arkansas, where they would give an entrance
exam. He said the college was very helpful to veterans and
if I needed to update any studies they would help me.

This was early summer. I was eager to get on with my plans
and I went right away to Ouachita. The school administrators
were indeed very helpful, giving all the veterans eight hours'
credit for military service. I passed the entrance exam except
for English. I signed up to study freshman Chemistry in summer school. For someone who had not been in a classroom for
two years and who had never seen inside a Chemistry lab - it
was an ordeal - a real test of my determination to stay in
college or fall by the wayside. Some didn't make it.

In the fall semester over thirty of us ex G.I.'s were required to take the English non-credit course. At last, being
in college was not the fulfillment of my dream, but the marvelous beginning of my pilgrimage.

As long as I could remember I had dreamed of being a phy-
sician. The thought probably was strongest during the dust
pneumonia epidemic in Duval County. Dr. Floyd, the one doctor in our area, worked day and night to care for the sick.
He was at my bedside many times; so at Ouachita I was a pre-
med student.

God's Plan

**For God has not given us a spirit of fear,
but of power and of love and of a sound mind.**
                                        II Tim. 1:7 NKJ

It was nearing the end of my freshman year, 1947. I volunteered to work with the Training Union Department of the Arkansas Baptist Convention for six weeks of summer field work. Preston Taylor, who was to have a very important influence in my life, was one of the thirty student volunteers. We all spent a week of training at Siloam Springs Baptist Encampment, in the northwest corner of Arkansas. Our leaders prepared us so we could assist small churches needing help to organize Training Unions.

We were to be sent out in teams - usually a young man and a young woman. The man was to work with young people and adults and the woman with the children. My teammate was Hazel Cain (the late Mrs. David Tate). As the week at Siloam Springs drew near to an end, I came to feel that I had not really made the full commitment needed to do the job. I would be expected to preach, and that terrified me. Preston and I went for a walk one afternoon; we talked a long time about the weeks before us. Up on a mountainside above the encampment grounds, I yielded my fears to God and surrendered fully to His will.

Hazel and I went to Hackett for our first week of work in the church there. Just the week before, the pastor was cruelly beaten on the streets of that small town. When I met him, he still had the bruises on his face. He abruptly said,

"Young man, you are in charge here for the week. I cannot
 help you in any way."

The next day I preached my first and second sermons, and a sermon every night that week. The wonder of it all was that there were several people converted that week.

After Hackett, Hazel and I served in the churches in Floral, Tichener, and Mt. Olive. I discovered that God had not given me a spirit of fear (II Tim. 1:7).

I found myself literally being thrust into the ministry. That summer as I went from church to church I found God at work in the churches and in the lives of the people. I came to understand that God had a mission and a plan for my life that I could not explain, apart from the preaching of the Gospel. From that first week in a very difficult situation until now there has never been any doubt in my mind about God's will for me. God had clearly said,

... This is the way, walk ye in it, ... Is. 30:21 KJ

JLK

When I returned to Ouachita in the fall of 1947 for my sophomore year I changed from pre-med to ministerial studies. The Philadelphia Church, a country church in Liberty Baptist Association, invited me to become their pastor. (Liberty Baptist Association is composed of all Southern Baptist churches in Union and Ouachita Counties, Arkansas.) The Philadelphia Church requested the Urbana Church, where I was a member, to call a council to ordain me. January 11, 1948 I was ordained in the Urbana Church, where my father had been baptized many years before, and where his funeral service would be conducted January 20, 1952.

After my ordination I became pastor of the Philadelphia Church. It was here that my mother attended when she was a little girl - even in the same building. Once the family went there to hear a Rev. Simmons preach. He had a "peg" leg since he had been injured in the Civil War. My mother was curious about how he would manage to kneel to pray before the sermon, so she didn't close her eyes or bow her head.

Grandmother Frisby, seeing this lack of reverence, took hold of Mom's one long braid and yanked it upward; so consequently Mom's head was bowed! (It was this preacher's son, Arthur Simmons of Urbana, who would contribute to the purchase of my boat passage to Brazil.) When I left Philadelphia my Ouachita classmate Clay Hale became pastor and he had a long and fruitful ministry there. The roots which nourished my faith and sustained me through times of testing grew long and deep.

I was a junior at Ouachita when I heard Dr. Samuel Maddox speak at Chapel. He was the son of missionaries to Brazil where he grew up. Now he was on the staff of the Foreign Mission Board, Southern Baptist Convention. Sam Maddox told how his father had preached one day in a Brazilian community. After the service a man asked him to go for a walk. They went out into a field where the Brazilian got down on his knees and dug up some images. Showing them to the missionary, he cried out,

"Oh, why didn't you come sooner? My parents died without hearing about Jesus! They died, worshiping these idols!"

I was deeply impressed. From that moment my preaching took on a missionary emphasis. At that time I was serving the Calion Church on weekends. One day Brother Pat Poole, a deacon of that church asked if I thought that some day I would go to the mission field. I said,

"I believe that God will some day require of me the kind of commitment that one must have to go to the mission field, but I do not believe that He will ever lead me to go to a foreign field."

The Calion Revival

The Calion Baptist Church experienced a great revival in 1949-50. The church had just completed the construction of a new building and it seemed that God wanted to bless the efforts of His people.

I was still a student at Ouachita, going to the church on weekends. My dear fellow student Preston helped me in the spring in a week-long evangelistic effort. Over twenty people trusted Christ as Savior; it was a tremendous blessing to the church. In the fall we had another great week with Lonnie Lassiter as the evangelist. This time we had another large number of conversions. Most of these were young people and adults and the results were long lasting.

The awakening went on for almost two years. During this time the membership almost doubled. Two deacons, Mr. D.B. Cummins and Mr. A.H. Hefner, surrendered to the ministry. Both were ordained and served in churches in several different states during their ministries. Harold Cummins, son of D.B. Cummins, later served in Kenya, Africa as a Southern Baptist Convention missionary.

Mr. Plez Major was wonderfully converted in the Calion Church. He is mentioned in Preston Taylor's book "Joy In Jesus," pages 81, 82. Plez Major was later ordained to the ministry and served churches in Arkansas and Montana.

I also baptized Donald Jackson who went to California where he serves as Associational Director of Missions. His older brother Edgar Jackson while not a member of the Calion Church, was no doubt inspired by his godly father, Mark Jackson, who was a pillar of the Calion Church for many years. Edgar served as pastor of churches in Texas, Missouri, Hawaii, and he finally served on the faculty of Hardin Simmons University, Abilene, Texas. The awakening that moved the church so mightily was largely the result of prayers.

Do it again, O Lord.

Oh, that you would rend the heavens!
That You would come down!
That the mountains might shake at Your presence -
                                        Is. 64:1 NKJ

The Commitment To Foreign Missions

I studied one year (1951-52) at Southwestern Baptist Theological Seminary in Fort Worth, Texas. There at Southwestern I made the commitment that led me to Brazil. I wrote home on April 24, 1952:

Dear Mom and George,

I don't know what you are going to think of this. Today at the close of the Missions service I found that I could not resist God's spirit as He spoke to my heart; so I went forward surrendering my life to foreign missions.

I don't know why God should choose one such as I am but He knows more about me than I do myself so as I yield myself along with all my misgivings, my failures and faults, I simply trust God to do with me and my weakness what He will.

I have always thought of missionaries as being people who were great, and that makes it even more difficult to see how God could possibly use me there. But at last I think I know the secret of it all. All this time I have sought to walk by sight instead of by faith.

"For in this we groan, earnestly desiring to be clothed upon with our house which is from heaven: If so be that being clothed we shall not be found naked."
II Cor. 5:2,3 KJV

I also realize that even Isaiah felt his weakness as God called him. But today I answer along with him,

'Here am I; send me.' Is. 6:8 KJV

I am to go before Dr. Cal Guy tomorrow for a conference and he will help me get started off on the courses that I should take in order to get prepared for the work and tell me something of what is to be expected.

There are a thousand questions in my mind that are not answered yet but I am beginning now to see what Paul meant when he said, "We walk by faith and not by sight."

Now I think I know what He wanted when our blessed master said, "Take no thought for tomorrow."

What comes my way from now on will be in His hands and all that I will do is just continue to walk by faith. I cannot tell what He wants with this wreckage of my life but whatever He wants with it I will no longer fret but gladly yield it all to Him.

Never have I had such assurance and peace of mind as I have
now for I can look back and see that God's hand has been at
work in my life all the way through. For who was I with no
high school diploma to attempt to go to college? The fact
that I did four years there and am now here; the fact that I
am anything is because of our Lord.

Had He not taken over when He did I wouldn't have finished
Ouachita at all - one year would have been the end of me there
and I would have ended up a one-horse farmer or an underpaid
sawmill worker. Surely God has dealt richly with me and as I
look back, knowing how I followed unwillingly, wanting to walk
by sight and not by faith - I marvel that he did anything with
me at all.

But now I seek to walk wholly within the circle of His will.
If He can do what He has in the past with me, then my future
is in His hands and it is His to do with it as He wishes.

A lot of people are saying how foolish it is for people to
do what I am about to do when there is so much sin here in
America and so many, many lost people doomed to spend eternity
in awful, awful hell. But there is no one in America who hasn't
had an opportunity to hear the glorious Gospel of Christ at
least once - that is enough for any man to hear it.

Good has been our opportunity here to turn to Christ. God
would have us to go to those who have never heard the story
of Jesus once, yet who are lost, that they may have an opportunity to trust Him whom to know is life eternal. Oh! That
the world could know the joy that I have in this hour as I
wait before Him.

Love, Jesse Rom. 1:15,16

> **So, as much as in me is, I am ready to preach the gospel
> to you that are at Rome also. For I am not ashamed of
> the gospel of Christ: for it is the power of God unto
> salvation to every one that believeth; to the Jew first,
> and also to the Greek.**
>
> **Rom. 1:15,16 KJ**

A Difficult But Necessary Decision

I returned to Arkansas for the summer and completed the Bachelor of Arts degree at Ouachita. My Ouachita transcript is not a thing of beauty. As I study my certificate bearing a graduation date August 8, 1952, I reflect on the very fragile background for college level work. That B.A. certificate reflects the patient endurance of the dedicated men and women of the administration and faculty, who labored with me through those precious college days.

Dad had died in January that year 1952. Mom was living in the house near Urbana which they built early in their marriage. She was caring for George's year-old son George Neal. George had gained full custody of him through his divorce. He left George Neal in Mom's care and went to Beaumont, Texas to work in the oil field. Mom never wanted to leave her home and kept hoping that George would return. Month after month she waited.

Time was running out for me because I needed to get ready to return to seminary for the fall semester. The thought of leaving Mom in such a difficult situation was very painful. I went for long walks in the woods as I wrestled with the situation. Part of me wanted to assume responsibility that did not belong to me.

Saturday morning I went down to the grove of huge pecan trees that Dad had planted before I was born. In the midst of those trees I settled the issue. The next day I attended church with Mom. After the services that night as I was leaving, the church treasurer, Mrs. Walter Pagan, handed me an envelope. It was a check from Mr. and Mrs. Frank Hudson. He was county judge of Union County. The check was sufficient to take care of my seminary expenses that semester.

The next morning with full assurance that God was leading, I caught the bus to Ft. Worth and enrolled for classes. In a few weeks Mom resolved to sell the home and moved to Beaumont where she bought a house on Delaware Street. George came to lead a more stable life and eventually came to know the Lord.

During three years of seminary studies I was pastor of the Ebenezer Church in El Dorado. This meant traveling over 660 miles (round trip) each weekend. Fellow students sometimes traveled with me and our friendships have continued for years.

Preston served the Trinity Church in Little Rock. He and his wife Dovie Jean later served as missionaries in Argentina.

Clarence Allison was serving the Fountain Hill Baptist Church near Hamburg. He and his wife Alta would go as missionaries to Kenya, Africa.

Jack Gulledge was pastor of the First Baptist Church in Strong. Jack would work with the Sunday School Board, Southern Baptist Convention, until his retirement.

During the summer months I lived on the church field, and upon graduation in 1955, I moved to El Dorado to give fulltime service to the Ebenezer Church.

George: My Brother

This is the way I remember my brother George, the third and youngest child of John and Ida Kidd. He was just one month old when we moved from Urbana, Arkansas to Texas. George was accident prone. When he was about eighteen months old he pulled himself up at the ironing board; the iron fell off and the point struck him on the bridge of his nose. So he always bore a small scar.

The next accident resulted in the first prayer I remember uttering. He cut his foot on a hoe and it bled. I was frightened and ran behind the house, asking God to spare George's life (or something like that).

When George was about eight years old, our family dropped out of church. Our paternal grandfather Jess Patrick Kidd came to live with us. He enjoyed being a rebel and this left its imprint on his youngest grandchild. Without the stabilizing help of church attendance, grandfather's influence was lasting.

In Texas when George and I were small, we played together. On the farm in the Ozarks we worked together, but even then we formed separate friendships. When we moved back to south Arkansas, I enrolled in high school; he was not in school.

Military service separated us for some years. When I returned from the army, I continued my education; George went to work in the oil fields. When I made my decision for the ministry he was resentful. When I pastored the Calion Church he enjoyed making a scene on Saturday nights at a local tavern. Frequently Mr. Russell, the town constable and deacon of my church, would say on Sunday morning,

"Well, Pastor, I had to run your brother out of town last night."

34.

JLK

When I started to seminary in Ft. Worth my brother moved to Beaumont and there were no more conflicts between us. I became pastor of the Ebenezer Baptist Church of El Dorado, traveling every weekend from Ft. Worth. One Sunday night after services when everyone had gone home, I had just turned out the lights and was locking the doors. I noticed someone walking toward me with difficulty. It was dark and I didn't recognize the person. Within a few feet of me George said,

"Jesse, I've come to make peace with you and with God."

The drilling rig where he was working had collapsed and he was caught in the wreckage. It was a miracle that he got out with just a broken arm and leg. As soon as he could travel he drove to El Dorado. In the darkness in front of Ebenezer Baptist Church, we wept together and he gave himself to the Lord.

When we parted I drove to Ft. Worth rejoicing all the way, arriving there at dawn. George returned to Beaumont where he and George Neal lived with Mom. The following Sunday he made a profession of faith in the College Street Baptist Church in Beaumont. The church asked me to baptize him. It was an answer to a lot of prayers. From then on our relationship was beautiful, but brief.

George was working on an offshore drilling platform when I went to Brazil March 1958. He was shipping out from Port Sulphur, Louisiana. He and six other men lost their lives in an explosion, October 15, that same year. He was one month short of his thirty-second birthday.

It was a great shock to the family. The most grievous part was that he left a seven-year-old son without a father. The fact that George had finally anchored his life in Jesus Christ has been a great comfort to us.

The bodies of the men were never recovered. At the appointed time the sea will give him up. This is the hope of all believers everywhere. This wonderful hope must be shared with the whole world where without Christ, there is no hope.

And the sea gave up the dead which were in it; ...
Rev. 20:13 KJ

From the time of my commitment to Missions, to graduation in 1955, there were many conferences with Dr. Cal Guy, professor of Missions at the seminary. I consulted with Dr. Elmer West and Miss Edna Frances Dawkins, representatives of the Foreign Mission Board, Southern Baptist Convention. They periodically came to the Ft. Worth campus.

I applied to the Board to be appointed, indicating my interest in Latin America. I was warned that they were not appointing single men to Latin American countries. Dr. West suggested that I consider Africa. I made a real effort to switch my interests to Africa, but I was fully convinced that God was calling me to Brazil.

When I finally concluded there would be no appointment by the Board I tried to put my calling to Foreign Missions out of mind, but I could not. The Ebenezer Church had seen me through most of my seminary training. They had built a nice residence next to the church, and the entire growth and development were encouraging. A lot of my preaching reflected the frustration I felt in my heart. Those dear people suffered with me; never was there a congregation so patient. Most of them have gone to their reward in heaven; I owe a great debt of gratitude to them - the living and the dead.

I never gave up the idea of being a missionary. I drove from El Dorado to Ft. Worth to meet with a representative of Wycliff Bible Translators at the seminary. I came away with great admiration for Wycliff but I wanted to be involved directly in Southern Baptist mission work.

The World Missions Conference

During a World Missions Conference in Liberty Baptist Association I met Walter McNealy, a member of the visiting team of missionaries. He had learned about my desire to go to Brazil and asked the Associational Director of Missions, W.F. Couch, to set up an encounter. We met at Immanuel Baptist Church in El Dorado where we talked a long time; he invited me to join him in Brazil.

"I can only offer you a place to stay and as long as I
  have anything to eat you will eat."

I was aware of his deep sense of calling to Brazil, and I understood that he was a mover and a shaker. Brother McNealy suggested that the Central Baptist Church of Volta Redonda, where he was pastor, provide the necessary invitation and documents (as required by the Brazilian government for an American to live and work there).

It was encouraging to have such an invitation, but at the same time I was appalled to think that I might spend the rest of my life working in that arrangement. God led me into some reading to strengthen my faith. I had been diligent in Bible study and sermon preparation, but I needed a greater faith. Books on the lives of missionaries fell into my hands.

"Praying Hyde," who was an English missionary to India
"The Small Woman," about an English missionary to China
    (made into the movie Inn of the Sixth Happiness)
"Through Gates of Splendor," about Nate Saint who died at
    the hands of wild natives in Ecuador, along with his
    fellow missionaries

I wrote in the flyleaf of my Bible this statement from "Through Gates of Splendor:"

He is no fool who gives that which he cannot keep,
    for that which he cannot lose.

There were other books: "Crowded to Christ" and "Born Crucified" - both by L.E. Maxwell, founder of Prairie Bible Institute in Alberta, Canada.

Ann Wollerman
Vivid in my memory was my experience in Ouachita when I had been treasurer three years for a mission fund which aided in the support of our teacher, Miss Ann Wollerman. She had announced one day in Chapel, "I am going to Brazil even if I have to hitchhike." The students contributed to the fund and I mailed her a monthly check. I received her letters and had them mimeographed and distributed. This fund continued until she was appointed by the Board.

Bruce and June Murphy
From my own church, Ebenezer, Bruce and June Murphy and their two little boys Bruce Edward and Fred Yocum, set out for California to study in Fuller Theological Seminary. I watched Bruce overhaul a 1949 Chevrolet for the trip. They had no job nor guarantee of support; their faith stirred me deeply. (Other children born later are Timothy, Todd, and Tammy.)

My concern finally reached the crisis point and I needed to determine,

"Am I called to be a missionary only if the pay is
    guaranteed?"

I shared that question with a friend one day and he rebuked me for my (so-called) arrogance. He thought I was being haughty. But I had to decide if God had truly called me. If so, I must go!

The Promises Of God

For all the promises of God in Him are Yes,
and in Him Amen, to the glory of God through us.
                                    II Cor. 1:20 NKJ

To step out on faith one must believe. It is necessary to believe that God is worthy of our trust. We must believe that His promises will not fail.

Someone said,

> God makes a promise
> Faith believes it
> Hope anticipates it
> Patience waits quietly for it

To answer God's call to walk by faith required a step-by-step transition from a casual belief in what I had been taught through the years, to a firm commitment of my life to faith in Him and His plan for my life.

There were countless hours of prayer and study of God's Word. Day by day His promises became more real to me. There was a growing confidence in the fact that I could trust them implicitly. I had been taught that "All Scripture is given by inspiration of God," (II Tim. 3:16 NKJ). God was equipping me for what He had called me to do.

I also believed that "the word of God is living and powerful, and sharper than any two-edged sword," (Heb. 4:12 NKJ). God's Word was operating in me to take away doubts, fear, and weakness. He was preparing me for service. The conclusion of it all can be summed up:

> **Your words were found, and I ate them.**
>   **And Your word was to me**
> **the joy and rejoicing of my heart;**
>   **For I am called by Your name,**
>   **O Lord God of hosts.**
>   **Jer. 15:16 NKJ**

A Ticket on the Steamship Del Mundo

November 1957, five years after I became pastor of Ebenezer Church, I resolved to take the step of faith that would lead me to Brazil: I resigned that dear church.

My last day passed with grace and poise, although it was not easy. After the Sunday evening service I met with the young people for youth fellowship. A call came that Mrs. Mamie Turlington had died. Only a few days before, she had lamented my departure, saying,

"Who is going to care for us when you are gone?"

39.

JLK

The family asked me to conduct the funeral service. It was almost more than I could handle as I thought back over the five years of my pastorate. Once I looked back at Brother John Burton who was assisting, thinking I might have to ask him to continue the service. But his presence and an encouraging look took me through. I was saying "Farewell" to a church that had borne with me through many difficult hours; I was saying "Goodbye" to Ebenezer.

When I sold my car and closed out my accounts, there was nothing left with which to buy a ticket to Brazil. I said nothing to anyone about it and took a bus to Beaumont (my trip was not a happy one). There was a lot of time to reflect about my missionary venture.

When I arrived at Mom's house she handed me two letters. One was from Mr. Arthur Simmons of Urbana (son of the preacher my mother went to hear in the Philadelphia Church when she was a child). The other letter was from the Stagg family of Eunice, Louisiana, and Beaumont. Each letter contained a check, the sum being adequate to pay for freighter passage from New Orleans to Rio de Janeiro, Brazil.

I booked passage on the S.S. Del Mundo from New Orleans. When it docked at Beaumont I put my freight and baggage on board and two weeks later, February 27, 1958, I myself boarded at New Orleans. My family wanted to give me all the encouragement they could and came to see me off: Mom and George Neal; Willie Mae and Rex; nieces Rexene and Curtis Ann and my nephew Johnny.

The Doubts - The Victory
As the ship got under way I realized that questions and doubts were still with me; they had not been left behind. About midpoint on the voyage I had some deep anxieties. Late one night when other passengers had gone to bed, I took my Bible and climbed to the top deck where I could be alone.

I wrestled with my own thoughts for a long time. Actually I was asking again all the questions I thought I had settled. A strong wind began to blow the pages of my Bible so I put my hand on it to hold it still. I looked down and a verse seemed to leap out:

I have been young, and now am old;
   Yet I have not seen the righteous forsaken,
Nor his descendants begging bread.
                              Psalm 37:25   NKJ

40.

JLK

I thought of my parents and all they had taught me. Whether I could lay claim to righteousness or not was for God to
judge. But I firmly believed that I could lay claim to that
promise because of who and what my parents had been. That
night any thought that I might ever have about my financial
security was forever settled. Never would I have to fight
that battle again.

The Message Of Love

When the ship docked in Rio de Janeiro March 19, 1958,
Walter McNealy and several from the Central Baptist Church
and its school were there to meet me. Brother McNealy handed
me a letter from the Liberty Baptist Association, back in
El Dorado. The churches there had set up a fund for my support! They had established a bank account in my name, and
their voluntary love gifts were to be deposited to my account.

Praise God, from whom all blessings flow!

Contributions began that March 1958 and continued until the
day I was appointed by the Board, March 13, 1969; eleven years!

II.

CARROLL, NEBRASKA

I was born January 26, 1922 in the farm home of my parents,
3 3/4 miles southwest of Carroll, Nebraska; the tenth child
of Robert and Ellen Gemmell. My cousin Alice Killinger Gifford
served as midwife. Dad recorded in his bookkeeping for January that Alice was paid $26.00 for "nurse and housework."

My sister Elizabeth recalls the wonder she knew as an almost-
ten-year-old when Dad showed her the new baby. My sister Jean
recalls that she was a sophomore in high school. She says
that my brother Ralph did a lot of the caretaking. Now they
are called siblings, but I simply called them brothers and
sisters:

Donald	born July 2, buried July 19, 1898
John Richie	born August 19, 1899; died September 18, 1935
Ralph Lewis	born August 31, 1902; died October 4, 1936
Mary Elsie	born August 19, 1904
Jeanne	born June 17, 1907; died February 2, 1998
Fred Gordon	born August 5, 1910
Elizabeth Ellen	born January 28, 1912
Allan Andrew	born October 31, 1914; died January 2, 1924
Jessie Martha	born March 31, 1918

Note: Jeanne (now Jean) was not given a middle name at
birth and she longed for one. She would select a possible
name and spend pages of tablet paper writing it. Dad told
her she could have one, but it must be Margaret. Thus she
was named after Dad's Scotch family.

Mother was almost forty-six years old when I was born; her
birth was January 28, 1876 at Avon (Fulton County), Illinois.
Dad was fifty-six years old; he was born June 15, 1865 in Glas-
gow, Scotland.

Our rural neighborhood represented the stable, industrious,
aggressive citizenry of Wayne County, or the backbone of the
development of Nebraska, which is called the "Breadbasket of
the World."

Immigrants from Europe had come to build their fortunes
and establish their roots in wonderful America. They and
their children formed the strengths of our farming community.
Their fiber was of "the old country" - Wales, Scotland, England, the Scandinavian Peninsula, Poland, Germany, the Ukraine,
and other European countries. Often while we waited for an
opening on the party telephone line, our neighbors were speaking in Welsh.

Dad's Census Report as Director of School District 62 (June
11, 1923), records these names: Griff Edwards, John Frances,
David E. James, Ole Olson. Ward Williams, Tim Collins, Edwin
Davis, John Davis, Herb Shufelt, Richard Ellrich, John M. Peter-
sen, Charles Linn, Elmer Fisher, and Homer Ross.

WAK

There was a consideration for people of other countries in-
grained in me from birth; also a high standard of honesty and
service to others; a pride in the community; a determination
to seek a better way of life. Neighbors helped neighbors.
Mrs. Roberts was usually the midwife for Mother. No matter
what the season or circumstance, all helped the one in need.
Whenever a neighbor or church member had a crisis, my parents
were there to help.

In our home the family altar was as much a part of our daily
life as the rising of the sun. We'd distribute the Bibles;
Dad nearly always read, then we knelt at our chairs and he or
Mother led in prayer. We always closed by praying the Lord's
Prayer out loud. (For me, there was a lot of peeking through
the chair back, and daydreaming.) When gathering for a meal,
and before the serving dishes were touched, Mother or Dad always
led in a prayer of thanksgiving to God.

Oat Thrashing

When oat thrashing time came the farmers formed a team,
moving from farm to farm to help each other. When the team
came to our farm, Mother needed all hands possible in the
kitchen to prepare the noon meal. We set up the washbowl outside - water, soap, and towels. Coming from the heat, dust,
and debris from the grain, the men eagerly washed up, lather-
ing face, neck, hair, arms, and rinsing with more cold water.

They hungrily served themselves at the tables set up in
the yard. Potatoes, fresh garden vegetables, homemade bread
and home-churned butter, fried chicken, or pork from the store
of canned food in our cellar. Gravy. Cake or homemade pie;
pie plant (rhubarb) sauce, and drinks of hot coffee or lemonade made from store-bought lemons.

After the noon meal the men soon went to their work. In
the hot afternoon we carried beverages to them in fruit jars -
lemonade, coffee, or water.

Gathering Eggs

When I was sent to gather the eggs, I was afraid that the
setting hens would peck me. Those others who were just linger-
ing on the nest could easily be chased off. The collected
eggs were laid carefully in my bucket. I enjoyed handling
the fresh eggs, delightedly "lifting" them from the hens'
hiding places or from the nests.

When the sky darkened, the wind arose, and the scent of
rain was strong, I was sent to round up the mother hen with her
baby chickens. If I couldn't get them in, Mother came running,
flapping her apron up and down to corral that squawking, skitter-
ish mama and her wild brood. Those minutes before the rain,
wind, or hail struck were tense and wild as the animals and
fowls were driven and herded into pens and barns.

46.

Fuel For The Stoves

The woodbox by the kitchen stove always seemed to be empty. My sister Jessie and I were often sent for fuel: manageable pieces of wood for maintaining continuous, steady heat in the cookstove; kindling for starting the fire; and larger, heavier pieces for the heater in the dining room. Sometimes we scouted in the trees west of the house or in the orchard to the east, looking for kindling and firewood. Dad valiantly tried to keep the stacks of chopped wood from dwindling.

Sometimes there was a pile of clean, dry cobs which the large corn sheller spewed out. Then there was the hand operated corn sheller. Ordinarily one person turned the handle and when the needed speed was reached, another fed the ears of corn, one after another. I considered it a challenge to hand feed _and_ to turn. Consequently my middle finger, right hand, is scarred from shoving one ear in too far.

When Dad moved the hogs from the hogpen so it would dry, we were sent to pick up the corncobs there. They were messy and the job was smelly, but when dried out, those corncobs made good fuel for the cookstove.

There were some disagreements between us two girls about who was to do what - when. Nonetheless, we have grown up into two agreeable, reasonable, women.

The Separator

The milk separator, which required daily washing, was my nemesis. Each part had to be washed separately - by cold water, then soapy water, then scalded in hot water. How many disks were there that fit systematically into the other? I could dismantle the disks, but I always required help in putting them back together.

My brother Fred whistled as he brought the buckets of fresh milk from the barn. There was a peace in the barn during milking time - the rhythmic ping-ping of the stream of milk into the bucket; Fred as he whistled; and the distinctive language that "bossie" liked to hear as the milker talked to her. Cats stayed nearby because they knew it was feeding time.

At the house some whole milk was kept out for drinking and cooking. The other bucketsful were lifted and poured into the separator basin. One container was set in place for the "skimmed" milk; another for the cream. A stand-by person needed to be there to switch containers as they filled, and to replenish the basin with whole milk. Fred whistled as he turned the separator handle in steady rhythm.

The cream was carried to the cellar to cool; some of it to be sold in town, rendering a needed income. Dad's bookkeeping February 1923 shows they sold 169 pounds, netting $25.42. They also sold four dozen eggs for $.98.

WAK

The skimmed milk was used for slopping the hogs or feed-ing the calves. Whoever fed the calves had to know their bus-iness. If the bucket were not held just so and if the calf were not coaxed by the hand in the milk, the calf would toss its head and the milk would spew all over. Fred let me hold the bucket only after the calf had been quieted. Fred was active in 4-H, raising hogs for sale and showing them and his calves at county and state shows.

Ashes

Sometimes I could be persuaded to carry out the ashes. For the cookstove you simply pulled out the ash pan and car-ried it outside, being careful not to burn yourself if the ash-es were still hot. For the heater you needed a flat, metal pan shallow enough to go under the stove, into which you raked the ashes. The ash rake was a long, slim handle with a rectan-gular piece of metal on the end. Care was needed if the stove were still hot. Then the ashes were dumped into the coal bucket.

Ashes were carried outside to be thrown into the yard. If it were windy you got a cloud of the gray dust in your face, so you learned to test the wind for direction. The job was not done until the floor around the stoves was swept and scrubbed.

Quarantine!

In December 1923 our family was scourged by scarlet fever and diphtheria. Ralph and John were away at school, and Elsie was quarantined at the M.S. Whitney home in Carroll. There had been a heavy snow leaving high drifts and Dr. Texley of Carroll could not reach us - even by horse and wagon. He came so far, and turned back.

The townspeople were able to send a nurse to help Mother. Allan Andrew, age nine, died January 2, 1924. Dad and neigh-bors chopped his grave in the frozen soil at the Carroll ceme-tery. For many years after, Dad would hold me on his lap and talk about his grief for his little, blond-headed Allan.

An infected place on my right thigh abscessed, and I still bear the scar. My abscessed ears have been years in healing. In winter they ran, and not having money to buy cotton swabs, I did the best I could with a white cotton rag, mopping at the running pus.

I had blond, curly hair, and since my head was tender, the suggestion of hairbrush, soap, or water, sent me flying under the bed, screaming. One day when my cousin Alice Killinger Gifford was visiting, Mother had her cut my curls. In my childhood and into early adulthood, cold weather brought in-fected and running ears. I was twenty-one in September 1943, when I moved to Fort Worth, Texas. The change in climate brought blessed relief for the ears and sinus.

WAK

In 1966 in Rio de Janeiro, Dr. Atherino performed a tympanoplasty on the left ear, which was considered successful. However, scarred eardrums are still a part of my life. Interest
and participation in music, and ministry through music - are
evidence of the miracle of God's lovingkindness to me.

Washday

How meticulously my mother cared for the family laundry!
Her day started early; heating the boiler of water on top of
the cookstove and mixing the rice pudding (washday lunch)
for the oven. The white things were boiled in the oblong-
shaped boiler, and stirred by a strong, wooden stick.

The soap had to be cut into small pieces and dissolved in
a little hot water - whether it were Mother's homemade lye
soap or P & G (Proctor and Gamble) store-bought bars. After
boiling the white things, the hot boiler was lifted from the
stove so the laundry could be processed through the washing
machine and rinse tubs. Our wooden washing machine was hand
powered. To move the agitator, you grasped the lever on the
outside and forced it back and forth, back and forth. Bluing was added to the first rinse water for the white things.
The laundry was forced through a hand operated wringer - and
this is where we children were needed - to guide the things so
they didn't bunch up. The rinse water in the aluminum tubs
was changed when it got too soapy.

All the soapy water was saved - not because of a shortage
but because it was so good for scrubbing. First, the Sears
and Roebuck, or Montgomery Ward catalogues were removed from
the toilet. The wooden seats, walls, and floor were scrubbed
until they were bleached. The kitchen floor, back porch,
and walkways were scrubbed forcefully. Between wash days,
the wooden washing machine had to have water in it so it
would not dry out and leak.

If possible, in winter the laundry was hung outside on the
lines to freeze - and it dried some. We watched from windows
painted by Jack Frost as the stiff, frozen clothing and linens
danced in the wind. To gather it, we wrestled with the unbend-
ing, wonderfully sweet smelling linens, overalls, underwear,
shirts, dresses, and long stockings, trying to get it into the
house to dry on lines strung in the kitchen and dining room.
I long for the distinctive scent of frozen long underwear and
flannel nightgowns.

Mother made an ironing board of the table by spreading sheets
or flannel blankets. The sadirons were grouped at the hottest
place on the cookstove. For testing, you wet a finger with
tongue, and sssst, lightly touched one. Then you attached the
handle and lifted it. Mother could fly through the ironing
with skill, making it all look beautiful. The sweet, clean
aroma filled the house.

49.

WAK

My brother John sent his dirty laundry home from Lincoln
where he was studying at the university. Once when Mother
brought his brown, canvas suitcase from the mailbox and dumped
the clothes on the floor, there was candy for the little sisters. Afterward, I was a careful watchdog of that suitcase!

The bag went back full of clean clothes. The shirts were
starched, ironed, and folded, smelling so fresh. Mother
watched for the mailman and carried the bag down the incline
from the house and out the lane to the mailbox. She often
shared her warm, freshly baked bread with the mailman. We'd
watch for him on the road, and meet him with her gift.

Butchering

When the weather was cool enough Dad made preparations for
butchering a hog. He sharpened the knives on the rotary,
foot-operated grindstone. We stacked wood in the kitchen by
the cookstove. Dad prepared the pulley for raising and lower-
ing the animal. Outdoor tables were built, where the meat
would be cut. Containers for the intestines and organs were
made ready. We washed glass jars and crocks and scalded them.
Water was heated for scalding the hog.

Dad would bring the animal to the slaughtering place and
slit its throat. After the bleeding and squealing slowed, a
hard blow to the head brought death. It was hung by its hind
legs and maneuvered into the scalding water, then placed con-
veniently for scraping. When Dad removed the intestines and
organs he was very, very careful not to cut the intestinal
membrane, thus avoiding contamination. At last, the clean
carcass was suspended and left to cool.

After cooling, Dad lowered the hog onto the cutting boards
and dressed it. Portions were set aside for the neighbors.
As soon as a pan of meat could be cut up, we'd run to the kitch-
en with it for Mother to process in the frying pans. She ren-
dered leaf lard into cracklings.

Mother filled the jars and crocks with fried meat and hot
lard. When sealed and cooled, we stored them in the cellar.
By evening we were exhausted, yet we relished the meal of
succulent fried tenderloin or liver.

WAK   **Women's And Girls' Life**

In summer we gathered fruit and vegetables and canned as
much as possible. Harvesting mulberries was fun time, when
we spread sheets under the tree and shook the boughs. One of
us would lay on her back to see how many berries she could
capture in her open mouth. A sauce dish of raw berries topped
with sweet cream and sugar was delicious!

We picked and processed cherries, apples, crabapples, plums,
and rhubarb. It was hot outside, and we complained about it
when we were perched on ladders, trying to balance ourselves
and a bucket, and picking fruit while the juice ran down our
arms. It was hot inside where the cookstove raised the temperature unbearably. We cooked apple sauce and apple butter,
jelly, fruit preserves, and crabapple pickles; cherry, rhubarb,
and mulberry sauce and sweet, tomato preserves. Then the filled,
sealed jars testified to the victories, and Mother carefully
counted them. This was next winter's tasty food!

The garden yielded tomatoes, lettuce, peas, new potatoes,
cucumbers, carrots, onions, and cabbage. Young field corn
was a delicacy. The fall garden yielded potatoes, rutabagas,
parsnips, turnips, squash, and pumpkins. We gathered the
black walnuts which fell under the trees.

Spring house cleaning was exciting. We moved the heater to
a corner, removed the stovepipe and cleaned and stored it.
The stovepipe for the cookstove was removed, cleaned, and replaced. Mother and my sisters tore off loose wallpaper, and
re-papered walls and ceilings. I could help a little bit.
I cooked the flour paste and spread it on the wallpaper, and
helped to measure the strips. When we completed a room we'd
bask in the clean, newly decorated appearance.

We children ran errands: borrow - or return - bread at the
neighbor's house. Take - or get - mail at the end of the lane.
Intercept a neighbor on his way to town, so he could do an
errand for us.

We helped care for and clean the house. It took two of us
to roll the living room rug, carry it outside, and wrestle it
onto the clothesline where we beat the dirt out with the rug
beater. The reservoir on the cookstove, the teakettle and
dishpan required filling with water. Mother had to prime the
pump at the sink if the leather dried or froze. There was a
pump outside, too. Lamp wicks required trimming, and the lamps
needed to be cleaned and filled with kerosene. The slop bucket
under the sink always seemed full, needing to be carried out.

It was nicer to be outside. Help plant potatoes, and harvest them. Help weed the garden or harvest vegetables and
fruit. Scoop snow and sweep the walk. Hang around the barns
and pens, watching the men, or escape to the hayloft, where
we dreamed and played, bouncing in the hay and savoring its
pungency. The swing hung from the cottonwood tree. There,
Jessie and I drew lines in the dirt, outlining our playhouse.

51.

Sleighride!

When the snow was right (especially if covered by frozen sleet) and we kids were home from school, we went sleighriding. My parents knew that as long as it was light enough, or if the moon were bright, they weren't going to corral anyone in the house. We only came in to change wet clothing for dry, or if darkness and hunger drove us inside.

The area around the dining room heater was crowded with wet mittens and pants, steaming as they dried. The kitchen cookstove had a warming oven above, where we kept the spiders (skillets) and salt and pepper. The top of that warming oven and the doors pulled down, made good, warm surfaces for drying wet mittens.

In school among your peers, if you wanted to gain more popularity, you sported a long sled. "Flyer" was a popular word used in the brand name, painted in bright caption on the varnished, wood body of the sled. The runners, of course, must be polished to a silver patina from use.

At our home school there was time at recess for only one slam down the hill and trudging back in time for the bell.

If you sit up on the sled you use the feet for guiding. If you lay on your stomach, you steer with your hands. The "name of the game" was for one sled to accommodate as many humans as possible; but if there were too many and the weight was unbalanced, the sled swayed until it ditched. And the bodies rolled.

If we didn't have sleds, or if they were being repaired, we'd try to find a big, tin sign. We could sort of hold up the two corners at the front to prevent them from digging in. "Happiness" was speeding down the ice-covered hill on a piece of tin! Often the sign slid one way and we went another!

When I was small someone hauled me out through the lane and up the first hill. Jessie sat me on the sled at the top of the field and before she could get on to guide it, I went slithering over the icey surface. Jessie yelled, "Lay down!" but I was too terrified and as I went under the barbwire fence it grazed my scalp. Jessie pulled me on the sled to the house as blood poured over my face. Fortunately the cut healed well, leaving a slight scar in the scalp.

The Carroll Baptist Church

Sunday School and church attendance at the Carroll Baptist Church were simply part of our Sunday. Also there were Young People's and Ladies' Aid meetings. Our transportation was horseback, buggy, wagon, wagonbox on sleigh runners, or Model T Ford.

Santa Claus came at the church. He brought the children wonderful presents. He brought a doll and a doll buggy for me. There were parties and wedding showers at the church.

There was always Mrs. I.O. Jones. She stood in front of us little ones as we sat in the pew with our legs swinging. She told us about Jesus; she talked funny because she was from Wales. She was short and she waddled when she walked but that didn't make any difference; we knew she loved us.

Mrs. Jones gave us pictures of Jesus and other people of the Bible. She helped us struggle to read from the Bible. She told us that Jesus loved us. We could believe that even though we couldn't understand why He had to die on the cross.

There were two Sunday School rooms in the church - one on each side of the platform. After Mrs. Jones's class, we graduated to the east room and as we got older we moved to the west one.

In Sunday School we gave our money for "the Lord's work." One day my sister Elsie, who was leading the Sunday School, told us that we were either blue or red. The blues were to compete against the reds in bringing visitors to Sunday School. I looked at my arms and thought, "Why is she saying that I'm colored? I'm neither blue nor red!"

School - Music - Literature

I started to school in September 1927, when I was five. The Gemmell school was on top of the second hill east of our house; named because so many of my family studied there. Dad served on the three-man school board. White sweet clover still grows on the grounds, and those steep hills have never been reduced! When I return to that vacant school yard the clover smells the same, the ground still has gopher holes, and the breeze is still strong.

Mother insisted that we eat a hot breakfast before leaving in the morning. Then we'd gather books, school supplies, dinner buckets; put on wraps (overshoes if needed), and start out the lane. Pulling the first hill was not so bad, but climbing the second, steeper hill was harder. We'd race against the "late" bell. We hung wraps, arranged dinner buckets in place and gulped a drink of water, hopefully arriving at our desks before the final bell.

WAK

I had heard "education" preached by Mother, so I knew that
discipline was expected. Miss Burson was my first teacher;
she was strict, and she wore long, dark colored skirts. When
she required that I stand in the corner, I was duly impressed
that her students didn't lean back and put their feet on top
of the desks. I have heard educated, prominent men state that
they treasured having been in one-room, eight-grade schools
where they learned invaluable lessons.

Mother's education philosophy reached our neighbor, Ruby
Davis. Elizabeth and Fred went to high school in the buggy,
going one-fourth mile extra to pick her up in the mornings,
and to take her home in the afternoon.

Music and literature were part of our lives. We literally
wore out the hand-wound Victrola record player on the light-
oak stand. Dad's bookkeeping shows he purchased many phonograph needles. We played the records until they were scratchy
and raucous:

    Madame Ernestine Schumann-Heinck
    Alma Gluck
    Harry Lauder singing Scotch songs
    Harry Lauder laughing and giggling
    Military Marches by John Philip Sousa

Elsie says that Dad gave the girls runt pigs to raise; the
proceeds from their sale helped pay for the organ. Elsie
studied piano with Dr. Phillips' wife and she says that our
cousin Edith Killinger taught the girls to play hymns.

Dad bought the upright Schiller piano in Sioux City, Iowa
for $265.00 on September 25, 1916. He brought it in the wagon
on its final miles. Elizabeth and Jessie studied piano from
the Etude music magazines which came in the mail. The keyboard
duets in them progressed from a simple tune to a very difficult
variation. As my sisters played, they started giggling and
heckling, continuing until they collapsed in uncontrollable
laughter! Rarely did they finish a duet.

The family sang together upon the slightest inspiration,
and always when we had company. Mother would coax until
Jessie and I sang duets or solos. Dad occasionally went to
plays and concerts in Wayne, the county seat, or in Sioux City.
He often read to us. One of his favorite poems was "Cuddle
Doon," in Scotch dialect, by Alexander Anderson.

Mother sang "Give The Flowers To The Living." Jessie and I
remember:
            Give the flowers to the living;
               Let sweet fragrance fill the air.
            Let us show appreciation
               Pure and white as lily fair.
Chorus: Music, flowers, sunshine hours, -

WAK

Box suppers in neighboring country schools were popular.
Readings, quartets, duets, solos and choirs were presented.
Once a girl dressed as a doll was carried onto the stage
in a life-size box. The bearers set the box upright; the
"doll" stepped out and mimed the song as the men sang. Jessie
recalls the words. (Remember, dolls' bodies were cloth stuffed
with sawdust.)

> I've got a pain in my sawdust,
> That's what's the matter with me.
> Something is wrong with my little insides;
> I'm just as sick as can be.
> Don't let me faint, someone get me a fan;
> Somebody run for the medicine man!
> Everyone hurry as fast as you can,
> 'Cause I've got a pain in my sawdust!

Boxes packed with sandwiches, cake, and fruit had been prepared by the women; each was about the size of a large shoe
box. They were artfully decorated with fluted crepe paper,
cutouts, and small objects, reflecting the season or a
theme. The boxes were to be auctioned off, with proceeds
going to the host school.

At refreshment time before the auctioneer sold a box,
he held it up and extolled its beauty and originality.
A buzz would pass through the room as people speculated
about who had made it. The husband or boyfriend would
have been briefed, so he knew how to bid and claim the
box. But pseudo rivalry and competition made the bidding
exciting. Finally, each family "won" its own box!

Hard times came and the folks had to leave the home farm. They lost the place and had to let Dad's life insurance policy lapse. It must have been March 1 of 1929 when we moved to Carroll; I was in the second grade. In town school there were four rooms for grades one through eight. I remember a favorite teacher, Miss Adams. She played the piano; at a parents' meeting she played a solo with her left hand! Music study was part of the school curriculum, and I loved it.

Dad kept as many farm implements and tools as he could accommodate on our rented place, along with his team of horses and some cows. He earned as much as possible by small jobs people asked him to do, and plowing gardens in the spring. Mother sold eggs and cream, and rented out some of the first-floor rooms.

We lived at the northern edge of Carroll, west of Main Street. We girls walked to school at the other end of town. This meant we crossed the railroad tracks four times daily. I respected that monster steam engine, learning to judge if I could "make it" before it descended upon me. I had greater respect for the weed burner as it passed on the tracks, spraying the weeds with a black, oily substance smelling like creosote.

We didn't have to go to Main Street to cross the tracks; we could do that near our house, but we'd have to pick our way through the black, oily residue left by the weed burner. Have you ever tried to clean creosote spots off shoes and clothing?

We barely had time to race home from school for lunch, gulp a few bites, and hurry back, trying not to be late. One winter morning the temperature was fifteen degrees below zero! However I escaped frostbite by covering my face with a heavy scarf.

When we didn't have cash Mr. M.S. Whitney allowed us to buy groceries on credit, hopefully to be paid off the next spring. Owing the Whitneys haunted me for years. I believe Mr. Whitney simply wrote off any final debt. Their son Charles and daughter Lauretta married my siblings Elsie and Ralph.

My brother John who lived in Colorado was thoughtful of Mother, Dad, Elizabeth, Jessie, and me. One Christmas he sent us a box of toys! What excitement! Some whirled; some spun; some ran; some tooted; they jumped, scooted, and crawled. Another Christmas John sent a complete set of pink dishes with flowers and gold trim. They were our treasured "good dishes."

My sister Jean and her husband Harold made it a Christmas custom to send home a box of homemade candy - divinity, fudge, penuche (brown sugar fudge) and carmelized popcorn. My brother Fred sometimes sent me school supplies; I proudly wore a pair of white mittens, a gift from him.

Jesus Christ, My Savior

We had a large, two-story house. I'd get one of the much used Bibles and sneak upstairs to read. I knew that hiding away from Mother's voice was wrong, but I reasoned that since I was reading the Bible, sneaking was all right.

No matter where I read of Jesus' suffering for man's sins, in the Old or New Testament, I had the same reaction; I'd cry. When I got to where Jesus was crucified, I'd cry hard. Then I'd cry for joy when reading about His resurrection. Finally, I'd turn to His last command in Matthew.

> **Go ye therefore, and teach all nations, baptizing them in the name of the Father, and of the Son, and of the Holy Ghost:**
> **Teaching them to observe all things whatsoever I have commanded you: and, lo, I am with you alway,**
> **even unto the end of the world. Amen.**
> **Matt. 28:19,20 KJ**

In the Old Testament I liked to read about Moses and the "children" of Israel. There were so many, many questions to ask Mother, who had a marvelous understanding of the Bible.

"If Jesus were a Jew, and said he was the Messiah, why did the Jews crucify Him?"

"Why couldn't Moses go into the Promised Land?" "Why not?"

I loved our church building. There was a mysterious beauty inside and outside - the stained glass windows; the blond, oak pews with carved arm rests; and the full basement with its huge furnace and complete kitchen. There were wide steps leading up to the front door that gave distinction to the light tan, brick building with its stately belfry.

There was a piano in the church auditorium, but we didn't have a pianist. Mother told me to play for Sunday School, and although I had not studied piano, I did the best I could; everything went well as long as the song was in the key of F!

Mother sometimes sent me to the church to clean it when a visiting pastor was expected. Once, as I went in the front entrance, the stairs leading to the basement caught my attention, for they were dusty and musty. So I decided to clean them first. With pan of water and rag, I mopped to the bottom. Then I thought the basement looked dusty and musty. With pans of water and rag, I scrubbed the whole basement on hands and knees. I thought this was honoring God's house.

At home Mother asked how I was progressing, and I promised her I'd dust and sweep the auditorium. I never got it done for it grew too dark. Mrs. Pearson had to come early Sunday morning to dust the pews and pulpit, to receive the preacher.

WAK

    We moved to another house on the same street, but east of
Main Street. Rev. Braistedt was pastor of the Wayne Baptist
Church (twelve miles away) and he came to preach. He was a
frequent visitor at our house. Once I was wrestling with a
washtub of dirty dishes - Mother had set them outside by the
pump, commanding me to wash them. Then up drove Rev. Braistedt!
I was so embarrassed to be found in a mess, and because I was
wearing overalls without a blouse.

    Rev. Braistedt talked to Mother and Dad about Jessie's and
my relationship to the Lord, then he talked to us together.
He explained carefully and tenderly:

Who Jesus was - the Son of God.

Why Jesus came to earth - to show people, as the Son of
God, what God was like.

What sin was - falling short of being and doing the best
that God would have us to be and do.

Why Jesus died on the cross - as a sacrifice to pay for
our sins.

He asked us if we believed that Jesus died for our sins. We
said "Yes."

He asked us if we believed that Jesus loved us. "Yes."

He asked us if we understood that since we believed, then
when we died we would go to heaven to be with the resurrected
Jesus. We answered, "Yes."

He explained that since we had expressed these beliefs, we
had "accepted Jesus Christ as our Savior and that He now lived
in our hearts." He then said we would pray together, and he
talked to God. In his prayer he thanked God for Jessie's and
Wilma's believing hearts.

    He talked to us about baptism, so we both planned to be
baptized. Easter is a beautiful time to do this, but that
day in Nebraska can be very, very cold. Baptism is done
thus: the pastor goes into the baptistry (or river) - into
the water. The one to be baptized then goes in and stands
in front of the pastor. With one hand supporting your back
and the other clasping your hands, he lays you into the water -
on your back. He then immediately lifts you to standing position. This is a testimony, or a demonstration of:

    1. Jesus' death
    2. His burial
    3. His resurrection

58.

WAK

I wrote to John November 25, 1933 telling him that I was baptized in the Carroll Baptist Church August 27, 1933 when I was eleven.

> "Last Sunday afternoon Rev. Braistedt, pastor of Wayne Baptist Church held COMMINION in our church, and Bonnie Herley, Verona Pearson, Fern Herley, Jessie and I received the hand of fellowship. All five of us were baptized August 27. Last Sunday we received our certificates of BAPTIZM too."

After the preaching and communion service that day, the church members shook hands with us, expressing welcome to the church - this was the "hand of fellowship." I recall these precious ones who were church members sometime during my childhood, some of whom could have been there:

Elizabeth	Mr. and Mrs. Hurley
Elsie	Mr. and Mrs. Robert Pritchard
Mother and Dad	Mr. and Mrs. James Eddie
Mr. and Mrs. Grant Young	Mr. and Mrs. Fred Wilcox
Mr. and Mrs. I.O. Jones	Grace Jones
Mr. and Mrs. Glen Wilcox	Mr. and Mrs. Ellery Pearson
Mrs. Hurlburt	

Home Life

Elsie was a skilled seamstress. As she sewed for her children June, Donald, and Merle, she often sewed for me. She used her tailoring skills and made a beautiful, tan wool coat for me. Elsie thoughtfully cared for our personal needs.

Ralph's wife Lauretta was artistic in her intricate embroidery, garment making, and crafts. She gave me a beautiful length of dress material - dark brown, crinkled rayon. She helped to choose a flattering style and then sewed the lovely garment, which I cherished.

How would one measure Mother love? There was almost no money, but Mother somehow ordered fabric from the catalogue for new dresses for me. She would talk the shoe clerk in a Wayne store into charging my new shoes, then she'd pay them out when she had money. One Christmas she didn't have anything for me except a naked doll; she was embarrassed that she had no clothing for it.

Dad allowed the cigarette salesman (Old Gold, I think) to paste and nail their huge billboard on the corn crib, highly visible from the road. Mother reacted in anger and resentment. She placed a ladder and put me to work to dismantle the abhorrent advertising. I needed to soak a small section until I could scratch or peal it away.

WAK
    There were thousands of nails. The claw hammer couldn't
catch the nail head until I dug at it with a screwdriver.
The nail couldn't be dropped to the ground, so it went into my
pocket. Balancing on the ladder with one hand was easy, but
handling a bucket of water, rags, hammer, and screwdriver -
was precarious and dangerous.

    Dad castigated Mother for putting me up on the ladder and
Mother railed at Dad for allowing the cigarette advertising.
The corn crib was never cleaned up, and remained a symbol of
the animosity between Mother and Dad. The atmosphere in my
home was bitter with their disagreements, and I wondered
how this man and woman could have lived together, producing
ten children. I felt guilty because there seemed no way I
could bring them together in love and understanding.

EAST OF TOWN

    When we moved 2 3/4 miles northeast of Carroll to an 80-acre
farm I was again in a one-room school. Elizabeth was my teacher;
also Mildred Grier who married before the end of the year;
Irene Sahs followed her. I passed the state exams for the
seventh grade in 1934 and the eighth grade in 1935 while attending that school - district 18.

    On the farm we found thousands of nails scattered in the
farmyard. Debris, old tools and machinery had been abandoned.
Dad didn't have time to pick up the nails so he encouraged me
by paying a few cents per bucketful. I'd work enthusiastically
for a time then the eagerness waned.

    I begged Dad to build a trapeze in the corn crib. Finally,
with his patience tried, he said he would build a trapeze but
it would be well built so as to be completely safe. He backed
the Model T Ford out of the crib and did what he had promised.
The imagination soared: the darling of the circus flying
through the air to the delight of the crowds below; daring impossible stunts and feats; bowing when at last she is steadied
on the high platform by her handsome partner!

    One thing Dad didn't seem to be able to teach me was to
drive a nail straight. As he built something he held the nails
in his mouth and moved rhythmically, driving one nail after
another.

    Dad taught me to sight a straight line. In the spring he
was busy plowing and harrowing, preparing the ground for planting. During those long hours in the sun and wind, Mother often
sent me to take a quart jar of water to him. Crossing the rough
ground to where he came to the end of the field, had no rhythm.
The rows didn't match my stride and sometimes I stepped on the
high part of the row, or in the low part. The unevenness set
the heavy jar of water swinging. When Dad met me he halted
the team of horses and thankfully savored the water.

60.

WAK
As he rested he explained how it was necessary to guide the team in a straight line. He did this by sighting a tree or fencepost in the distance. As he added row on row he continued sighting so the rows would be straight. I have always carried this lesson with me, for often I realize I am unconsciously sighting a line, detecting the irregularities.

Snowstorm

One winter when Dad and I were alone, a prolonged snowstorm set in. Dad only left the house to go to the barn to care for the stock. Upon returning he stomped his feet and shook the snow from cap, coat, mittens, overshoes, eyebrows and mustache. Dad and I ate well because we had cans of roast beef in the pantry, and Mother always baked bread and pies before she went to visit friends.

In the night the storm spent its fury and morning sunlight sparkled on a silent, white, cold world. Dad mounted the wagon box on the sturdy sleigh runners, then he put the wagon seat in place. We dressed warmly: long underwear, sweater, pants, coat, mittens, cap, overshoes, and scarf about the face.

Dad hitched the team to the sled, lifted me onto the seat, and tucked the horsehide blanket about me. We set out for town cross-country since the fences and roads were buried in drifts. Dad stood in the front and had to brace himself against the force of the galloping horses as he guided them by the taut reins.

Spring brings melting snow, flooding streams, and thawing ruts in the road. The Wurdeman girls and I always walked home from school together since they lived further. One spring day we came to the bridge at the bottom of the last hill to my house. How enticing was the snow which had filled in between the stream's banks. The other girls jumped from the bridge, landed in the snow, got up and returned. I jumped, but I went in feet first, and panicked as I realized I was packed tightly in the snow, with my feet in water. My companions thought it funny, and danced with glee. I could turn slightly, and finally persuaded them to go to the house for help. Dad came running and extended his strong right arm, pulling me free to safety. What an embarrassment!

David The Shepherd

When the grass in the pasture dried up we had to herd the cows on the road. Mother helped get them onto the road and I was to control how far they wandered. The heat was unrelenting, as were bugs and flies. I had read in the Bible about David as he cared for sheep. I believe God spoke to me, saying that I, too, was precious; He was very personal to me in the sun on that dusty, sweaty roadside.

61.

The Pilger Missionary Society

Mother took me to Pilger where we went to the afternoon meeting of the Missionary Society at the Baptist Church. (Pilger is about 45 miles from Carroll.) The women were studying about mission work in Africa that day, and the study magazine was passed around so we could look at the pictures. I thought, "I'd like to do mission work in Africa when I grow up."

****

My parents were still living east of Carroll when I started to high school in 1935. Elizabeth was teaching school two miles west of Carroll, so we rented a "light housekeeping" room. It was upstairs, furnished with bed, dresser, woodburning stove, table and chairs, and kitchen cabinet. The stove had space for two pans, and the bathroom was outside.

Mother brought what food she could from the farm. Elizabeth was up and away early in the morning, walking to school. We didn't eat too well because I was not interested in cooking. Elizabeth married Christmas day December 25, 1935, and the rest of that school year I stayed with Elsie and Charles.

Though He slay me, yet will I trust Him.
                                   Job 13:15a   NKJ

For I know that my Redeemer lives,
   And He shall stand at last on the earth;
                                   Job 19:25   NKJ

John

There were two tragic deaths in the family within little
more than a year. I was a freshman at Carroll High School in
September, 1935. Someone came to the school and spoke to the
principal who then came to me, telling me I was needed by my
family. As we left I was told that my brother John had died
September 18. I knew that Ralph had taken Mother and Dad to
Fort Collins, Colorado to be with John after his surgery for
ruptured appendix.

Elizabeth and I traveled with Elsie and Charles in their
car to Grand Island where we met Jessie, who came from Lincoln.
We spent the night with the Smith family, parents of my brother-in-law Harold; then traveled on to Fort Collins. We lovingly greeted Edith, John's wife who was caring for their two
small children Laurel Anne and Allan.

At the funeral Martha Norris, sister of Elizabeth's fiance
Charles Norris, sang "Sweet Peace, The Gift of God's Love."
There were many carnations, and for years I could not bear
the perfume of carnations. John's and Edith's Christian
friends thoughtfully testified that John was in heaven.

My parents' pride and hope had been in John. He was district manager for Union Central Life Insurance Company. He
was converted at the age of twelve, and taught a boys' Sunday
School class fifteen years. He sang in the church choir and
was a deacon. He belonged to the Ft. Collins civic chorus
and was a Mason and a Lion; also, Scout Master.

When we returned home shortly after the funeral, family and
friends far and wide shared with Mother and Dad their faith
in God's wisdom and mercy and their confirmation that John
was in heaven with Jesus.

Mother told me that shortly before John's death, the doctor
told her and Dad they could spend time with John (although
they knew he was dying). John begged them to live and witness for Christ and to be sure that Christ was a reality in
their lives.

By October 1936 we had moved back to Carroll - that was when Fay Hurlburt came to the high school to get me. As we walked home she told me that my sister-in-law Lauretta had telephoned from Park River, North Dakota, telling her parents that Ralph had been killed instantly in an automobile accident October 4, about forty-five miles west of Park River.

She and the three baby girls were being brought to Carroll. Funeral services were to be in the Wayne Baptist Church. Again, we were suffering together in grief. Christian messages of condolence poured in, and the townspeople were there to help.

After John's death Mother and Dad had depended heavily on Ralph, and he was a loving, compassionate son. How could such a promising young man be cut down? He was in Civil Service as an Associate Soil Scientist in the Federal Agricultural Department. He was in charge of the Soil Department (Soil Conservation Service) at Park River, North Dakota.

In 1912 he was baptized in the Carroll Baptist Church. He served as Sunday School superintendent, president of Lincoln, Nebraska, Baptist Young People's Union, and secretary of that organization for northeast Nebraska. At the University of Nebraska he was president of the Palladian Literary Society. When he and Lauretta lived at Wayne, he was a junior deacon in the Wayne Baptist Church.

The brother I knew often chugged into our lane at the home farm in his Model T Ford truck. I'd excitedly run to him and he'd swing me upon his shoulders, calling me by my nickname, "Billy." While he attended the University in Lincoln he worked during summers in the state Soil Survey Department, in the areas of Clay Center, Stanton, Long Pine, Hebron, Hartington, Niobrara, Valentine, Trenton, Loup City, Ord and Stuart. Ralph took "us kids" on a wonderful outing at a cabin near Long Pine: Lois Killinger, cousin; Wayne and Doris Gannon, second cousins; Jessie and me. Jessie and I remember this as a high point of our youth.

Lauretta chose to live in Carroll and care for her three small daughters Joyce Arden, Janice Renee, and Lynel Gay. My parents' grief was comforted by her nearness and her devotion to the three girls.

The loss of the home farm was a terrible blow; but nothing compared with the loss of two wonderful sons. Although Mother and Dad grieved, they were absolutely steadfast in their faith in God. They had looked to John and Ralph in hope and confidence; but they looked beyond to their God, proclaiming that He was in His heaven; that He was the Good Shepherd; that He had provided Jesus, Savior of both Ralph and John.

During high school days there wasn't much going on at the
Baptist Church besides Sunday School and occasional preaching,
so I sang in the adult choir at the Methodist Church and went
to Epworth League Sunday evenings. There, I learned about the
founding of the Methodist Church.

The Vacation Bible School at that church needed one more
faculty member, so for two weeks I taught the Intermediates
from Genesis. Mother and Dad helped me in preparation; they
got me up in the mornings, and on my way to the church. Mother
always prepared lunch.

High school days were exciting and challenging. I played
trombone in the band, then moved to clarinet. Glee club was
more fun. June Pearson and I were the only Baptists.

My father was an avid reader. He subscribed to the Saturday Evening Post, Omaha World Herald, Capper's Farmer, Wayne
Herald, and the Nebraska Farmer. When he read interesting
articles, stories or poems he'd explain them to me. We spent
hours at the kitchen table studying a map, a story, a picture.
He loved stories in Saturday Evening Post about sailing vessels.

I have a copy of "One Hundred and One Famous Poems" - cover-
less, dog-eared, with loose pages; and I imagine that some
of those rhyming lines have almost been "read off the page."
"A Psalm of Life" by Henry Wadsworth Longfellow and "The Raven"
by Edgar Allan Poe, call to mind that Dad nurtured my interest
in that book. He had given me Robert Louis Stevenson's "A
Child's Garden of Verses" one Christmas before I could read.
1919-1923 he was Director of the 3-man board of District 62
school (as recorded in the Director's Journal).

During my high school years Dad spent many hours beside
me on the piano bench. I didn't have a boy friend and he
didn't have a farm to maintain. I couldn't read sharps and
flats so he sounded out the melody and I'd try to match with
the right keys. The Scotch songs were dear to him:

    Loch Lomond   Annie Laurie
    Auld Lang Syne   Robin Adair
    Comin' Through The Rye   The Campbells Are Comin'
    Flow Gently, Sweet Afton   The Blue Bell of Scotland

Others:
    March of The Men of Harlech (Welsh)
    All Through The Night (Welsh)
    Drink To Me Only With Thine Eyes (English)
    Believe Me, If All Those Endearing Young Charms (Irish)
    Londonderry Air (Old Irish Melody)

WAK

   We'd sing through the Community Song Book, never omitting
"The Bulldog On The Bank," then we'd use the hymnal. Dad sang
the melody or switched to tenor or bass. He loved music in
spite of his hearing loss - deafness in one ear. He told me
that when they lived on the home farm, one day he had a severe
pain, and although the doctor treated it, he never again heard
with that ear.

   Mother haunted the Carroll public library which was open
Saturday nights. She must have read about every book there,
but she preferred novels; one was Ben Hur. Mother also ordered
denominational literature from Judson Press, and she liked
to receive whatever was published about mission work.

   The encouragement by my parents and their expectation of
high grades, comprised a help that many high school students
missed. When I graduated from Carroll High School in spring
1939, I was valedictorian of the 20-member class. The scholarship granted tuition at any of the four state teachers colleges.

COLLEGE AND SEMINARY

Wayne State Teachers College and Teaching

In September 1939 I enrolled at the State Teachers College at Wayne. I lived in the home of Dr. and Mrs. S.A. Lutgen with four other college girls. We did house cleaning, cooking, and dishwashing for room and board. One year of the Normal course qualified me to teach a country school. Securing a school was quite competitive, so I was fortunate to be awarded a contract to teach the Gemmell school, 1940-41. There were thirteen students in the eight grades.

Before the academic year started, I went to Wayne to buy the textbooks at the specified book store. The Nebraska course of study was on the odd/even year. At the age of eighteen I was responsible for all even-year studies on four different levels: reading, mathematics, geography, english, etc. I was accountable for three seventh and eighth grade students preparing for Nebraska state exams in the spring. Howell Roberts was in the eighth grade and being very intelligent, placed third highest in the county. The other two passed.

I boarded in the Howard Ellenberg home about 2 1/2 miles from Carroll. I'd walk home Friday evening and back on Sunday afternoon. Mrs. Ellenberg (Gertie) was a fine cook and housekeeper. She always made a nice lunch for me to carry to school. (Later Gertie completed college and became a mathematics teacher.)

There were no young men lined up to strike up a friendship with me and loneliness without companionship was part of that school year. I left for school early in the morning so I could do the janitor work before the children arrived. In cold weather the teacher started the furnace in the morning, maintained it through the day, and banked it for the night. She also scooped the drifted snow at the door. I stayed after 4:00 P.M. to correct papers and make lesson plans, arriving at the Ellenbergs hopefully before dark, often carrying work to do in the evening.

There was the annual meeting of Wayne County teachers in the fall, led by the county superintendent Mr. Decker. The course of study for each of the four age levels was given to us in visual form, showing the required material for each week. I loved the actual teaching; the children were easy to work with and I loved watching their development. My sister Jessie, an experienced teacher, was my main source of help. Nonetheless, I was scared. I fearfully waited for the annual, surprise visit by Mr. Decker. I was afraid that something terrible would result from his evaluation, based on a once-a-year, ten-minute visit!

WAK

Chairman of the three-member school board, Mrs. Herman Brockman was thoughtful, considerate, and very conscientious. But characteristically, youth was unwilling to accept suggestions or to seek counsel. Without thinking of the possibility of negotiation, I spanked a sixth-grade boy, Ronald Sundahl, for disobedience.

I had admonished the children that they could take one slam down the hill on their sleds - but no more - during the fifteen-minute recess. Ronald took two. I suppose this episode was why only two of the three board members wanted me to return for a second year. I was heartbroken, but now I believe that if I had gone back I would have matured.

Ronald, the recalcitrant, was a good student. I was told in later years that he committed some crime and that he was punished by death in the electric chair (this was no comfort).

The next year, 1941-42 I taught in a school southeast of Wayne. I didn't have a car so I relied on Jessie for transportation. That year I went with a group from the Wayne Baptist Church to a Young Peoples' meeting (possibly in Beatrice). We rode in a covered pickup. The theme song was "Are Ye Able?" and the highlighted Bible verse was

And I, if I be lifted up from the earth,
     will draw all men unto me.
                    John 12:32   KJ

****

For the summer of 1942 Jessie and I went to Kansas City, Kansas to be with my sister and her family, Jean and Harold Smith and their children Marilynn, Roger, and Sharon. I had decided not to continue teaching, so I wrote to my director, asking to be released from my teaching contract.

I got a job doing housework by the day; next I packed crackers and cookies at the National Biscuit Company. This was war time when transportation was problematic. I rode with two veteran women employees, and for the first time in my life heard indescribably filthy language, abusive to my whole being. I then worked as typist at the North American Aircraft Corporation on the night shift.

Southwestern Seminary
Diploma Course

**There is a river whose streams
  shall make glad the city of God,
The holy place of the tabernacle of the Most High.
God is in the midst of her, she shall not be moved;**
                                    Psalm 46:4, 5a   NKJ

Jean and her family attended Emmanuel Baptist Church on Quindaro Boulevard, near their suburb. They loved their pastor Dr. Homer Huff, then in the military as a chaplain. I went to Emmanuel too, and one Sunday morning I had decided that the interim pastor Dr. Sipes was not interesting, so I started to walk home after Sunday School. A thought suddenly came to me with such clarity that I stopped, to fully perceive the inspiration.

**You must complete your college. You are chosen
of the Lord to serve Him in Christian work.**

It was so clearly impressed upon me that I was deliriously excited, hurrying to my sister's house and blurting out the revelation to her. Jean was raising her family in a very difficult city. Harold was a chemical engineer with the Union Pacific Railroad and traveled. The war only made life more burdensome; so Jean could not have been very excited. I sought information from Central Baptist Seminary in Kansas City, Kansas; Moody Bible Institute and the Northern Baptist Missionary Training School in Chicago.

But my inquiry to Southwestern Baptist Theological Seminary, Fort Worth, Texas, was more personal. My brother-in-law Charles Norris had finished his theological course there and Elizabeth had completed her Diploma studies - they were still there, in the process of deciding where they would move to, in Missouri.

I decided for Southwestern, and August 1943 I boarded the train for Fort Worth. I had money for $15.00 tuition, some books, and one month's room. Upon arrival I rode to the Seminary on the Hemphill city bus. At the end of the line with temerity I stepped onto the campus - bleak and seemingly uninhabited. A blisteringly hot wind was blowing, and not a blade of grass stirred - it was hot and dry. Elizabeth received me in their Seminary duplex on Townsend Drive. Later she took me to Barnard Hall on the campus, where I would live.

I ventured downtown, hoping to find employment. I opted not to work at Leonard Brothers department store, and I was hired by the Fort Worth Star Telegram to attend the classified ad counter. I believe I was hired because the paper's owner Amon Carter was a benefactor of the Seminary. When he strode through the lobby to the elevator he was immaculately clothed - always wearing his ten-gallon hat. In recent years his son was credited as a benefactor of the Seminary.

WAK

I worked eight hours Monday and Saturday and four hours
Wednesday and Friday. It took eight hours riding the city
bus, so the total is thirty-two hours weekly! But the reality
of being in the Lord's will was exhilarating and I got A-plus
in Church History, B-plus in Old Testament, and eight A's and
three B's that year.

For joining Travis Avenue Baptist Church, I wrote to Lala
Pearson in Carroll, asking for a record of my baptism. She
wrote back that it was not in the church minutes, so Travis
Avenue accepted me upon my declaration that as a Christian,
I was baptized in the Carroll Baptist Church.

The Trunk Room
One room in Barnard Hall girls' dormitory was called the
Trunk Room where the girls stored empty suitcases, makeup kits,
and trunks. It was a mess with all those things stacked hap-
hazardly from floor to ceiling, but it was the only place on
the campus where I could be alone to talk to God.

Nightly before lights out, we gathered on each floor for
prayer time. We shared our burdens and the leader asked someone to lead in prayer. But this was not satisfying, and when I
could find time I'd go into the Trunk Room and talk to God.
There I'd unburden my most intimate thoughts, many times in
tears: leaving my family; not being able to help my parents
financially; thankfulness for being at Southwestern; my salvation; how to witness for Jesus; my nieces' and nephews' salvation; and my sins - asking for forgiveness.

I had to square away with God about my salvation. I was in
the midst of young people who could talk openly and persuasively
about how, when and where they became Christians. They could
explain clearly what Jesus meant to them, while I was mutely
tongue-tied. God led me to conviction that I was saved when
Rev. Braistedt talked to me in 1933 and that my name was reg-
istered in the Book of Life in heaven.

When Barnard Hall was built it was meant to stand many years,
and there it still is, in its stately architecture. Inside,
it has been remodeled and modernized many times. It's a symbol
of many things to those who stayed there, but for me it's the
prayer place where I unburdened my heart before the Lord and
tried to listen to Him.

The spring of 1944 I talked with Dr. T.B. Maston, professor
of Social Ethics, who encouraged me to enroll at Howard Payne
Baptist College in Brownwood, Texas. That summer I worked
nights as typist at Fort Worth Consolidated Vultee Aircraft
Corporation, saving money for college.

WAK

There is a fellowship among the 1943-44 seminary students that will last until our deaths. My dearest friend then was Irene Johnson. She introduced me to "goobers" (peanuts), Stamps Baxter music, her rural church near Lewisville, dinner on the ground, and the real, genuine Texas drawl. Irene and her husband Hershel Bennett came to our silver anniversary celebration October 11, 1992, and now she is with Jesus.

Howard Payne College

**I will lift up my eyes to the hills -
From whence comes my help?
My help comes from the Lord,
Who made heaven and earth.**
                                    Psalm 121:1,2 NKJ

The motto at Howard Payne was "The College Where Everybody Is Somebody." Classes were scheduled for mornings so students could work. Cap Shelton, beloved coach, welcomed me there when I arrived August 1944. We talked about employment, and he took me to Miss Gladys Hicks, Dean of Women. She offered me the job of Assistant Dean of Women - I was to help manage the girls' dormitory which housed one hundred girls. This job paid a full scholarship; I would be responsible for books and personal things.

Days of glory! Days of suffering!

    Up at 6:00 A.M. to ring the 6:20 bell
    Room checks and office hours during the day and evening
    Room checks at night
    10:00 P.M. bell
    Lights out at 10:20

It was amazing that I was staying on the Dean's List (recognition for good grades) without burning midnight oil!

The uncertainties and clouds of war were part of life. Some students were writing to friends, sweethearts, or husbands in military service. Mrs. Morris Day, my teacher, had lost her husband in the Bataan March. One day no specific prayer request was on my mind, so in my quiet time I prayed for an unnamed soldier in an unspecified place. I still wonder if that soldier's name was Jesse Lee Kidd.

71.

The students endeavored to make everyone into Somebody,
and I entered into the challenge with vigor.

   Life Service Band. We planned and carried out mission
      projects. As Librarian I chaired the annual retreat
      October 18, 1945.

   Volunteer Mission Band. We supported home and foreign
      missionaries with prayers and money.

   Alpha Chi. A national honorary scholastic society composed
      of the highest ranking ten percent of the junior and
      senior classes of denominational colleges. Founded in
      1922 to give recognition to superior students in reli-
      gious colleges where there are no fraternities and so-
      rorities. Corresponds to Phi Beta Kappa.

   Who's Who Among Students in American Colleges and Univer-
      sities. Students from junior and senior classes who
      distinguished themselves in scholarship, citizenship,
      and leadership. They were nominated by the faculty and
      presented to the student body for election.

   Girls' Octet. I sang bass; we sang in churches, at the
      USO, and a chapel service at Camp Bowie.

   College Women's Sunday School Class, First Baptist Church.
      I was president.

When Dad was eighty, the family called me home from school
because of his sickness. Dr. W.A. Dodd, my dear Bible Professor, loaned me money for bus fare, and by the time I arrived
home Dad had rallied so he was able to eat. Dad's problem
was terrible pain in his head and the doctor knew of nothing
to alleviate it. His hearing, sight, and equilibrium were im-
paired. Afterward, he could read only with great difficulty,
and his hearing loss was almost complete.

   Later, when I was again visiting Dad, he explained how he
managed to walk across the room. He chose his objective,
then sighted to right or left of it, and if he aimed there,
he arrived at the desired point.

   Howard Payne had accepted all my credits:

Wayne State Teachers College: 33 credits for 1939-40
Wayne State Teachers College   9 credits for summer, 1941
Southwestern Seminary   22 credits for 1943-44

That way, I completed the degree plan in January 1946, graduating with majors in Bible and Secondary Education and a
minor in Business Administration.

WAK

<u>First Baptist Church, Stephenville, Texas</u>

That January I moved to Stephenville to be Educational Secretary of First Church. I was to work in the office, handling Sunday School and Training Union records, correspondence, Sunday service bulletin, and addressing the weekly paper. I was to minister to the young people of the church as well as to Baptist students at Tarleton State College. Texas Baptist Student Department supplemented my salary.

Here was practical theology: Stephenville was in Erath County; there was an unwritten law that the sun would not set on a Negro, in that county. I wondered how I could support that philosophy since I was a mission volunteer to go to a foreign field.

I pestered H. Marshall Smith, the pastor, with questions about the workings of the church and he was a thoughtful, patient teacher. The principles that he explained were put to good use in Brazil, even until my retirement.

The Russell family were members of the church; Mr. Russell was U.S. congressman. Their daughter Laverne was studying at Baylor University; she later married Ralph Rummage and they served as missionaries in Rhodesia (Zimbabwe).

Southwestern Seminary
Master of Religious Education

**Be diligent to present yourself approved to God,
a worker who does not need to be ashamed,
rightly dividing the word of truth.**
2 Timothy 2:15   NKJ

The Stephenville church wanted to enable me to start on the Master's degree, so they voted for me to start January 1947, commuting sixty miles to Fort Worth to attend classes Tuesday through Friday. Boyd O'Neal was pastoring the church's mission which later became Calvary Church. I rode with Boyd and Irma, arriving at the Seminary Monday evening and returning to Stephenville after classes Friday afternoon. At Southwestern, I stayed at Barnard Hall.

I reluctantly interrupted studies to journey to Carroll for my folks' golden wedding anniversary March 11, 1947. Elsie, in her inimitable way, prepared hospitality for our family and friends. The Methodist Church prepared the banquet.

To my complete amazement, at that banquet my mother and father kissed each other - the first time I had ever seen that! Jean had prepared a sixteen-page program for each guest, honoring family history and customs. She gave each one a decorative, tiny porcelain shoe with gold wings.

73.

WAK

I received a working scholarship from Texas Woman's Missionary Union, so starting September 1947 I could live on campus.
The dear people at Stephenville gave me a lovely personal
shower. They had their hearts in mission work, and they were
interested. I missed those precious ones.

The golden wedding trip had been costly; because of absence
my Old Testament Survey grade was D. Now I worked very hard
to bring my grades up. In that Bible class my attendance
was perfect, exam grades added up to A, and my notebook made
A, so I received a semester grade of Dr. Daniel's rare A's!
Students in his class kidded each other,

"Don't drop your pencil. By the time you retrieve it, Dr.
Daniel will be in another book of the Bible!"

Two of my classmates in all my courses were David Gomes
and his wife, Haydée. We were seated alphabetically, and
"Gomes" and "Gemmell" were together. They were Brazilians,
and David delighted us with his mixed-up English. Haydée
avoided speaking in English. They went back to Brazil where
David became executive secretary of the Brazilian Baptist
Home Mission Board. When I saw them in Rio, Haydée was speaking beautiful English and David still spoke it mixed-up!

Edna Frances Dawkins was a representative of the Southern
Baptist Convention Foreign Mission Board, and she came periodically to meet with us foreign mission volunteers. It was
she to whom I sent the paperwork for an appointment. I wrote
my autobiography, and sent twenty-five names for reference,
along with my declaration of doctrinal beliefs. All the forms
were complete, as well as the physical and psychiatric exams.

The studies for Master of Religious Education were completed
January 7, 1949 and I stayed on at the Seminary, hoping for
appointment by the Board in the spring. The Board customarily
met in April when missionary candidates who were graduating
from the Seminary were appointed. They had sent plane fare
to travel to the Richmond, Virginia, headquarters, for the
ceremony. Then came the letter,

"You have not been fully approved. You may return the
check we issued for plane fare."

How can I put into words my disappointment? God's call to
be a foreign missionary didn't go away when I was not accepted
by the Board. In fact, the call was more insistent, and I
was more frustrated. I was ashamed to tell the people in
Stephenville that I had been turned down, and I felt a heavy
sense of guilt. Dr. Cal Guy, professor of Missions at Southwestern had accompanied my application. One Sunday he spoke
at Broadway Church in the morning service, and I thought to
greet him. But when I got to his side the only thing I could
do was to cry.

> . . . giving all diligence, add to your faith virtue,
> to virtue knowledge, to knowledge self-control,
> to self-control perseverance, to perseverance godliness,
> to godliness brotherly kindness,
> and to brotherly kindness love.
>   2 Peter 1:5-7 NKJ

For some months I worked in the business office of Williamson Dickie Manufacturing Company in Fort Worth. Dr. Floy Barnard, professor at Southwestern, recommended me to work in the national headquarters of Woman's Missionary Union in Birmingham, Alabama. So I moved to that city of steel works. The ladies at 1111 Comer Building (downtown) welcomed me royally, and I started as secretary to Miss Juliet Mather, Editorial Secretary. Woman's Missionary Union is Auxiliary to the Southern Baptist Convention, promoting missionary education.

Miss Mather was a genius, ahead of her time. When she stopped traveling among the churches promoting Missions organizations, she became Editorial Secretary over all literature being published. Her correspondence circled the globe, as she was loved by home and foreign missionaries. She was sought as an inspirational speaker, simply because of her love for Missions. Being a woman who worked best under pressure, she always expressed appreciation for my assistance:

    Transcribe correspondence and maintain files
    Type copy for Royal Service, monthly magazine for women
    Research manuscripts
    Prepare monthly Prayer Calendar: home and foreign missionaries on their birthdays (place and type of service)
    Type copy for annual Week of Prayer for Foreign Missions
    Also copy for annual Week of Prayer for Home Missions

Hopefully Miss Mather taught me some lessons. She had me pack used clothing and send it to her needy friends in the Orient. We wrapped simple, thoughtful gifts for lonely neighbors in her apartment building. She invited me to eat watermelon at the humble stand near the train station, where she chatted amiably with the owners.
                    ****
When I went north to visit the folks, it was convenient to go to Elizabeth and Charles' house in Missouri so we could travel together. In the early 1950's we started together to Carroll for Thanksgiving. Charles Jr. and Michael Eugene, their sons were with us. West of Kansas City we were caught in a terrible snowstorm, and we were lucky to find a hotel room. After two nights the storm abated and snowplows had cleared the highway, so we traveled on. At home, a high drift was even with the roof of our house.

WAK
    Storms seemed to schedule their ferocity for our Nebraska
trips. I was terrified in one rain storm. Elizabeth, an experienced driver, knew to sight the edge of the highway and
drive on. I drew back in the seat in fright as she pressed
down on the accelator with determination.

                    * * * * * * * * * * * * *

    Since Miss Mather was planning to retire, I secured employ-
ment at the Employers Insurance Company in Birmingham, where
I worked from 1953 to October, 1956. I took an Economics
course at the University of Alabama, Birmingham: study of
Economics from the Industrial Revolution in England to modern
America. This course actually influenced my later decision
to work in the business world.

    Miss Mather retired and she went to Japan to teach English.
Arlen Bradford who was a missionary there at the same time,
tells this story:

    He went from Tokyo to Fukuoka to be with some friends. He
needed some information and thought he would ask Miss Mather,
who was in her classroom and teaching, at the moment, Revelation 3:20 in English.

        **Behold, I stand at the door, and knock:
        if any man hear my voice, and open the door,
        I will come in to him, and will sup with him,
        and he with me. Rev. 3:20 KJ**

The students heard Arlen knocking at the door. When Miss
Mather opened it, Arlen was greeted with the students' glee-
ful, hilarious laughter!

The Encouragers

    Shelby Collier, minister of music at First Baptist Church
in Birmingham, urged me to sing a solo in church, and one
Sunday evening I squeaked through a song. It seemed that my
quaking voice transformed into slight, wet feathers that lay
limply at my feet; it was embarrassing. Shelby persisted and
there was some improvement, but one disaster was - disastrous.
The organ and piano accompaniment were in different keys, but
somehow, I got through the song.

    My pastor, Dr. T. Sloane Guy, was an encourager. I was
not married, and this was the time before the meaningful term
"Single" had come into use. I noticed an ad for supervisor
of office filing systems, for Remington Rand. I had seen
Blanche, state Remington Rand consultant, as she came to Woman's Missionary Union, helping with filing systems. I applied
for the job and was hired by the Atlanta, Georgia office.

WAK

This meant I would go to Atlanta, leaving the children's
Sunday School class I taught, my church relationship, and the
civic chorale. I was to sing one last time in church. At
the proper time in the evening worship I stood at my place
in the choir. As I opened my mouth, a large, full voice filled
the church to the high, vaulted ceiling. Diction, pitch, and
strength of the voice were that of a well trained performer.
It was I who sang, but the voice was transformed.

Afterward as we changed to street clothes in the dressing
room, one dear lady questioned,

"Why haven't you sung like that before?"

Silently I reasoned that my Lord chose the manifestation
to say,

"Wilma, in this new venture, you have sought My direction
and you are in My will. Now go on your pilgrimage with vigor!"

"Pilgrimage With Vigor"

He who dwells in the secret place of the Most High
   Shall abide under the shadow of the Almighty.
I will say of the Lord, "He is my refuge and my fortress;
   My God, in Him I will trust."

                              Psalm 91:1,2 NKJ

As I left Birmingham in October 1956, I realized that I
was leaving the security of my church family, and that more
than ever, God would have to go ahead of me and lead. I had
to be completely dependent upon Him. The Atlanta office
planned my assignments as a trainee:

1. Mobile, Alabama: Alabama State Docks. I assisted the
   organizer who was working in *Subject Files, in the administrative office.

2. Jacksonville, Florida: Atlantic National Bank. I worked
   under the organizer of Central Information File.

3. New York City: Home Office. One week, studying Subject
   Filing.

4. Ocala, Florida: Chamber of Commerce, Marion county.

5. New York City: Home Office. Cross Training in Remington
   Rand products and systems, for one month. There were eighteen women in the class.

*Subject Files: Paper records usually in letter or legal size
   folders. While some files are arranged in numerical, alpha-
   betic or other order, Subject Files are arranged by descrip-
   tive caption. Example: "Executive Committee Minutes"

77.

WAK

I was also sent to Richmond, Virginia to assist a supervisor working in the Commonwealth of Virginia Highway Department. She was a heavy drinker; I tried to witness to her, and I never knew what happened to her. Otherwise, the Remington Rand supervisors under whom I worked were highly professional and loyal to their employer, qualities which left their impression on me.

There came an economic crunch and I'd spent a lot of the company's money in training. The branch manager for Remington of North Carolina invited me to live in Charlotte to serve as state consultant, so I eagerly accepted.

In 1958 I moved to Charlotte. The salesmen for filing systems and supplies arranged with potential customers for me to make surveys of their filing needs. After we'd prepared the written proposal the salesman and I presented it to the prospect, hoping to make a sale. I worked in Charlotte and traveled the state, including Asheville, Winston Salem, the Raleigh-Durham-Greensboro triangle, Chapel Hill, and Wilmington on the east coast; once to Norfolk, Virginia.

****

I joined Elizabeth in Missouri and we traveled together to visit Mother and Dad at Carroll. Dad required constant care, and Mother was distraught since she was his main caregiver. We puzzled on how to help her. On the trip back south as we passed through Omaha we stopped at the Joslyn Memorial Art Museum to inquire about art supplies. They sent us to a nearby store where we bought a few brushes, tubes of oil paint in basic colors, some canvas boards and the wooden artist's box. The store mailed the package for us.

I would love to have been there when Mother opened the package. She had always told us that as a young girl she had painted, but the cares of motherhood had deterred her ever going back to it. She started painting on anything she could find: cardboard, pieces of wood, scraps of cloth; and her color blending was fantastic.

I have "The Plow" which she painted January 1965 when she was almost eighty-nine. It won "Superior" rating at the Nebraska Federated Woman's Club art contest. She joyfully entered her works in local shows at Blair, Nebraska, when she lived there. Painting gave her new life as she depicted scenes from her childhood. People who visited her until her death in 1967 were blessed by her art work.

Dad became deathly sick and my boss generously allowed leave for me to go home. By then he had rallied and I returned to Charlotte. Elsie and Charles, the main caretakers, and others nursed Dad until his death September 12, 1958, at ninety-three.

God gave me a voice but I wasn't aware of it until an encourager, Shelby Collier, brought it to my attention. My voice
has been described as contralto and as mezzo-soprano; not Wag-
nerian, dramatic, or lyric - but simply mezzo.

Even when Mr. Collier encouraged me to start singing church
solos in the early 1950's I did not put much value in it. When
I moved to Charlotte, North Carolina in 1958 I joined St. John's
Church. It was puzzling when I was not invited to sing in the
services, so I talked to Paul Langston, Minister of Music. He
explained,

   "You need voice training."

   "How can that be accomplished since I am a working woman
    and not involved in a college where there are voice teach-
    ers?"

   "There is one highly qualified teacher in this city whom
    I would recommend for you - Fran Shafter."

Fran agreed to teach me on Saturdays in her home studio.
She had studied at Juilliard School of Music in New York. She
soon explained that we would work on eliminating the bad singing habits acquired in church choirs. That was an affront to
me, and I argued vociferously but agreed to work with her.
The technique she instilled in me by patient endurance has
been valuable until today. The training led to performances:

August 30, 1959: Alto soloist in the oratorio "Elijah"
at First Church, Charlotte.

Fran kept on with the teaching and tried to convince me
of my talent, which was a long process. I joined the Charlotte Oratorio Singers comprised of volunteers who presented
at least two major works annually.

Spring 1960, Oratorio Singers
"Jubilate Deo" by Giovanni Gabrieli
"Psalm 150" by Heinrich Schuetz
"Hymn to St. Cecilia Op. 27" in which I was a soloist

Spring 1960: "Woman's Life and Love"
German love songs by Robert Schumann, in my voice recital

October 30, 1960: "The Lord Is A Sun And Shield"
J.S. Bach. Written for the Reformation Festival of 1735.
My church choir sang it on Sunday morning, and that after-
noon with Covenant Presbyterian Church choir

December 1960 (my letter): Oratorio Singers
"A German Requiem" by Johannes Brahms, with the Charlotte
symphony orchestra

WAK
    Christmas, 1960
    "Christmas Oratorio" by Camille Saint-Saens
    Sung by my choir of St. John's Church

    January 21, 1961
    "Judas Maccabaeus" by Handel: the Oratorio Singers

                    ****

May 13, 1961: joint voice recital, in which I sang:

Grauenliebe und leben.....................Robert Schumann
    Er, der Herrlichste von Allen
    Ich Kann's nicht fassen, nicht glauben
    Susser Freund, du blickest

Nel cor piu non mi sento....................G. Paisiello
Sento nel core.....................Alessandro Scarlatti
Ave Maria - "Otello"......................Giuseppe Verdi

The Deaf Old Woman....................Missouri Folk Song
Barbara Allen...........Knott County, Kentucky Folk Song
The Barnyard Song.......Knott County, Kentucky Folk Song
Sourwood Mountain......Harlan County, Kentucky Folk Song

                    ****
December 9, 1962
I sang in the Sunday morning service at St. John's
"Behold! A Virgin Shall Conceive" and "Thou That Tellest
Good Tidings to Zion," from "The Messiah" by G.F. Handel

January 19, 1963: Oratorio Singers
"King David" by Arthur Honegger. 110 choristers and 50-pc
orchestra

When I was being hired by the Foreign Mission Board I felt
I needed to resolve my involvement with music. I knew nothing
about music in Brazil so I talked to the Lord about it.

    "The music, study, experience, performance, joys and friend-
    ships. Here is everything. I have no expectations or de-
    mands; it's all yours. If going to Brazil means giving
    up music, that is exactly what I do here and now."

    Now to Him who is able to do exceedingly abundantly
        above all that we ask or think,
        according to the power that works in us,
                            Ephesians 3:20 NKJ

Since landing in Brazil the first time until this moment,
I have been singing, listening, developing, and teaching -
music! In Brazil there was always a challenge and opportunity
to witness for my Lord through music. How magnanimously the
Lord blesses!

I HAVE HEARD THY VOICE

> I am Thine, O Lord, I have heard Thy voice,
>   And it told Thy love to me;
> But I long to rise in the arms of faith,
>   And be closer drawn to Thee.

I had sung the hymn many, many times, and now it was to become real. It seemed that life would happily go on as it was, with supportive friends in the Oratorio Singers and St. John's Church. But one day at church Mr. Ernest Anderson, a deacon, thoughtfully said to me,

"Pride goeth before a fall."

> **Pride goeth before destruction,**
>   **and an haughty spirit before a fall.**
>   **Proverbs 16:18   KJ**

In 1962 I was hospitalized March 19 to April 14 for infectious hepatitis. James and Dot Nordan, good friends, took me to their home from the hospital, until I could manage in my apartment. I was so weak I couldn't open a can of food. There were long hours of resting and recuperation; many of them spent in meditation, prayer, and Bible reading. At last strength returned and I was able to return to work.

There were two events that brought me to the point of actually submitting to my Lord's will; I am not writing about them because they are between God and me. I hastily made an appointment with Roberts Lasater, Associate Pastor of my church, and confessed that my Lord had spoken to me.

As I tried to tell him how God had manifested Himself and that He wanted me in His service, the tears flowed and flowed. Bob waited and listened, compassionately understanding. We talked some more and he suggested that I carry on with life, keeping my eyes open for the Lord's leadership.

> Where can I go from your Spirit?
>   Where can I flee from your presence?
> If I go up to the heavens, you are there;
>   if I make my bed in the depths, you are there.
> If I rise on the wings of the dawn,
>   if I settle on the far side of the sea,
> even there your hand will guide me,
>   your right hand will hold me fast.
>   Psalm 139:7-10 NIV

In February 1963 I was going to Atlanta to attend a company meeting. When we sales people boarded the plane in Charlotte, we needed to move back in the aisle to claim the only seats available. I recognized Miss Edna Frances Dawkins of the Foreign Mission Board among the passengers.

> "Miss Dawkins, it's so nice to see you. You probably don't remember me. I'm . . . "

She held up her hand to silence me.

> "Don't tell me your name. You're Wilma Gemmell."

We chatted and I went to my seat in the back, then during the flight I returned, and we talked. Edna Frances knew Betty Gilreath of my church, and she asked if I would talk to Betty and other Missions Education leadership about a need in Rio de Janeiro: the financial office of the mission work in Brazil needed a secretary. I agreed to talk to Betty.

The plane was flying to Atlanta, but I knew my destination was Rio de Janeiro, Brazil. I still had the conviction that God had called me, so I considered this encounter to be in God's plan and that I should again apply for appointment by the Foreign Mission Board. Miss Dawkins had handled my application in 1948-49, and she again worked with me through the process.

June 1963 I wrote to Mother:

"I was in Fort Worth taking physical and psychiatric exams for the Foreign Mission Board, and they met yesterday and elected me as an Associate Missionary to serve a five-year term in Rio de Janeiro where the Brazil Missions headquarters is. There, I will be a secretary. I'll probably sail from New Orleans around August 15.

"Every moment since February has been filled with correspondence and working - I did not share this since I wanted to be sure that I was doing the right thing - I wanted time for the Holy Spirit to work in me. Now I am sure, and this is the task I have undertaken."

****

WAK

I was in Orientation for new missionaries June 27 to July 5 at Mars Hill College, Mars Hill, N.C. I was the first Missionary Associate hired for Latin America, and even though I was in Orientation with career missionaries, I did not go to Board headquarters in Richmond for the appointment service. You see, I had passed the age limit of thirty-five; I was forty-one.

The six of us Gemmells had been paying for Mother's care in the Crowell Memorial Nursing Home in Blair, Nebraska, where Mother chose to live after Dad's death in 1958. Our contributions made it possible for her to continue there. Now Mother was free of the cares and burdens which had characterized her life, and she was known at Crowell as the Popcorn Lady, who shared popcorn with others. She was Daisy, who wrote letters for patients and visited others in the building. She helped those with difficulty walking or eating.

As a missionary I would be expected to tithe and there wouldn't be enough salary to help support a mother. June 23, 1963 I wrote to my four sisters and one brother:

"Now I must ask that you will carry responsibility for Mother. I shall be able to contribute some - I have a 20-year policy maturing this fall which I plan to cash and place in savings and loan so the interest could go for Mother. I feel I am leaving a big blank wherein I should be carrying my part of the load.

"I think you can appreciate my position somewhat if you could know what went on this year before I learned of the Rio job. Since Christmas I struggled with sickness, then the opportunity for new work presented itself, and I followed through. Strength and health kept returning.

"Every moment has been filled with this endeavor since I started it in February. The Board in monthly meeting elected me - so I turn my face toward Brazil - and the marvelous challenge there."

****

Since the missionary term was five years I appealed to Dr. Frank Means for the Board to pay my travel to visit family. He consented and I drove to Dexter, Missouri to the Norrises. Michael Eugene went with us as we started north.

First, Jessie and Paul Back at Red Oak, Iowa
At Malvern, Iowa we were with Fred several days after his wife Doris had died
We picked up Mother at Blair
At Carroll we were with Elsie and Charles Whitney

Mother was eighty-seven years old when she embraced me and courageously bid me, "Go and do mission work, with my full blessing."

83.

WAK
    Leaving Nebraska, the Norrises and I started to New Orleans
and all went well until coming into steamy, Louisiana heat.
Without air conditioning, we all got hot; I drank a lot of
Coca Cola. In New Orleans I stayed in the hotel and the
Norrises were at the Seminary. I checked with Buchholdt and
Kutruff to confirm that they had loaded my freight on the
ship. The next morning, August 29, I called Charles,

    "I can't lift my head off the pillow. I'm sick!"

    "You're just upset because you're leaving the country.
     Get up out of that bed and get your bags ready!"

    I did exactly that, and the three Norrises came to carry
me to the ship. There was excitement at the Poydras St. wharf
where passengers, families and friends, stevedores, porters,
and officials mingled. The Dixie Land band played. Elizabeth,
Charles, and Michael went with me to my stateroom, then we
mingled with others of our party.

    When all visitors went ashore, I must have been more con-
cerned with the new adventure than with the goodbyes. Elizabeth,
Charles, and Michael Eugene stood on the wharf until the S.S.
Del Norte moved out of sight. I threw streamers to them until
I knew that shore was beyond reach. We moved past other wharves
until the banks of the Mississippi appeared and we came along
the extremity of Dry Tortugas at the Florida Keys at 8:30 P.M. -
the last sight of the U.S. coast.

    Our group of new Southern Baptist missionaries was large:

South Brazil Mission
Bill and Martha Ann Davenport   4 boys
Norvel and Hattie Welch   4 children
Marshall and LaVerne Flournoy   3 children
Marilois Kirksey
Wilma Gemmell
Equatorial Brazil Mission
Erling and Carrie Valerius   3 girls
Sidney and Ruth Carswell   4 children
C. Glyn and Sally McCalman   2 children
   They were returning missionaries, escorting us.
Gene and Exie Henson   2 children
North Brazil Mission
Glen and Audrey Swicegood   2 children
Mary Witt

This shows nineteen adults and twenty-four children; perhaps
my roster is not complete. We were a large part of the total
of 119 passengers. We thoughtfully and considerately tried
to get acquainted. Sunday August 30 we had Sunday School for
our group. That evening we had vesper service in the lounge,
when I sang "Draw Near To Me" by J.S. Bach.

S.S. Del Norte

We missionaries and children who boarded August 29, 1963 have a unique relationship.

"We went to Brazil together on the S.S. Del Norte."

When we are with each other we pick up that relationship, sharing our lives.

September 3 we stopped at Bridgetown, Barbados, where there was time to disembark. The welcoming band played music of haunting timbre. One instrument was the top of a steel drum with bubbles beaten to different depth; sounding the tones of the scale. Played with a soft mallet, the marimba-like sound was reverberant. Marilois Kirksey and I took a ride through a sugar cane field in an open, horse-drawn cart.

For the costume party on board ship, the passengers searched every available recourse and at the hour for the party we gathered: clowns, hula hula dancers, Carmen Miranda, cowboys, bride and groom, and robots.

I had brought a voluminous New York Times and a packet of straight pins. By tearing, folding, shaping and pinning, there evolved a garment with hat - "Miss New York Times," which tied with the beatnik for Most Original.

The dining room was decorated in varying motifs for the sumptuous meals: Chinese, Italian, International, Spanish, New Orleans, and Captain's Farewell.

The McCalmans would disembark at Salvador and I would leave the group at Rio. The others would continue sailing to Santos then go by land to Campinas, where they were to start language study.

Upon arriving at Rio de Janeiro, I would have traveled 2,908 miles on land and many, many nautical miles!

Guyana

Venezuela   Suriname
                             French Guiana

                                              Atlantic Ocean

Colombia

Ecuador   **BRAZIL**

Peru
                                        Montes Claros
                                              *

Bolivia
                                        Belo Horizonte
                                              *

                    Paraguay   Volta Redonda *
                                              Rio de Janeiro

Pacific Ocean
                                        Lajes
                                          *

                    Argentina   Uruguay

Chile

N

SOUTH
AMERICA

III.

VOLTA REDONDA, BRAZIL

March 19, 1958, that memorable day, my ship S.S. Del Mundo
arrived at Rio de Janeiro. Missionary Walter B. McNealy was
there, and after greeting me he introduced me to the representatives of the Central Baptist Church and its school.
(It was then that I learned that my home Association, Liberty
Baptist, would support me). The city of Volta Redonda was
seventy miles inland but it took about two hours to drive
because of traffic and road conditions.

I met Mrs. McNealy when we arrived. It was soon apparent
that she and Brother McNealy were equally devoted to their
calling to missions and to Brazil. Their long working hours
bore fruit in a way that never ceased to amaze me. They served
the Lord with devotion in leadership of Central Baptist Church
and its missions; and the school Colégio do Instituto Batista
Americano which the church owned. The McNealys were on call
day and night and were unshirking; never have I known two more
dedicated people.

Their only son Walter Jr. was a student in Baylor University then, and today he is a successful businessman in New York
City. Their daughter Mary Jean was twelve years old. She is
married to Wilson Borosvski who is Minister of Music of First
Baptist Church, El Dorado, Arkansas. My relationship with
the McNealys was pleasant. God in his goodness used them to
open the door to Brazil, and I cherish the years spent working
with them. What a blessing!

The Baptist School, Volta Redonda

The best job description for anyone working with the school?

**Whatever your hand finds to do,
    do it with all your might,   Ecclesiastes 9:10a   NIV**

With over 3,000 students ranging from kindergarten through
junior college, there was always something to do. Those of
us in Administration started the day at 7:30 A.M. and worked
until 10:30 P.M. when adult education classes closed.

The school being owned and operated by Central Baptist
Church, there were four Bible-centered assemblies daily, two
each morning and afternoon. First, one age group of students
marched into the auditorium and upon their leaving the second
age group entered. Every daytime student heard the Gospel
every school day. I worked with the age Junior High and up.
The students sang choruses and hymns lustily and we invited
visiting speakers for added inspiration. Through the years
many students came to know the Lord, and many families were
reached.

Mrs. McNealy (Dona Geny - "Dona" is a title of respect)
tells that often when buying food in the open market, she
would hear an unidentified voice singing a chorus. She knew
it was a student, letting her know they were there among the
crowd of shoppers. In pioneer Baptist mission work one of the
best methods was the establishment of schools.

Sônia Vidares

Sônia loved school, especially enjoying the assembly programs when we sang together and had stories from the Bible.
One day after an assembly when the plan of salvation had been
carefully presented, Sônia talked to me and trusted Jesus as
her Savior. We were privileged to see her develop in every
way as she grew in faith. One day she said she'd like to have
a Bible, so we gladly gave her an inexpensive one.

Occasionally we invited Sônia to Sunday services at the
church, but she never came. Then one day at school we were
concerned to see that her face was bruised. When I thoughtfully questioned her, she would not reveal anything. Day by
day she became silent, withdrawn, and reserved - so unlike
her exuberant self.

Once after Sunday School I noticed Sônia in the auditorium,
sitting with her parents. As I greeted them Sônia's mother
explained,

"Today is Sônia's fifteenth birthday."

(In Brazil the fifteenth is the coming-out day for young wom-
en.) They had been asking Sônia for weeks how she wanted to
celebrate her fifteenth birthday and finally she said that
all she wanted was for them to go with her to the services
at the Baptist church.

At the close of the service Sônia's mother hurried down
the aisle to me, weeping.

"I must see you. Would you please come to our home this
afternoon?"

When I arrived at the house the mother was still crying.

"I am the most wicked person who ever lived. Sônia came
home from school one day with a Bible. I was afraid of it,
for we have always heard that people who read the Bible go
mad. I took it from Sônia and hid it, forbidding her to
read it. Months later I awoke in the night, noticing a
light in the bathroom. It was Sônia who had found the
Bible and was reading it. I snatched it and beat her on
her face with it, leaving her badly bruised."

90.

JLK

I remembered those bruises. While her mother continued
lamenting, Sônia left the room and returned shortly with a
stack of papers. When I finished talkng with the mother and
praying with them Sônia asked,

> "Pastor Jesse, I want you to take these papers with you.
> When you have some time would you read them?"

Several days later when I settled down to read what Sônia had
written I was amazed. The poems of praise to God for his
goodness expressed her devotion as only a young girl could
write. I wondered if the thoughts and inspiration came to
her at school where she received nurture. Sônia had written
the precious lines while undergoing awful persecution at the
hand of her mother. I thought of the words of Jesus:

> **Blessed are those who are persecuted for
>   righteousness' sake,
> For theirs is the kingdom of heaven.**
> **Matthew 5:10 NKJ**

Sônia grew up to be a devoted Christian wife, mother, and
teacher.

Roberto and Trouble with Images

Roberto, age twelve, studied at the American school. One
day after the assembly we talked, and he indicated he wanted
to trust Jesus as his Savior. I counseled him about this and
we had prayer together. He made a very sincere decision.
Later Roberto sought me out,

> "Pastor Jesse, I have a problem. Here at school you teach
> us to pray. On Sundays my mother and father go to the
> cathedral, requiring me to go with them. But then I have
> a problem because I no longer want to pray to the images
> in the cathedral. What am I going to do?"

> "Roberto, we do not teach you students in this school to
> be disobedient to your parents. On the contrary we teach
> you that one of God's commandments is to honor your father
> and mother. Roberto, next Sunday when you go with your
> parents to the cathedral and it comes time to pray to the
> images, just shut your eyes. Forget the images and talk
> to God just as you have learned to do here."

Roberto was a good student and grew in his faith. Considering
all the Bible has to say about images, it is remarkable that
in the Latin world there are so many churches where so much
attention is given to all kinds of images.

> **"Honor your father and your mother, that your days
>   may be long upon the land which the Lord your
>   God is giving you.   Exodus 20:12 NKJ**

Vacation Bible School

The young people of Central Church worked with me in open-air Vacation Bible Schools during school vacation. I took two teams of workers to neighborhoods in the morning and two in the afternoon.

Children of all ages came - toddlers to twelve years, and even older. Their enthusiasm was unbounded, and they loved hearing the Bible stories and singing choruses. Many of these children were hearing about the love of God for the first time. What's more, they were taking the message home with them. Their joy multiplied our own joy. What a blessing to return day after day to the same place to find the children waiting for us. We reached them, then their parents became interested and wanted a continuous work - several churches were begun that way.

Dona Geny (Mrs. McNealy) was our excellent source for teaching materials of any age. She had prepared and maintained a library of illustrated Bible stories for any setting:

    School assemblies
    Vacation Bible School
    Bible retreats and camps

Her first love was missionary education for all ages, although she was gifted in promoting exciting, interesting parties and celebrations. She had lively encampments and meetings for her own church as well as leading these local people into associational, state and national efforts. Some of the young people that Dona Geny trained were appointed as missionaries by the Brazilian Baptist Home and Foreign Mission Boards.

Floriano: The Testing
Floriano was a community forty kilometers from Volta Redonda on the Rio-São Paulo highway. We had the Vacation Bible School under a large mango tree. This was the last day and the leaders had small sacks of hard candy for the children.

Each day we had noticed five little boys sitting against a high stone wall across the street, forbidden by their parents to join us. We noted they sang along with us and repeated the Bible verses. I decided to pass the candy to them, but just as I turned to cross the street that great stone wall came crashing down upon the boys. We desperately pulled debris from the rubble, hoping that the boys were not injured. But one of them had a terrible gash on his head.

JLK

It was in God's mercy that just at that moment Brother
McNealy drove up, and we sped to the hospital twelve miles
away. The doctors did all they could but the child died.
The next day was Saturday, and I remained in my apartment all
day wrestling with my thoughts and pondering the tragedy. I
seriously wondered if I should think of returning to the States.
Sometime during the night a wonderful peace came to me and
the words, "Lo, I am with you always," kept repeating in my
thoughts.

The next day, Sunday, some of the young people and I customarily went to Floriano in the afternoon for open-air services
on the town square. I assumed there might be violence and
questions to be answered. I told my companions that they need
not go with me - I would go alone. I was moved by their supportive spirit when they asserted, "If you go, we will go."

When we drove up to the town square there was an unusually
large crowd and we wondered what their attitude would be. Were
they going to be hostile, or just curious? No one spoke a
word as we set up the sound system and the little folding pump
organ. We conducted our service as usual. A teacher from our
school preached a simple message, and when he gave the invitation several people came forward.

The grandparents of the dead child, with whom he had lived,
were there and wanted to talk to me. This is the gist of
what they said.

  "We were foolish to prohibit our grandchildren from attending your service. You were trying to help us, and we
   didn't understand. If they had been with the other children such a tragedy wouldn't have happened. We were so
   foolish."

What a consolation to know that today a Baptist church stands
near the scene of that awful tragedy. It's a memorial to the
Savior who promised, "Lo, I am with you."

Clown

We decided to start a Sunday afternoon open-air service
on the town square in Quatís, an ancient town located off the
main highway. The corps of dedicated young people from Central
Church went with me Sunday after Sunday.

The local priest became unhappy and disturbed when the
crowds grew and there was a lot of interest. He arranged for
a clown to come to the services and distract the people. The
word for "clown" in Portuguese is palhaço, or straw man. This
clown wore huge coveralls stuffed with straw. He was disturb-
ing the services, and his antics were frustrating.

93.

JLK

   After a few Sundays I decided it was time to act. A friend
had a ten-year-old son, Silas, who was very active and courageous. I talked to my friend and he agreed to let Silas
be part of a plan to be rid of the clown. The next Sunday we
were all at the town square for services. When we were setting
up, I talked with Silas,

   "Take this box of matches and if the clown comes today,
    go and stand by him and start striking the matches."

I instructed him to be careful not to get too close to the
straw man, for we didn't want an accident. Right on time the
clown appeared and started his antics, so Silas quietly and
slowly slipped near him and struck one match, lighting it.
When he started to light another match the clown seemed to
get the message and he hurried away, leaving our group to continue uninterrupted.

   **Praise be to the Lord my Rock,
      who trains my hands for war,
         my fingers for battle. Psalm 144:1 NIV**

   Years later when we lived in Santa Catarina I received an
invitation from Silas to officiate at his wedding. It seemed
impossible to go back to Volta Redonda because of my responsibilities, but it would have been great to do this for a courageous ten-year-old who was grown up.

Austelino and Nair

   The McNealys were home on furlough so as a new missionary
I had many first-time experiences without their wise counsel.
Austelino, a bright young engineering student in his early
twenties, was dating Nair, a lovely girl. They came and talked
with me about their wedding plans, and I suggested that they
have a conference with Dr. Jaimovich the medical doctor who
was a friend of mine.

   A couple getting married may choose to have the civil ceremony at the specified government office. There, they and their
witnesses sign the required documents and the official declares
them man and wife.

   Some couples have a church wedding, simple or ornate. They
may have completed the civil ceremony previously, or they may
engage a representative from the government office to bring
the official book. The witnesses sign the book as part of the
ceremony.

   The ornate ceremony for Austelino and Nair was my first wedding in Brazil, being in Central Baptist Church. They were a
fine couple. The flowers and decorations were beautiful, and
the ceremony came off just right. Sometime later, they told
me when they knew they were going to be parents.

JLK

As the date for the birth drew near, Nair's fear of child-birth increased. Dr. Jaimovich arranged for her to have a semi-private room in the hospital owned by the National Steel Mill, a very special privilege. That way Austelino could spend every hour possible with Nair. Dr. Jaimovich had even arranged for two beds in the room, and Austelino being very practical, used one. Nair was to move into the maternity ward shortly before her delivery.

But there was a catch to the whole arrangement - the nurse on the midnight shift was not advised. On her routine check she entered Nair's room and slipped her hand under the cover to take the patient's pulse, taking hold of Austelino's muscular, hairy arm. The tray in her other hand and everything on it flew to the ceiling as she screamed,

"There's a man in this bed!"

The pandemonium soon settled. Anyway, Nair was comforted by Austelino's presence. Then there is the Lord who said,

Fear not, for I am with you; . . .
Isaiah 41:10 NKJ

Nair had her baby and later this precious family moved from Volta Redonda and I lost track of them. How I cherish those first-time experiences!

My First Funeral in Brazil

My first Sunday in Brazil it was my privilege to attend the afternoon mission service in the Kaiser home. The invalid mother and her four young adult children lived in their humble home at the edge of Volta Redonda. A married son and daughter-in-law lived next door. They had a marvelous witness in their community and church, and I would get to know the family well.

Mrs. Kaiser had Parkinson's disease so she had difficulty in speaking. As a new missionary I didn't know the language so of course there was little communication. However, when I became discouraged with language study, all I needed was a few minutes seated by Mrs. Kaiser's bedside to feel refreshed and ready to return to the struggle of learning.

Jeremias the youngest son was about twenty-five years old, and later he became a pastor. Early one morning he knocked on my apartment door saying his mother had died during the night and requesting me to help with the funeral service. As we drove to his home I asked him to tell about his family and how be became a Christian. I was nervous as this was my first funeral service in Brazil and I wanted it to go well.

95.

JLK

Jeremias's Story

The family lived in the mountains of the state of Minas Gerais. One day his father was seriously injured on his job and died within a few days. His mother was suffering from Parkinson's disease even then and she was destitute. She determined the only thing to do was to give her children away except one of the girls. Jeremias was given to the doctor who had tried to save his father, perhaps as sort of a payment for his services.

One day when Jeremias was going about his duties of cleaning and dusting the doctor's office and waiting room, he suddenly started to cry loudly and uncontrollably. The doctor rushed to his side, wanting to know what was the matter.

"It's that book, Doctor!"

"What book? What book could disturb you so?"

"Doctor, when my father was alive and we were all together, he used to read to us from that book. It's the Bible!"

The doctor was deeply moved and comforting Jeremias he said,

"That being the case, I'm going to enroll you in school and when you learn to read I'll give you that book."

The next day Jeremias started to school and being a bright student he learned quickly. When the doctor was satisfied with his ability to read he presented him with the Bible and a legal document releasing him from all obligation. Without the document Jeremias was bound to remain there until the age of twenty-one.

"Now Jeremias, you are free to go. I want you to go and find your mother and take care of her."

Jeremias returned to the mountain community to find his mother, then he located his sister and a brother. They moved to Volta Redonda where the two young men found employment in the steel mill. They also enrolled in the Baptist school, where they continued their education.

I preached my first funeral sermon in the language of Brazil, Portuguese, standing by the rude, open grave. It was rather formal, as I would have preached in a funeral home back in the States. But Jeremias was inspired by what the Lord had done for him.

When I had finished he leaped upon the mound of dirt soon to fill his mother's grave, and preached another sermon. He told how the Word of God had re-united the family after it was hopelessly scattered. He recalled how good God had been to bring the family together around their invalid mother.

96.

JLK
Together, the children cared for her until her death. Jeremias witnessed to the saving grace of God through Jesus Christ His son. He affirmed that it was the Bible that brought his family back together, after the children were given away and scattered to the four winds. God's Word was precious to him.

> **I have not departed from the commands of his lips;**
> **I have treasured the words of his mouth**
> **more than my daily bread.**
> **Job 23:12 NIV**

Jeremias gave an appeal there by the open grave and seven people confessed faith in Christ.

Late Night Caller

It was almost midnight and I was getting ready for bed after a long day, when someone knocked at my door. Reluctantly and wearily I opened the door and there was a young man in his early twenties. He told me his name was Aurélio and asked if I were the American missionary. He drew a ragged volume from under his arm.

"I found this on a trash heap. I've been reading it and it disturbs me. They tell me you can explain it."

I saw immediately that it was a worn-out Bible. Inviting him in, I took a new Bible off the shelf. I asked him to have a seat by me and I compared pages of the ragged Bible with the new one so he would see they were the same.

Then we started at the beginning much as Philip did with the Ethiopian in Acts 8:35. We frequently turned to John 3:16. About 2:00 A.M. he turned to me with a look of wonder on his countenance.

"Do you know where the little town of Rio Claro is?"

"Yes, I have been through that town on my way to Ungra dos Reis down on the coast."

"You passed by the cathedral where I attended catechism when I was little. One day when we boys were unruly the priest scolded us. He showed us the trap door in the floor and threatened us that if we wouldn't be good he would open it and we would be eaten by the angry dragon God had under there.

"Until tonight my only concept of God was that he had an angry dragon who would eat me if I didn't be good. I didn't know that God loved me!"

JLK

I never saw anyone so excited about the sublime discovery of a love that is greater than our sins. Aurélio later moved to the coastal town Ungra dos Reis and gave his life to proclaiming God's love. This young man had known about church, religion and God all his life, but what he knew held him in the bondage of fear. He had not been led to know Jesus who said,

And ye shall know the truth, and the truth shall make you free.

John 8:32 KJ

This experience shaped my thinking. Just because I was in a land of great cathedrals I should not assume that everyone knew the Savior. The trappings of religion may serve only to obscure the truth. Men and women so desperately need to receive salvation.

IV.

RIO DE JANEIRO, BRAZIL

Brazil at last! For most of our party, we first stepped
on Brazilian soil at Salvador, Bahia when the ship docked
there. Some of us were taken to the home of Roy and Patricia
Fowler; others to James and Maxie Kirk's house.

Patricia was in the last months of her pregnancy, but she
was a gracious hostess, serving ham and cheese sandwiches and
Champagne guaraná. Not real champagne, but the brand of guaraná, a drink made from the seeds of the guaraná shrub, sold
in brown bottles.

Roy loaded his jeep with TWELVE of us for a drive around
the city: Bahia University, Kate White Domestic School, and
two missionary residences: James Kirk and James Lingerfelt.
We went downtown, then stopped at Zion Baptist Church. The
choir there was in rehearsal and they sang for us in beautiful, mellow tones, and fascinating rhythm and diction. Then
Roy carried us back to the ship.

Rio de Janeiro

When we arrived at Guanabara Bay September 12, 1963, it
took hours to dock. The pilot ship met us; the officials
boarded, transacted business, and returned to the "pilot"
which at last pulled us to the dock. All of our missionary
party disembarked; everyone except me would sail the next day
for Santos. There was a host of American missionaries to welcome us.

I stepped onto the dock and waited. One of the men came
and stared at me a few moments then went away. Shirley Jackson approached and introduced herself, then she led me, with
my cabin baggage, to Customs. After passing through Customs
she tipped the porter. Mr. and Mrs. Victor Davis drove us to
the Mission apartment building.

At 512 Rua Uruguai in Tijuca suburb, we entered the gate
and drove up a gradual incline to the Woman's Missionary Union
Training School, a two-story building set out by tall palm
trees growing at the side of the driveway. We made a left
turn and drove up the steeper incline to our destination, the
four-story apartment building with background of lush, tropical plants and trees.

Whenever one came from the hot street and approached the
building, cool, soothing breezes wafted down from the hills
in back. Small monkeys swung in the trees, sometimes daring
to land on the front balconies; orchids grew in the back, and
higher up in the hills were the beautiful blue butterflies.
I learned not to park a car under the jaqueira (tree) because
when the watermelon-shaped jaca fruit fell, it dented the
automobile.

WAK
From the third floor balcony one could see the South Brazil Seminary which was several blocks away, and higher. The view was open: past Uruguai Street to see part of Dona Delfina Street. Further down, Uruguai was at intersection with Conde de Bonfim. We could see over and beyond the Training School, but now in the 90's highrise buildings block the view. This property (the school and Mission apartments) is simply an island of green surrounded by highrise apartment buildings to the front and sides, and mountains to the rear.

In the Mission building I lived in the first floor, right front apartment. Katherine Cozzens with whom I lived was preparing to go on furlough, so I ate with Shirley Jackson and Catherine Chappell.

The Sounds
512 Uruguai is in a long valley where sounds reverberated and were amplified. Late at night a club turned up its speakers and blasted away, granting us only a few minutes' sleep in early morning. Singing of hymns and choruses from the Training School; a pet parrot squawking; a rooster crowing; an argument; a radio; singing. Blasting from a construction site. At the nearby nursery school, children in play or argument, singing, and teachers teaching. Automobile traffic. Jackhammers. Beating of sledgehammers on cement or wood as workmen remodeled - a relentless, jarring sound. Maids within our apartment building, talking and singing. Our location and weather conditions sometimes seemed to conduct the cacophony within our very walls. Being new, my senses were sensitive to unfamiliar sounds, sights, and smells.

People - People - People
In Rio where the seacoast is slap up against mountains, people are "stacked." Buildings are constructed on mountainsides - always one more level UP. In visiting a given address you might find a gate in a wall beyond which live any number of people. You stop at the gate and clap the hands loudly, the custom of announcing your arrival. Random visiting in most apartment buildings is prohibited. Arriving in the lobby, you consult with the porter on duty or announce your presence by inter-com.

The stacking of people in limited space necessitates ingenious methods for utilizing every square inch. As Brazilians build so as to capture a breeze, they appropriate the slightest movement of air for drying clothes. I enjoyed using the light-weight, aluminum clothes rack mounted on the ceiling, lowered and raised by pulleys. You lower the rack, pin the laundry on, raise it to the ceiling, and walk under the clothesline! I always considered it a miracle that clothes did dry in the rainy season, even at sea level.

102.

WAK

I miss the _tanque_, the common, permanent part of the residence; combination clothes tub and washboard with water faucet and drain; usually located in the back, in the place called the _área_. Here the clothes are washed, dried, and ironed; dishes, pots and pans are washed, and the mop and floor wax are stored here. In the apartment where I lived Pearl Stapp (who was on furlough) had an automatic washing machine and I had a small, agitator washing machine for personal laundry.

Hospitality
The missionaries customarily invited newcomers for a meal. I was hosted by Ernest and Billie Wilson, Boyd and Joan Sutton, Victor and Ruby Davis, Samuel and Emanetta Qualls, Lester and B. Wayne Bell, Edgar and Zelma Hallock, F.B. and Nonna Huey, Jerry and Johnnie Key, Dr. A. Ben and Edith Oliver, Fred and Mariruth Hawkins, Jo Stover, Nadine Brewer, Virginia Terry, Bill and Jerry Ichter, and others. Norvel and Hattie Welch invited me to stay overnight in their home in Niteroi, across the bay. I was being introduced to the art of hospitality. The meals were served with the very best the family had; it was an honor to be received in the homes. I hastily wrote to Mother, asking that she make some cloth napkins, as I didn't have any.

Language Study

Dona Edith Guertner, wife of the Seminary business manager, was my first teacher. She started me in a Brazilian pre-primer. Each Wednesday afternoon I walked several blocks from 512 Rua Uruguai, mounted the 125 steps UP to the Seminary (the back route), then traversed the courtyard to the Guertner house. Being a thoughtful, merciful woman, Edith offered delicious, refreshing, chilled water or fruit juice before the class.

My letter of September 24, 1963:

"Now I have started to leave the Mission property, walking last night to the first _praça_ (shopping area) and maybe later this week to the second one. It's good to get away from the apartment and to walk and look - look. There are babies everywhere - curly-headed, fat, and so adorable. I wish you could have seen the nursery Sunday - I went to Shirley Jackson's church. Babies and pregnant women everywhere.

"There are family groups shopping - walking - talking - standing - arguing. People everywhere every hour of the day and night. A small boy going to the bathroom at a tree. People carrying water from the springs (at one of our schools) on their heads or by a yoke across their shoulders. A horse tied at the corner grocery, with produce on its back to be sold to the merchant. Corner grocers are numerous. The charm is in the people. They seem happy, bouncing, animated, and talk - talk - all day long."

Fellow missionary Marilois Kirksey was in Rio and we drove together to Campinas. The highway around São Paulo was under construction and there were no detour signs. Marilois and I had come to Brazil together, so we were sort of in the same boat. Several times we stopped to ask directions. We thought they said, "À direita" (turn right), but each time we did this we knew we were off course. Finally Marilois decided they were saying "Vai direto" or go straight ahead. Then we went on to Campinas, having circumvented the populous city of São Paulo (today the population is about 18 million)!

I wrote January 7, 1964 from Campinas:

"I am living with Marilois Kirksey on the seventh floor of Edifício Progresso, a modern downtown apartment building. Mary Witt and I exchanged living quarters during language school vacation. I'm taking five hours per day with individual teachers at the language school. The teachers are all mature, lively, hard-working, and delightful. I have never done anything that was such a pleasure!

"Last weekend Marilois and I went on a 450-kilometer motor trip, staying overnight at a resort in the mountains. Saturday night at Poços de Caldas, a resort town ringed by mountains."

Back in Rio, I studied weekly at the Berlitz language school downtown. In my limited Portuguese I tried to witness to my teacher, explaining that the word oração not only was a grammatical term, but the word for "prayer" and that we can pray directly to God. He didn't accept that idea; I was too limited in the language to understand his reasoning.

Daily Bread

Shopping for food, household items, clothing and school supplies - well, anything - required astute detective work, patience, and bargaining know-how. We lived among millions of people; today the World Book Encyclopedia gives the Rio population at 14,062,000. Consider these factors:

Ongoing street, residential and commercial construction
Growth of population
Inflation which rose daily
Changing government policies
Strikes and labor problems
A revolution
Marketing and merchandising methods were just beginning to modernize

You can imagine the challenge to the missionaries: living on the missionary salary, and trying to carry on mission work!

WAK
The _feira_ (weekly street market) was set up before sunrise,
when the vendors prepared their stalls. The _feira_ was a ka-
leidoscope of color, voices, fruit, vegetables, household wares,
meat, fish, all kinds of food, and a hord of small children
vying to carry your baskets. I really felt I was being integrated into Brazilian life when I bought the heavy, canvas,
basket-bag for carrying purchases at the _feira_ and store.

At Praça Saens Peña, the nearest shopping center, there
were jewelry stores, pharmacies, clothing stores, Casa Sloper
(clothing, jewelry, perfume), Casa Olga, where you bought
stockings and lingerie, and a dime store (which was so crowded
I feared to enter). Downtown you bought exotic flowers at
the flower market, chocolate at Casa Kopenhagen, and umbrellas
at the umbrella house.

Stationery stores were often crowded by uniformed school
children and youth buying school supplies. There was a super-
market near the apartment building which was quite crowded.

Clayton Anderson Company produced American-style peanut butter and margarine, so we missionaries hastily passed word along
about what stores stocked those rarities! The Baptist Good
Will Center received nice flour in the relief food from United
States. Zelma Hallock, missionary serving there, helped us
to exchange rice for the flour, since the Brazilian housewife
preferred rice. At the apartment building Zelma was the ear-
liest shopper, often arriving home with her purchases when I
was arising. The Hallocks entertained many guests - missionaries, Brazilians, and their children Jackie's and Charlotte's
friends.

Later when we lived in Lajes and Montes Claros, we were
fortunate in that vegetables and fruits arrived weekly at the
municipal market. In Belo Horizonte they came almost daily;
and weekly to the neighborhood markets. After purchasing vegetables and fruits they had to be washed, adding clorox or io-
dine. Then they were packaged for storing in the refrigerator.
Such things as cream of mushroom soup, canned beets, cherry
pie mix, prepared pie crusts and canned tomatoes were not available, so as a homemaker I was constantly learning culinary
skills!

Certain Brazilian foods bring the nostalgia:

Creme _de_ _Leite_ (canned milk for substituting whipped cream)
Cashew nuts, freshly roasted
Peanuts - roasted and ground or, whole, carmelized in sug-
    ar syrup and sold hot, on the street
Corn Meal - the coarse texture used to make _polenta_
Fruits: pineapple, oranges, limes, mangos, bananas of many
    varieties, _goiaba_, _papaya_, _fruta_ _de_ _conde_
Sweetened, condensed milk carmelized in the can
Goiabada - thick guava jelly served in slices, with a
    slice of cheese (quality of cottage cheese)
105.

WAK
    Foods (Continued)
    Avocados - large. When ripe, the pulp was whipped with
        lemon juice and sugar, making a pudding
    Cheese Bread: specialty of Minas Gerais state
    Ice Cream - brand name <u>Kibon</u> (How Good)
    <u>Guaraná</u> - drink made from seeds of the <u>guaraná</u> bush
    Green Cocoanut: split open so you can drink the milk and
        spoon up the tender pulp

    Nurturing the family and home is very important for the
missionaries. The home is the center of our life. Being away
from our own country, we are deprived of participating in many
civic activities which give stability. I always tried to cast
an absentee vote for President. The missionary home is refuge,
nourisher, strengthener, witness, and furnishes the emotional
"glue" that identifies our personalities. I felt that home-
making was a vital part of being a missionary, and I was aware
that my Brazilian friends recognized the value I placed upon
caring for our home.

<u>Finance: South, North, & Equatorial Missions</u>

    I was to work in the office of the Treasurer, located at
the Praça da Bandeira. We tried to combine transportation,
arriving at the office at 8:30 A.M. We usually went home for
lunch from 11:30 to 1:00 o'clock, then left about 5:00 P.M.
Maida Bridges was the bookkeeper and Opal was a clerk. Missionary Shirley Jackson was a secretary and Francisco, faithful Brazilian layman, handled the street work as well as being
janitor.

    Missionaries Sam Qualls and Claud Bumpus were Treasurer and
Auditor, respectively, of the three Brazil Missions: South,
North and Equatorial.

    This office was established on Brazilian soil in accordance
with the laws of the country. The permit to do business was
inspected at random by Brazilian authorities. This office received funds from the Foreign Mission Board at Richmond, Virginia, and disbursed them in accordance with business practices
established by that Board. The entire business was audited
annually by qualified auditors.

    Documents were received from the Board indicating transfer
of dollars. The task was then to get the money to the recip-
ients indicated, in Cruzeiros. Since the rate of exchange was
always inflationary, timing was urgent.

    Besides sending out the monthly payroll, this office dis-
bursed Cruzeiros to institutions, Baptist state conventions,
and special payments to individuals. We handled financial
affairs for arriving and departing missionaries. Sometimes
Sam, Claud, and Victor Davis, Area Representative for Brazil,
would huddle in conference, to solve unforeseen problems.

WAK

Compared with modern American office systems, this was quite a contrast. Telephone service was by an extension of the Baptist Publishing House. Long distance calls were nerve wracking; later modernization by satellite service was bright contrast. Finally, the office got its own telephone.

Sending money to different locations (before the days of electronic transactions) was done through the bank indicated by the recipient. Francisco went to those banks to buy the transactions, battling long lines of customers. We might receive a Mayday call from a missionary, "I haven't received my payroll!" Then we researched our records so he could negotiate at his home bank. The office purchased a Pitney Bowes postage machine for mail. Francisco battled crowded bus traffic during the day, and crowded trains back and forth to his home.

After several weeks as a new worker in the office I began training as bookkeeper and undertook this responsibility when Maida went on vacation. Afterward I became secretary, a responsibility until October, 1967. Since I had experience in the organization and retention of paper records, I worked on the handling of active and stored records.

The enlarged office staff made it necessary to move several times to rented space, then the Treasurer's office located in the South Brazil Mission quarters on the top floor of the modern, eleven-floor building at Praça Saens Peña.

Vacations

Missionary Alma Jackson arranged for my first vacation in the home of Dr. and Mrs. Rassi in Goiânia, capital of Goiás. These friends of Alma's received me in their home and family life. Mrs. Rassi spoke English, although neither the four children, her mother, nor her husband did.

Another vacation was in the home of missionaries John and Jean Poe and their four boys and one girl, who lived in Blumenau, Santa Catarina. Jean explained about the cold weather: the coldness that I noticed was only the first wave - it would intensify later when they would bring out their winter clothing. In Blumenau we visited the Schmidt Porcelain Company where they made china, and I bought a beautiful white, cotton damask tablecoth with twelve napkins woven in that city.

Missionaries Albert and Thelma Bagby of Pôrto Alegre, Rio Grande do Sul, invited me to their home for a week. Albert was a concert pianist, son of pioneer missionaries William and Ann Bagby. He was director of the Baptist school, and Thelma assisted. This wonderful couple had JOY and the gift of spreading it. Their friendship had the quality of a perfectly formed pearl, with glow of a muted patina.

107.

Why Is Everyone Whispering?

Katherine Cozzens went on furlough and Miss Pearl Stapp returned so she and I were living in the apartment at 512 Rua Uruguai. Miss Pearl was the daughter of missionaries and had lived in Brazil since she was a child. She taught Theology at the Training School, and was deeply loved by the students, as well as by her Brazilian friends.

Miss Pearl had a heart condition and was not feeling well. One noon when I came home to lunch the maid excitedly told me that Miss Pearl "looked funny." She was in her bed, having died only minutes before. Emanetta Qualls who lived across the hall came and called a doctor so as to establish a death certificate. Others in the building came and we were tiptoeing quietly and whispering. Emanetta's daughter Elizabeth, a fourth grader, asked,

"Mother, why is everyone whispering? Miss Pearl can't hear you anyway."

Jackie Hallock, Edgar and Zelma's son, thoughtfully went to the yard, selected an orchid, and placed it in a vase in Pearl's room.

We women washed the body and dressed it. When the beautiful, ornately carved, wooden casket arrived her students placed her in it. The men who brought the casket carried it to the Training School, just down the hill. The girls and missionary ladies covered the sheet up to Miss Pearl's hands, with the purple funeral flower. Then a white, fine netting covered the body.

The officers of the Mission contacted the family and funeral and burial arrangements were made for the following day. In Brazil, the body is to be interred within twenty-four hours. Shirley Jackson went to the office and sent telegrams to all missionary personnel of Brazil.

An official U.S. government limousine arrived at the Training School at 2:00 P.M. the next day for the funeral. Gordon Mein, assistant U.S. ambassador to Brazil had come, for his missionary parents and Pearl and her late husband Charles F. Stapp had worked together in the North Brazil Mission.

Mission cars and a few Brazilians' cars made up the entourage to the cemetery. No hearse; no limousine to carry family. The casket was placed in the same repository with the remains of missionaries Albertine Meador and Mrs. A.B. Deter.

My letter to Elizabeth September 27, 1964:

"Let me tell you about the cemetery. It is almost solid concrete, with the receptacles for receiving the coffins on top of the ground. Mrs. Deter's and Albertine Meador's bones had been removed from their coffins five years after death, placed in two little boxes, and sealed. These boxes were removed and Pearl's coffin was lowered. Bars were fit in place, then we threw in small bouquets and single flowers. Two heavy slabs were placed and cemented at the edges, and the boxes containing bones were placed on top. The temporary, tin cover of all would be replaced by the permanent, marble slab after the name was engraved."

After the loving act of placing a missionary in her final resting place and granting dignity to the deceased, we drove from the cemetery into the roaring, bumper-to-bumper traffic. The noise and rush startled me into the reality of the press of the demands of living.

I was on the committee to correspond with Miss Pearl's sister about caring for the missionary's possessions. One of her directives was for us to care for her hymnal. We decided to give it to Jes Sutton, son of Joan and Boyd. Jes flashed a smile of gratitude.

Church Membership

I chose to join First Baptist Church of Rio, so I made an appointment with the pastor Dr. João Soren and I was required to attend the next business meeting to be voted into the membership. I traveled to church with Nonna and F.B. Huey, but when they went on furlough I was on my own. The church was after the "Y" of Conde de Bonfim and Avenida Frei Caneca. The landmark for getting off the streetcar was a prison.

In Sunday School class I could only listen and try to recognize meaningful words. The conviction that I was in God's directive will was thrilling, and just to enter the church was exciting. I didn't want to be anywhere else doing anything else.

I began to participate in the choir, but I found the music quite illegible since it had been hand written and printed on an alcohol copier. The choristers helped me to know when to stand, sit, pray, sing, remain silent, and when to go home. When I learned some Portuguese I indicated to the choir director, Marília Soren, that I could prepare a solo. The choir sang from the balcony of the vast auditorium, so when I sang my first solo I realized it was a real test of ones ability to communicate. But the song went well and I felt liberated -

"Now! I can tell others about Jesus!"

WAK

Some of the youth at the church indicated they wanted me to take them to downtown Rio for an <u>Ar Livre</u>. I didn't know what that was, but I promised to take them Sunday afternoon. I realized as we started out that my passengers were not accustomed to traveling in Rio in a car, and they could not direct me. Somehow I managed to get to the designated park downtown. There they set up the sound system; someone preached and we sang; then another youth preached. We passed out religious tracts to the bystanders, some of whom stayed to listen to more preaching and singing. Thus I learned about open air evangelistic services, used very much. (I found my way back to the church afterward).

The Green Dauphine

The first Mission car assigned to me had a French name, and the temperament of a French lady. While driving in Rio traffic it would simply stop. However, after trying vainly to get it started again, some energetic, hearty men would converge on us, give a good shove, and off we would go to shouts and laughter - my green Dauphine and I!

Once when backing from a parking lot downtown I hit a car. A lot of people gathered and began to discuss the accident. When they realized that I couldn't talk much in Portuguese, they merrily waved me into traffic and on my way!

Driving in Rio was not too hard because you couldn't get anywhere very fast. It took at least an hour to get from our resident community to downtown, because of congestion. The city government secretly worked out a plan to re-route traffic and to eliminate the illegal parking of thousands of cars. One night while we slept they relocated traffic signs and deflated the tires on illegally parked cars.

Can you imagine the chaos that morning when thousands of workers could not find the buses they customarily rode; when we motorists couldn't find routes to our destinations; and when all those cars had flat tires? The final result after the confusion settled, was that traffic flowed.

Annual Mission Meeting

Mission Meeting in July, 1964 was in a hotel at Patí dos Alferes, a town near Rio. The 127 missionaries and their children were there for a week. This was the first time to meet away from the city of Rio which was delightful because the Rio people were free from entertaining the visitors. There were business sessions and recreation in the daytime, as well as Vacation Bible School for the Missionary Kids (MK's). The evenings were for inspirational time. The children and youth looked forward to this annual time when they could be with their friends, and they often formed deep relationships.

110.

Missionary Robert Johnson Sr. was coming through Rio as a fraternal representative from the North Brazil Mission, so he drove my car to Patí dos Alferes since I did not have a Brazilian driver's license - just a permit.

Many of the missionaries were quite new, and there were a number of enthusiastic, called, individualistic people. Harrison Pike was elected moderator, and was an astute follower of "Robert's Rules of Order." Richard Plampin was parliamentarian.

At the Salvador Conference in 1963 (Intermission Committee of Americans meeting with Brazilian Baptist leaders) the Brazilians initiated a plan for the national evangelistic campaign. Missionary Earl Peacock was to direct the 1965 campaign, and this undertaking was part of the sessions at Patí dos Alferes.

As an Associate Missionary I did not have voting privilege; in later years this was granted. Nonetheless, I enjoyed the meeting. Shirley Jackson had warned me that the weather could be cold, so I had bought two pairs of stockings at Casa Olga - one teal blue and one black, the only colors they had. Later I was puzzled why a missionary lady seemed to be unfriendly. Many months later she confessed that when she saw me in those stockings she decided I was "way out" and she didn't want anything to do with me!

The Atherino Clinic

The physical exam the Foreign Mission Board required in 1963 had confirmed what I already knew - that my left eardrum was perforated. Now the problem of hearing intensified, and I could not bear the increased irritation by any sound. Dr. Atherino, ear specialist in Rio, recommended a tympanoplasty, so late in 1966 I entered his clinic.

The surgery was done by general anesthesia and a blood vessel above the left ear was utilized. Dr. Atherino warned Frances Bumpus not to let me lie on the left side during recovery from the anesthesia. She had the courage to keep on bodily throwing me, to keep me on the right side. I have realized that when Frances' husband Claud came home that day expecting a hot lunch he had to settle for probably a self-made, cold sandwich.

WAK   I WILL PRAISE YOU, O LORD

> Trust in the Lord, and do good; Dwell in the land,
>   and feed on His faithfulness.
> Delight yourself also in the Lord,
> And He shall give you the desires of your heart.
> Commit your way to the Lord, Trust also in Him,
>   And He shall bring it to pass.
>   Psalm 37:3-5 NKJ

Music was one avenue by which this learner could find expression. In Rio, Katherine Cozzens presented the Baptist hymnal "Cantor Cristão" to me. She cited several familiar melodies and taught me the words phonetically. She introduced me to Eurico Freitas who was the Training Union Director in the nearby Itacuruçá Church. He graciously consented for me to sing in Sunday evening Training Union assembly, my first venture in singing in Portuguese, and only a few weeks in Brazil!

In those early years, as soon as I could get enough of the rhythm and pronunciation of a song, I sang it - in Sunday School, Training Union; in a wedding, or worship service. Once I sang at a wedding at São Francisco Xavier Church, using (I thought) acceptable Portuguese. Afterward a lady said,

"That was such beautiful Latin!"

Any hour, one could get classical music on the radio. An undated letter of 1963:

> "There was a Bach program at Itacuruçá Church Sunday evening. I sang a solo from "The Passion of Our Lord According to St. Matthew," translation by Dr. João Soren, pastor of First Church. The Brazilians don't just sit - they absorb the music - and communicate back."

November 20, 1963 I wrote of being invited, with other missionaries, to the residence of Assistant U.S. Ambassador Gordon Mein and his wife. They lived on the fifth floor and had plate glass sliding doors opening onto the balcony. While standing on the balcony I felt I could reach out and pluck the illuminated statue "Cristo Redentor," as it seemed to hang in the air atop distant Corcovado Mountain. That night I sang "Getting to Know You" from "The King And I." Glaucia Vasconcellos accompanied me.

> "How Lovely Are Thy Dwellings" - Psalm 84, by Samuel Liddle
> "Come Ye Blessed" - Matthew 25:34-36, by John Prindle Scott
>   I sang these in Portuguese at evening worship, First Church, November 24, 1963.

113.

WAK   **<u>Music</u> <u>Literature</u> <u>And</u> <u>Education</u>**

There was only limited choice of printed music in the Baptist Book Store in Rio. Some of the titles:

"Cantor Cristão" with music; 15th printing 1961
"Cantor Cristão" text only
"Côros Sacros" in separate volumes, compiled by Artur Lak-
    schevitz. Combined into one hardback 1967
"Pérolas" (Pearls); miscellaneous; compiled by Alyna Muir-
    head 1956
"Antemas Celestes" choir selections (difficult); compiled
    by Alyna Muirhead. Published again in 1980
"Hinário do Grande Coral" choir music published for Bap-
    tist World Alliance evangelistic crusade in Rio
    June 26 - July 3, 1960
"Melodias de Vitória" miscellaneous; published by Seventh
    Day Adventists 1955
"Os Ceus Proclamam" (The Heavens Declare) Volume I; com-
    piled by João Wilson Faustini 1962
"Cânticos Para Crianças" compiled by Edith A. Allen; 3rd
    edition 1964. Mrs. Allen composed many of the songs.
"Cânticos do Natal" Henriqueta Rosa Fernandes Braga 1947
"O Festival de Música Sacra" compiled by Alyna Muirhead
"Hinos de Louvor" compiled by Grace Cowsert 1950

★★★★★★★★★★★★★★★★

In 1971 the revised "Cantor Cristão" was published, 36th edition - eighty years since the first edition. Missionary Joan Sutton enlisted her music students at the Rio Seminary to research the documentation: authors, composers, translators, source of text and melodies, metric patterns, and indices; also the music and texts were corrected and updated.

In 1990 the new hymnal, "Hinário Para O Culto Cristão" was published - the first new hymnal since the "Cantor Cristão."

Joan and Boyd Sutton at the Rio Seminary and Fred Spann at the Recife Seminary were pioneering in establishing music curriculum for their schools. In Rio the Suttons established a degree plan patterned after Southern Baptist Seminary, Louisville, Kentucky. As this developed there were more positions of Minister of Music in churches, and denominational posts, than there were graduates to fill them. Also, Brazilians were composing and publishing sacred music, available nationally.

Several other music missionaries were at work in the South Brazil Mission when I arrived (others came later):

Bill Ichter, Director of Music, Brazilian Baptist Convention
Gene Wilson, Director of Music, state of Rio Grande Do Sul
    (appointed in 1963).

114.

The chorus of the song says, "Wherever He Leads I'll Go," an expression of my attitude during the learning years in Rio. The youth of First Church could always use a soloist when they did street preaching on the sidewalks of the crowded downtown area. I sang from the hymnal.

At my first annual Mission Meeting, July 1964, I joined other missionaries for street preaching in the town Patí do Alferes, and sang a hymn.

Bill Warren, pastor of Copacabana Church in Rio (English speaking) invited me to sing on a Sunday morning. Gordon Mein was worshiping there, and he was very attentive to the music. Bill asked that statesman to lead in prayer, and I heard the Missionary Kid now grown up and in the U.S. Diplomatic Corps pray,

"Lord, help us in our daily work."

Later, when Gordon was Ambassador to a Central American country, he was murdered on the street. The missionary family mourned the tragedy.

As one mingled with the crowds of Christmas shoppers, it would suddenly surface to the consciousness, "That loudspeaker is playing music about snow - in this high 90's heat!"

"I'm Dreaming Of A White Christmas"
"Jingle Bells"
"Rudolph, The Red-Nosed Reindeer"

When I was a member of São Francisco Xavier Church in Rio I directed the Adult Choir a few months. The people of the church enthusiastically worked to evangelize, and I sensed the warmth of a loving people. Some members were from the nearby favela (ghetto). The pastor Marcílio Teixeira was studying at the seminary, and the bond of friendship offered by him and his wife Helena was precious.

Sometimes in visiting churches, I encountered the most fascinating paradox. On Sunday night, the principal worship hour, at the time for the choir to sing, the choristers and director took their places at the front of the church. The leader, who did not have a pitch pipe or tuning fork, hummed the pitches for soprano, alto, tenor and bass. He repeated the pitches until he felt they were ready to sing. (No one had music.)

Then the choir sang an intricate, long anthem, with special passages for some or all the four voices. I marveled at the rhythm, the timbre of the voices, and the harmony. But the puzzle was that I sensed those people who sang so beautifully, didn't read music!

The Encouragers

A smile - a thoughtful word - a good suggestion; all this from my encouragers Joan and Boyd Sutton. Boyd was directing the music studies at the South Brazil Seminary in Rio, and Joan was a teacher there. I admired their dedication to music; Boyd's ability as a tenor soloist blessed my life. Joan had been reared in Brazil; as a child she traveled with her missionary parents John L. and Prudence Riffey, to the churches.

She asked to borrow my copy of "The Messiah," then she expertly penned in the Portuguese text to the alto solos, and returned it as my birthday present! Joan was respected in Brazilian academia as an authority of the Portuguese language. She had many requests from Americans to translate English music texts, to which she would promise,

"Send me your music, and I'll place your stack alongside the other stacks. I'll do it when I can."

I extol Joan the teacher, pianist, conductor, violinist, composer, linguist, strategist, arbitrater, but most of all, my friend. Finally, I think she had the brain of a mathematician/scientist - and the compassionate heart of a missionary.

Associacão Canto Coral

The Association (for the) Singing of Choral Music was composed of music lovers who met regularly and prepared concerts. They were a part of the government's promotion of fine arts. Cleofe Person de Mattos, professor of sight reading was the director. Boyd Sutton was a member and he helped me to join. Dona Cleofe trained us, preparing for the programs, which were usually led by other conductors. I loved the challenging repertoire; I list some of the music we sang in Rio de Janeiro.

August 19, 1964
Music of William Byrd, conducted by Sir Thomas Armstrong, head of Royal College of Music of London

October 18, 1964
"King David" by Arthur Honegger and "Dance of the Dead" with orchestra. Municipal Theater

September 16, 1966
"The Messiah" in English, with orchestra
Municipal Theater

We heard a startling sound while the tenor soloist was singing a sustained note in "The Messiah." That Sunday afternoon the theater was full, even to the balconies. When his voice cracked we in the chorus didn't react, but we heard a rustling, as of a wind passing through. It was the movement of the people reacting to the unusual break. However, the performance continued and the rustling subsided.

WAK

My friend Anna Campello taught music at the Rio Seminary, having studied in São Paulo, and graduated from the Baptist Seminary, Louisville, Kentucky. Anna, Elza Lakschevitz and I were all single and we had a camaraderie. Later we all married.

Anna helped me prepare a recital to give in the auditorium of the Associação Canto Coral.

RECITAL DE CANTO
de Wilma Alice Gemmell
Anna Campello, Piano
dia 5 de dezembro de 1964 as 16 horas

Messias..G.F. Handel
   "Then Shall the Eyes of the Blind Be Opened"
    Recitativo e Ária
   "Behold! A Virgin Shall Conceive"
    Recitativo e Ária

Judas Maccabaeus.....................................G.F. Handel
   "Father of Heav'n!"

"An Die Musik"....................................Franz Schubert

"Der Alpenjager"..................................Franz Schubert

La Favorita......................................Gaetano Donizetti
   Ária "O Mio Fernando"

Canções Brasileiras

"A Sombra"......................................Francisco Mignone
"Modinha"...Jayme Ovalle

Folclore Americano das Montanhas

"Black is the Color"...............................Arr. J.G. Niles
"The Deaf Old Woman"..........................Arr. Katherine Davis

Canções Americanas

"Oh Lovely Night"................................Landon Ronald
"Sea Moods"......................................Mildred Tyson

****

Some of the members of the Associãcao had gone to the Municipal Theater to music where they learned it was canceled. They drifted over to our program - augmenting our audience!

117.

V.

WONDERFUL NEW DIMENSION

> **For who is God besides the Lord?**
> **And who is the Rock except our God?**
> **It is God who arms me with strength**
>   **and makes my way perfect.**
> **He makes my feet like the feet of a deer;**
>   **he enables me to stand on the heights.**
>   **Psalm 18:31-33 NIV**

For some weeks I sensed that something was tugging at my consciousness. One day at work I wrote on a piece of paper:

"All right, Lord. I understand that You are directing me to return to the States. I WILL be obedient even though I don't understand. After years and years of sensing Your call to serve You on a foreign mission field, I came to Brazil to work in this office. Do You realize I haven't completed the five-year term? But You are telling me to return to the States; so, yes, I'll do Your bidding."

I thought Bob Baker, seminary teacher in Rio, might be a good counselor. The family was leaving Brazil and Bob was in Rio to sell their furniture. We agreed to talk at the Alvin Hatton residence on Dona Delfina Street. There, Katie led us to the back porch, where the rock embankment ascends to the Seminary. I had talked to the Lord about this meeting, asking Him to reveal His will.

I explained to Bob that the Lord was indicating that I return to the States, but to what? What would I DO in the States, and would I take my Beautyrest mattress and springs with me? And my refrigerator? After all, I was forty-five years old! Bob sat in silence for interminable minutes. Finally he spoke:

"Do you know Jesse Kidd?"

"No, not personally, but I know there is a person by that name since our office insures his car."

"Jesse Kidd is a good missionary. If I were you I would go up to Volta Redonda where he lives."

That was the end of the conversation, so I thanked Bob for his taking time to meet with me, and we both left.

(I handled the automobile insurance records in the Mission office. The insurance company required that the chassis number be taken by impression and sent to us, and we also required the license number and model description. Hence I was spending a lot of time on this. Jesse's blue Chevrolet Veraneio was in the group policy.)

WAK

I had promised God that I would follow His leadership, so after pondering on the conversation with Bob, I called Mrs. Walter McNealy, the missionary at Volta Redonda, and asked if it were convenient for me to come and visit them.

  "We'd be delighted to have you. Just let me know the hour
  of your bus arrival and I'll meet you."

Senhor Francisco of the Treasurer's office purchased the ticket and on a Saturday in April, 1967 I boarded the bus for the two-hour ride. Mrs. McNealy (Dona Geny) met me.

  "Tch, tch, you don't wear slacks in the interior."

As we got into the microbus (van), she said,

  "We'll stop at the school and talk with Mr. Kidd. He usually
  eats Saturday lunch with us."

We stopped at the Colégio do Instituto Batista Americano and I waited in the van. As Dona Geny and Jesse stood in the door of the school talking, I was impressed by the thought,

  "This is your future husband."

  Dona Geny was known as a marvelous hostess and cook. She decorated their rented house with beautiful curtains and area rugs so one was not concerned that the solid wood furniture was new or old. Color, fabrics, pictures and plants tastefully arranged reflected a warmth and delight to the visitor. For meals the table was set artfully and Dona Geny sat at the head.

  Jesse ate lunch at the McNealys Saturday and Sunday. Sunday afternoon I took a bus back to Rio. On Monday I was so disturbed that I called the office pleading sickness. I called Dona Marcolina, my language teacher, asking to meet with her. She lived near the Seminary, and it was convenient to go there by bus. I explained the events of the weekend; and that God had chosen Jesse Kidd as my husband.

  "Do you think it reasonable that I return to Volta Redonda
  and ask him to marry me?"

Dona Marcolina loved and understood me. Thoughtfully she said "Yes," so again I went through the same steps: get the bus ticket, call Dona Geny, and make the journey. Again I arrived for Saturday lunch, and again Jesse was there. As I sat at the table for lunch on Sunday I observed Jesse's personality and said silently to God:

  "You've brought me this far, and if anyone is the innovator
  it will be Jesse Kidd, not I."

After lunch, Jesse asked me if he could carry me back to Rio.

122.

Dr. Henrique Mayr had been my gynecologist since I came to Rio. He was the son of German immigrants and spoke English with an accent. He had practiced in Santa Catarina before moving to the Copacabana area of Rio. He cared so much for his patients that he made it a practice to visit with each one who had an appointment before getting to the medical part.

In May 1967 he was my surgeon for hemorrhoids in what we called the German Hospital, noted for its cleanliness and expert nursing staff. Several missionary friends were in my room during recovery from anesthesia, and I couldn't speak to tell them I was cold. They were having such a good chat, but finally they covered me with a warm blanket. As my eyes began focusing I identified a bouquet of a dozen roses from a special visitor.

Joan and Boyd Sutton invited me to their home when I could leave the hospital. After several days there Jesse came for me and took me to the McNealy's home in Volta Redonda. He devised a bench so I could lie down in the back of his Chevrolet. These were days of pampering and sleeping. About six o'clock in the morning I could hear Mrs. McNealy leaving to do the daily food shopping.

One morning after breakfast Brother McNealy asked if we could remain at the table and just talk. He told me how they had worked with Jesse since he came March 19, 1958. He verified that Jesse followed his missionary calling to Brazil even though he was not appointed by the Foreign Mission Board.

"I know Brother Kidd closer than a brother. We've been together through many hard situations and trials. Sometimes we'd be on the road many, many hours without proper food. We fought the battle to get books and supplies ready for the school sessions.

"You can count on Jesse. He maintains respect for us and we for him. The students at the American School love and respect him. The people at the church love him too.

"I can vouch for him."

I listened thoughtfully and attentively to Brother McNealy even though Jesse and I had already determined that we loved each other.

I had heard Jesse speak of Ebenezer Baptist Church, his last pastorate near El Dorado, Arkansas. I could tell he loved those people. He related that his support was a love offering the churches of Liberty Baptist Association (south Arkansas) sent monthly. He shared that Lonnie Lassiter of Greenwood, Arkansas had promoted the purchase of a Volkswagon van (Kombi) and he had traded it for the Chevrolet he now drove.

123.

The highway between Volta Redonda and Rio de Janeiro had long, tiresome detours since it was still being repaired after the 1966 floods; but that did not deter our courtship. One evening when I had gone to see him, Jesse carried me to his school for a program in the gymn. The young people were seated in the bleachers, but that is not where we sat. Jesse escorted me to a front seat on the playing court, in full view of the students.

In December 1964 I had moved away from the Mission apartment to 451 Avenida Paulo de Frontim, apartment 401. This was just a few minutes from the bus station, so it was convenient to travel to Volta Redonda to be with Jesse on Saturday evening, returning Sunday morning to direct the Adult choir at my church, São Francisco Xavier.

Once, as I was stepping up to the bus at the Rio station, a delicious, comforting, blanket of warmth enveloped me, and I had the intense impression,

"I'm going home!"

How could that be? Dad died nine years before and Mother was approaching death at Crowell Nursing Home in Blair, Nebraska. But I could not deny that experience.

We bought our wedding rings at Casa Matos, a jewelry store on Rua Ouvidor, near the flower market in downtown Rio. We were shown samples and the rings were ordered.

Rua Ouvidor
In the book "Amazon Throne, the Story of the Braganzas of Brasil" by Bertita Harding, the arrival of the Portuguese Regent Don João and his wife Carlota Joaquina is described. In March 1808, they came into the port of Rio de Janeiro and weighed anchor. Rua Ouvidor is mentioned as the main artery of the town: Rua do Ouvidor (Street of the Royal Audience). In our time it was a narrow, cobblestone, walking street, where no automobiles were allowed.

When I drove back to Rio after attending the 1967 Mission Meeting, I stopped at Volta Redonda to be with Jesse. The next day, July 12, he was at my apartment. We each placed the wedding ring on the other's right, ring finger, according to the Brazilian custom for engagement.

Jesse mentioned an American style engagement ring, but since I didn't know his income I said I was happy with the wedding ring. On a visit to Rio he boldly announced that we would look for an engagement ring. We picked out a diamond at Casa Hugo, where the Americans often traded. Mr. Hugo called in a jeweler and we described the "mirror" setting. I had often admired Jo Stover's ring of that design. So I wore an engagement ring on each hand.

My sisters had written about Mother's deteriorating health
so I wrote to her May 11, 1967:

"I cannot list all the blessings you have brought to my life
but I want to humbly express all my appreciation for what
you have given me and done for me. I don't think you will
ever know what it has meant to me here in Brazil - to get
your many, many faithful letters and your encouragement.
I know periodically when to expect your letters - and they
always come."

                  ****

I wrote to my family July 22, 1967:

"I wish to put in writing my gratitude for your thoughtfulness and for all you have done. I'm so sorry that Jessie
and Paul had the hospital experiences at this time; each
one of you in the things you did and said, performed a
ministry and you were blessings."

                  ****

On July 27, 1967 I wrote to my four sisters and one brother:

"What can I say about Mother? I have left the care and the
loving to you so much - however I have a peace within me in
my trust to all of you. It is more difficult for you than
for me to see her fail so fast, for her life has been more
closely entwined with yours than with mine. I can only en-
trust her to God's purpose and strength - in these which
appear to be her last days."

                  ****

Mother died August 1, 1967. The girls and Fred took care
of the funeral at the Baptist church in Blair, as well as her
burial in the Carroll, Nebraska cemetery. Mother specified
before her death that she didn't want a sermon eulogizing her;
but an evangelistic one. The family carried out her wish.

After our marriage the following October Jesse and I were
traveling in Nebraska, and we stopped at the Crowell Home in
Blair. We sat with the director chatting, and mentally I recalled Mother's ministry to others; I thought of her seated at
her easel, painting in oil, in her room here at Crowell. All
the accumulated, unexpressed grief burst out in agonized crying and sobbing. It was good to grieve.

That is, "So long." We planned to fly to Charlotte, North Carolina, October 9 so I moved from my apartment in town to the Mission apartments at 512 Rua Uruguai, living with Virginia Terry. Virginia would keep my bed, sofa, and chest of drawers in her apartment. I also had a dining room suite.

The ground floor of the building was divided into storage units and the missionaries graciously shared space with me for household and personal things, wedding and shower gifts. We knew we would come back, but we didn't know when.

How lovingly the missionary family celebrated!

September 29: Linen shower by Minnie Lou Lanier and Catherine Chappell
September 30: Miscellaneous shower by Katie Hatton and Dona Marcolina, my language teacher
October 7: Coffee given by Marilois Kirksey

When we boarded the plane to leave about midnight October 9, the missionaries were there at the airport waving Boa Viagem! Also some from my church São Francisco Xavier, as well as Jesse's dear friends from Volta Redonda.

* * * * * * * * * * * * * * *

St. John's Church just couldn't do enough for us. Someone met us at the airport and carried us to Heart of Charlotte motel where one of the members hosted us. Dot Nordan, a very special friend, called and offered herself and her car for any of our needs. Dr. Leslie McLeod cared for the marriage documents so all we had to do was go to the courthouse and affix our signatures.

Irene Kimball would meet Elizabeth when she arrived from Dexter, Missouri - receive her in her home and take her back to the airport. There was to be a wedding in the chapel Saturday evening, and it was arranged that our ceremony would be at 12:00 noon since the flowers and candles would already be in place.

Kays Gary, writer for the Charlotte paper, published an article about the flap going on at St. John's, and from then to our departure the telephone calls, letters, cards and gifts deluged us.

At noon on Saturday October 14, 1967 the weather was perfect. Dr. Broach my pastor handled the ceremony beautifully, and we were blessed by the presence of Elizabeth and those wonderful friends who gathered in the church's beautiful chapel. The ladies had a reception, where we could chat briefly with the guests.

126.

It was April 1967 and I had been in Brazil over nine years. Wilma Alice Gemmell came to visit the McNealys in Volta Redonda and they invited me to have lunch with them and their guest in their home. I do not say that it was love at first sight; I just knew I had met the one to be my wife. (That took some getting used to!)

God in His own time and way had blessed my willingness to wait on Him. In spite of the extensive road construction because of the 1966 flood, I often made my way to Rio de Janeiro. Wilma lived in an apartment on Avenida Paulo de Frontim and later she moved to the Mission apartments at 512 Rua Uruguai, located on the same grounds as the Training School for young women. They locked the gate nightly at 10:00 P.M. One Friday night I let the time get away and discovered the gate was locked. I had to climb over the six-foot-high stronghold (it was not made for climbing to get in or out).

We were married in the beautiful chapel of St. John's Baptist Church in Charlotte, North Carolina, the church where Wilma was a member when she left the States. Dr. Claude U. Broach, the pastor, performed the ceremony in the presence of Wilma's - and now my - friends and Mrs. Elizabeth Norris, Wilma's sister. Dot and James Nordan were special friends; Dr. Roberts Lasater was Associate Pastor of St. John's. There were many who were pleased to work out the details of preparing for the ceremony at 12:00 noon October 14, 1967.

As soon as we could get a car we traveled so I could meet Wilma's family. There were four sisters and one brother: Elizabeth and Charles Norris of Dexter, Missouri; Jessie and Paul Back of Red Oak, Iowa; Fred and Cora Gemmell of Malvern, Iowa; Elsie and Charles Whitney of Carroll, Nebraska; and Jean and Harold Smith of Salt Lake City, Utah.

Wilma had twenty nieces and nephews so we touched base with some of them: Janel and Larry Howard of Hannibal, Missouri; Merle and Bonnie Whitney of Wayne, and June and Milton Stanley of Norfolk, Nebraska.

I had an appointment to fulfill in El Dorado, Arkansas late in November: Training Union Mobilization Night (M night) of Liberty Baptist Association. There I introduced my bride to the dear people who had supported me during my time in Brazil. After we settled in an apartment in El Dorado we were given a shower by the Liberty Association December 4.

We traveled to East Texas to be with my family. My sister Willie Mae and her husband Rex Mathews lived at Hemphill. Their children Johnny and Patty Mathews in Nacogdoches; Rexene and Del Setters in Pineland; Alice and Raymond Neal in San Augustine. Curtis Ann and Ted Kehtel were in Germany. We had been with my nephew George Neal Kidd in El Dorado.

JLK

How is it that we grew together in fellowship and love within our marriage despite the stresses and demands of mission work?

<u>God</u> used our daily practice of Bible reading and prayer together. Even before we were married we spent time together, reading the Bible and praying.

<u>God</u> used the lives and examples of our parents: Robert and Ellen Gemmell and John and Ida Kidd. They had tried as best they could to follow the Lord and to be examples to their children.

<u>God</u> gave us the support of colleagues and friends who loved us and prayed for us.

While on a furlough we were in a group of missionaries meeting at the Sunday School Board in Nashville, Tennessee. The leader asked the couples to think on the questions,

"How did you as a couple get together? How did you stay together?"

We shared this:

"There have been very few days in our years together that we have not had our daily time of prayer and Bible study together. We kept our daily appointment with Him, even under difficult circumstances. We have given Him time to work out His will in us."

Submit to one another out of reverence for Christ.
Ephesians 5:21 NIV

God has given us many wonderful years together.

He who finds a wife finds what is good
and receives favor from the Lord.
Proverbs 18:22 NIV

I did not find Wilma; God brought her to me. She is worth far more than the rubies mentioned in Proverbs 31:10.

Love that does not grow but remains static soon becomes insipid. It dies unnourished, uncared for. Love must be nurtured, then it grows. Falling in love may be a one-time event, but love that grows and endures is a process. It becomes richer, deeper, and always more rewarding.

The relationship of a couple that has been built on love and its diverse elements becomes a haven, a fortress. The storms that come are no threat to the relationship - it is their tower of strength.

128.

VI.

TOGETHER WE SERVE

It was good to be in the United States, where we could communicate in English, and contact with our families was so convenient. Our first home was in El Dorado, then we moved to Arkadelphia, Arkansas where we studied at Ouachita Baptist University in the spring of 1968. The churches eagerly invited us to tell about mission work.

But our thoughts were on Brazil. The McNealys had been profuse in their invitation to Volta Redonda, and the door was still open. However we felt we should approach the Foreign Mission Board and seek an appointment. Jesse accepted the interim pastorate of Marrable Hill Baptist Church in El Dorado about May 1968, while we were in the appointment process. We stayed until leaving for Brazil July 1969.

Associate Missionaries

We went to the Little Rock, Arkansas airport to meet with Louis Cobbs, secretary for Missionary Personnel of the Board. We told him of our desire to return to Brazil under the Board; it was Louis who guided us through the appointment process.

Physical and psychiatric examinations
Updating our histories of education, employment, and auto-
    biographies
Stating our doctrinal beliefs, calling, and commitment
We each gave twenty-five names for recommendations

By chance we encountered Jesse Fletcher, who had been with the Board.

"Jesse Kidd, I hope this appointment goes through. There are several thick files on you at the Board, bulging with correspondence from Arkansas."

We went to the headquarters in Richmond, Virginia along with other appointees, when the Executive Board was in session. Each of us spent a few minutes with the members. Mrs. Carl Bates asked Jesse how he felt about being a Southern Baptist (I think she assumed he had been an "Independent"). Jesse replied,

"In my years as pastor in Arkansas and as a missionary in Brazil, I have always been a Southern Baptist."

Our hearts were warmed and strengthened in our five days with Louis Cobbs and others of the staff. We were appointed Associate Missionaries to Brazil March 13, 1969. We excitedly anticipated reuniting with missionaries and Brazilian co-workers, and starting a new assignment somewhere within the South Brazil Mission.

WAK

We sailed from Everglades, Florida July 1, 1969 aboard the S.S. Brasil of the Moore McCormack Lines. The missionaries of the South Brazil Mission who were passengers:

Norvel and Hattie Welch and four children
    State of Rio
Richard and Lee Grant and two children
    Language School, Campinas, São Paulo
Gerold and Verla Golston and Jeremiah (Equatorial Mission)
    Language School, Campinas, São Paulo
Richard and Carolyn Plampin
    Deter Bible Institute, Curitiba, Paraná
Dan and Mary Burt and three children
    Moving from President Prudente to Campinas, São Paulo

There were other Southern Baptist missionaries:

Don and Sheri Richards and four children
    Palmeiro dos Índios, Alagoas
T.S. & Anita Greene and children
    Argentina
Mark and Cecile Alexander and child
    Argentina
John David and Laura Cave and children
    Buenos Aires, Argentina
Tom and Marceille Hollingsworth
    Buenos Aires, Argentina

Tom and Marceille were our dinner partners, whom we enjoyed so much. Two American Ambassadors were on board: John Lodge for Argentina (brother of Cabot Lodge) and Charles Elbrick for Brazil.

Return

We docked in Rio de Janeiro July 8, and spent that night and the next in the Othon Palace Hotel downtown. We six couples for South Brazil traveled by chartered bus to Caxambú, São Paulo where the annual Mission Meeting was in session. My letter of August 14, 1969:

"We were there July 10-13, experiencing the spirit of jubilant strength and fellowship. We cannot describe the joy of coming to OUR PLACE."

I sang "I Walked Today Where Jesus Walked" by Geoffrey O'Hara on the Sunday afternoon music program. Dona Clarice, with whom I had studied voice in Rio, was at the hotel that day.

We lived in the Claud Bumpus house in Rio until August 12. Then the O.D. Martins invited us to live in their home in Campinas until we decided where we would live and work. Quirks happen: when we packed to move from their house we took all their dictionaries - of course we embarrassedly returned them.

132.

One Sunday we returned to Volta Redonda, and there was hugging and kissing with old friends and co-workers. It was there Jesse embarked on his mission career in Brazil. Nine years they had labored together developing preaching points, missions, churches, and laboring in the American School where the Gospel was taught and preached every school day.

There was a delicious meal in the home of Antônio, business manager of the school and Central Church, prepared by Dona Jurema, his wife. Dismantling Jesse's apartment took three days. (Recall that this was Jesse's "place to sleep" which Brother McNealy had offered to him back in El Dorado.) This apartment on the third floor of the school is where Jesse counseled many students and played games of Chinese checkers. It is said that once when the checkerboard tipped and all the marbles scattered Jesse innocently exclaimed, "I've lost all my marbles!"

In Rio, Marcílio Teixeira and Helena invited us to their home. Marcílio was my pastor at São Francisco Xavier Church. Helena, with her tender, loving, compassionate, spirit was a dear friend.

My letter September 28, 1969:

"It seems very, very strange in returning to Brazil to discover the deaths we die. We are foreigners, and always will be; we speak with an accent; we will never be full citizens. There will always be some aura of the unknown that we sense. And we know the reality that an official from the American Embassy was kidnapped not far from my old residence."

The Lord's Choice

We were responsible for discerning God's will for where we would live and our job classification. The missionaries on the field helped us plan field trips and they graciously hosted us, providing transportation and information.

The first trip was to Lajes, Santa Catarina. Marshall Flournoy drove from Florianópolis to meet us there, then he took us to Curitiba where we boarded a bus back to Campinas.

The next trip was to Três Lagoas, Mato Grosso, where Ben Hope met us. From there we traveled by train to Campo Grande where we met with the missionaries of Mato Grosso in the Ernest and Billie Wilson home. Then we flew to Cuiabá the state capital, where we were received in the Charlie and Betsy Compton home. We had Thanksgiving dinner there.

Then to Brasília where we were met by Paul and Betty Noland. We visited with James and Jewell Lunsford. We flew to Uberaba in the state of Minas Gerais. Bill Richardson had driven there from Belo Horizonte to meet us. He took us to Uberlândia and Araguari, then to Belo Horizonte where he and Kathy lived. We took a plane back to Campinas.

Dan Burt showed us the area of President Prudente in western São Paulo.

In all the places we had visited we were introduced to the Brazilian leaders; the needs were shown; we met many Southern Baptist workers and missionaries of other groups. We were to be sensitive to God's leading us to our place of service.

LAJES, SANTA CATARINA

We finally determined that Lajes, Santa Catarina was our place of service. We went back there and Marshall Flournoy drove from Florianópolis on the coast to help to rent a house owned by Stuart Lang, an American. He was in management at Klabin paper mill at Otacília Costa, thirty miles from Lajes. Then we returned to Rio for the actual move.

The moving van contained Jesse's household from Volta Redonda, my household, our personal things and wedding gifts which had been stored, and freight we brought from the States. We traveled in a Jeep with station wagon body, arriving in Lajes before the van.

The rented house was two-story, pink stucco, near the center of town, two blocks from the principal cathedral. As soon as we unloaded and stocked the kitchen with basic food, Jesse left for the annual state Baptist convention at Pôrto União. When he returned he started visiting the churches, meeting workers, and assessing his plans. I was setting up the household.

The most popular spot in this large house was the dining room where the windows gave bright afternoon sunlight. Many hours of our lives were spent at the table: meals, study, preparing children's materials, visiting with callers, music work, bookkeeping, and our morning prayer time together.

The Finance Committee of our Mission was sympathetic to the need to repair the house. Jesse ordered bars for the windows, and built screens. (How many missionaries have been tested with the challenge of glass, bars, screens and shutters for one window)? Jesse spent a day cleaning the muck in the cistern and water boxes on top of the house. The electric pump for water needed repair. The roof leaked.

Workers painted the first floor, garage, and stairwell. A workman surveyed the windows, broke out nine incomplete panes, left, and we never heard from him again. We installed iron bars so pedestrians wouldn't walk on the cistern. The kitchen cabinets were so high they were inaccessible, so they were lowered.

WAK
"Curtain" is defined in the dictionary: "Theater. The descent of a curtain at the end of a scene, act, or play." The curtains I sewed for our house symbolized the beginning of a new scene, not the end.

First, we bought all the curtains (sight unseen) from the Mission house in Blumenau for $75.00. They were of a very fine, gray broadcloth, enhanced by an additional layer of sheer beige nylon. I dismantled the gray ones, measured, cut, sewed French seams, then hemmed top and bottom. I engaged the "curtain lady" to thread the cord in the top for gathers, and sewing on the little wheels (these would be threaded on the rod). Then I washed, starched, and ironed them.

Second, Dona Hilda, wife of the house owner, left the dining room curtains: flowered cotton satin, fully lined, and in excellent condition except for fading and rain spots.

Third, we brought many yards of unbleached muslin in our freight.

Fourth, we had to buy new fabric for one room.

These curtains kept us warm on the drafty, cold days, and served as window shades. Since I had used French seams, they lasted until the day we left Brazil October 29, 1988.

Pioneer Life

Nothing in our years in Volta Redonda and Rio de Janeiro had prepared us for Santa Catarina. We were impressed by the courage, pain and suffering of Spirit-led Baptists and the trials and hardiness of many pioneers we met. We felt we had moved to a country quite foreign to our other experiences. I very much needed more language learning, as well as honing music skills - especially playing hymns from the hymnbook, "Cantor Cristão." But we experienced the joy of establishing our home and marriage.

Letter of March 16, 1970:

"Being downtown, you might think you were at your television viewing a wildwest movie of gold rush days. Hammers banging, slush of hand-mixed cement; cathedral bells bonging; horses clattering on cobblestone streets of slick, gray slate; the horse-drawn milk wagon with cans gnashing against each other, stopping at houses where they ladle out the milk; trucks loaded with wood, groaning through the city (wood is the main product).

135.

Letter of March 16, 1970 (Continued):

"A store building burning. Gun shells slipping into waist belts and the gun into the holster; cowboy boots are pleated down to the ankle, and they squeak. Uniformed school children bursting from classrooms and crowding onto the sidewalks. Rains have started, relieving the plague of dust, and umbrellas have sprouted everywhere.

"At the city market Wednesday through Saturday, there are sweet Concord grapes from the state Rio Grande do Sul. Pork meat on top of the counter. A slaughtered hog arriving in the luggage compartment of the bus."

****

In Campinas we had choice, fresh vegetables produced by Japanese gardeners; here the vegetables arriving at the market were days on the road. Fortunately we had brought good kitchen equipment such as a Sunbeam mixmaster and an electric roaster. To have fresh greens, we located a lady who raised spinach.

Our friend of the Presbyterian Church thoughtfully brought us honey. But somehow he thought that since we were foreigners he needed to holler at us. Once he came to the front door and handed the container of honey to me. I didn't remember its density and weight, and I nearly dropped it! This dark and strong honey came from the bracatinga flower.

The first winter in Lajes, we ignored the advice of the Brazilians, which was to only build the fire in the fireplace or wood-burning stove in the evening, not trying to maintain warmth throughout the day. Consequently I had a bad case of bronchitis, which returned every winter. Many of the people wore thongs without stockings, and their only winter comfort was a sweater.

Jesse requested a car heater from the Mission. But when the matter was treated by the Executive Committee, one Rio missionary said,

"When they vote to put air conditioners in the Rio missionaries' cars, I'll vote for the heater."

Jesse's letter of June 14, 1971 reflects that the request was finally granted.

"We have found a firm here in Brazil that makes heaters for cars. I sent an order by telegram."

The cats congregated at our house during cold weather. When the fireplace warmed up the inside of the house, the outside got warm, at the chimney. At night the cats gathered on the cement walk at the chimney and carried on a cat convention while we vainly tried to sleep!

WAK
     When we went to the town São Joaquin, we confirmed that
it really is the highest point in Santa Catarina, for the
gusty wind was very cold. The area seemed desolate and barren,
but we discovered some apple orchards. Japanese horticultur-
ists were caring for the trees, training the branches on ar-
bors. Apple production in the country would increase, so
Brazil would not have to import so many Argentine apples.

The Baptist Church of Lajes

     The church's property extended the complete width of the
block, street to street. The old house which served for meeting opened right onto the street; this was 3 ½ blocks from
our house. The pastor Miguel Rocha Campos, his wife Teresa
and their two boys lived in the house. The parlor was set
aside for the auditorium, and the other living quarters were
used for Sunday School rooms.

     There were thirty-nine members. Three were studying at
Deter Bible Institute in Curitiba: Helen Engel, Miriam Johnson, and Otília Silva. About half the men were literate.

Children's Building
     On Sundays the children had just a small space for their
classes. Tiny babies, crawlers, and toddlers were gathered
in their mothers' laps. Some money became available, and
Jesse supervised building the wooden structure which we called
Children's Building. The tables and chairs were child-height,
and there was room for the children to move about.

     Jesse's letter of June 14, 1971:

   "Our church is going to try something different for the next
   two months of cold weather. All services will be conducted
   in the afternoon. I felt so sorry for the little children
   yesterday. Some were crying from the cold during Sunday
   School, but still they came."

     We framed and mounted pictures from my collection for chil-
dren. My brother-in-law Charles Norris, Director of Missions,
Stoddard Association in southeast Missouri, had given us a number of the large pictures for Juniors. As I catalogued and
labeled them I learned Portuguese, and it was a blessing to
use them with the children in Sunday School. They loved having the Brazilian Baptist quarterlies because they were well
written, with handwork and puzzles.

JLK
New Church Building
     A new auditorium had been started on the opposite side of
the property. This was the street where the most modern homes
of the city were built, and there were palatial houses on both
sides of the church's property.

137.

The men of the church and I studied the abandoned walls. Adão Ramp of the group was a builder, and with his encouragement we decided to proceed. We studied the original plan and altered the design to blend better with the modern homes on the same street. We built new scaffolding, then we cleaned each mouldy, dirty brick inside and out, using steel brushes. The walls were thick, and at least fourteen feet high. When we began to plaster the walls we found they were so uneven the plaster had to be at least two inches thick.

On the facade where the roof came to a point over the door the height was about twenty-four feet. A company in Curitiba made a type of stained glass windows, and they helped me develop the design for the windows above and to the sides of the front door, using five colors.

I drew the windows to scale, and there was enough space above the door for a large, red, glass cross in the center window. We put this in the design, knowing people would respect it and refrain from throwing rocks. The company which made the glass sent a workman to install the panes. Except for the red cross the colors were distributed at random.

There was a park across the street from the front of the church with a shallow pool about 1 1/2 acres in area. It was called the tanque because in pioneer days it was guarded so the women of the city could wash their clothing there without being molested. At night the stained glass windows of the church were reflected in the tanque, in beautiful, shimmering color.

Elizabeth and Charles

My sister Elizabeth and her husband Charles Norris came to visit us, arriving July 31, 1972. I met them in Rio de Janeiro and traveled with them to São Paulo then to Curitiba. Jesse met us there and we drove to Lajes.

Charles blessed the people when he preached in all the churches of the Planalto - with Jesse interpreting. Carlos Frichenbruder, a young man, made a decision to preach the Gospel when Charles spoke in the Papanduva church. Years later we learned that he had been true to his decision; he had studied in the seminary in São Paulo and was working on textbooks for Theological Education by Extension.

Elizabeth and I trained so we could sing two duets in the language, and wherever Charles preached, we sang. The people lovingly received our family, and we were so honored to have them for the month of August.

Our Personal Report
to the
Foreign Mission Board
June 16, 1971

Lajes is in the area called "Planalto," a plateau inland from the coast, at a higher altitude. Reporting on Baptist work, we realize Lajes is:

    60 miles from the nearest church south
    70 miles from the nearest church east
    105 miles from the nearest mission point west
    110 miles from the nearest church north

The Planalto has 220 miles of paved roads, and 1,500 miles of graded, dirt/gravel roads. The area covers about 1/3 of the state, with 320 cities, towns and communities.

Lajes is second in population, in the state of Santa Catarina. The church here has thirty-nine members, meeting in an ancient house. It invites the city of 130,000 to come and hear the message of hope and salvation. Two years ago a new building was started, but the work stopped for lack of funds and the four incomplete walls stand, roofless.

There has been a Sunday School and radio ministry in Joaçaba, western Santa Catarina, for ten years without aid of a pastor. The leader is an aging Russian immigrant. The church in Pôrto União is thirty eight years old, having had a pastor for only seven of the years.

Pastor Walfrido Sousa Cruz leads a fast-growing church in the area called Papanduva. Walfrido was a house painter when God called him to the ministry. Being married with a family, he was unable to go to a seminary, so he studied Theology at home. His church membership is diverse: Polish, Latvian, German, Ukrainian, and Brazilian. Walfrido's transportation is motor scooter - this being the only one owned by the state Baptist convention.

Ratio of Workers to Churches
There are eight Baptist churches, five mission points, and several preaching stations. They all are receiving pastoral attention, though some is part-time. Five pastors and one evangelist live on the field, and the couple sent by the Home Mission Board is starting new work in Chapecó, to the West. Only one of the pastors and Heronete, Home Missionary, are Seminary graduates.

One mission point meets in the back room of a store; two other groups meet in residences converted to churches, while three of the churches have reasonably good buildings.

Personal Report June 16, 1971 (Continued)

Economic Expansion
Two large paper mills have been built in the Planalto and
another is under construction. The population around these
mills mushrooms, measured in the tens of thousands. The city
of Correia Pinto, fourteen miles from Lajes, has 20,000. We
do not own a lot or chapel in any of the three population
centers. Other, diversified industries are entering. A new
east-to-west highway is being paved, linking the western part
of the state with Florianópolis, state capital on the coast.

The city of Curitibanos finds itself located at the crossroads of that new state road and a federal highway, thus becoming a strategic city in the Planalto. There is a mission point
there, and after seven years of hoping and praying, it still
doesn't have a permanent place of worship.

What Did We Do?
Jesse preached wherever he was invited to supply for the
national worker. He conducted revivals, led in Stewardship
studies, and taught Bible Institute courses. I was interested
in helping the people in the churches to develop in congrega-
tional singing and worship through music.

We can report that Monte Castelo Church has a resident
pastor, and that the Lajes church called a new pastor. Three
girls from Lajes were studying in the Deter Bible Institute
in Curitiba, and during holidays they led in Vacation Bible
Schools in some of our churches and preaching stations.

The Challenge
The Lajes church received a letter from the mayor of the
city Garibaldi, requesting that Baptist work be opened there.
This was a thrilling letter, but there weren't workers or
recourses to attend their request.

It's cold in the Planalto. It's reached below freezing
for nearly a week here in Lajes, with a hint of snow. We do
not expect or hope for many workers from tropical or warm cli-
mates. We feel we must lay the foundation and then those new
Christians will continue evangelizing in the more difficult
areas of the state.

Santa Catarina is one of the most challenging mission fields
in Brazil. The state of Rio de Janeiro has one Baptist for
every 60 people; here, it is one Baptist in every 2,500 persons.

We face the challenge of the Planalto with just regular
Travel, Literature, and Small Equipment allowance. We have
not received funds for Bible Institutes, evangelistic emphases,
promotion of Vacation Bible Schools, Religious Education, radio,
mimeographing, music instruments and materials. We've tried
over a year to receive a Public Address System from Mission funds.

140.

Personal Report June 16, 1971 (Continued)

Personal Commitment

When we try to be more philosophical, we wonder if we have
placed too much emphasis on the lack of funds and equipment.
How does the national pastor feel on Sunday night after the
meeting, when the missionary loads up all his gadgets and
drives away? Does our PERSON have any value? It is worthy
just to catch a bus, with Bible and a supply of evangelistic
tracts, and go to one of the churches to walk with the pastor
a week, just offering OURSELVES.

* * * * * * * * * * * * * * * *

Telephone

We didn't have one. At the telephone office we entered our
request for long distance with the operators, and waited for
the connection. Brazil didn't have satellite communication,
and the waiting might take hours and days. Jesse and I spelled
each other at the telephone office. The local radio stations
devoted certain hours for announcing messages even to far-flung
places. Also bus drivers carried written and verbal messages,
as well as parcels. We were thankful for these networks so
thoughtfully carried out, and we often used them.

We devised a plan for making the trips to Florianópolis on
the coast, for meetings with other missionaries of our state.
We drove from our house to Blumenau by gravel road, where we
spent the night. The next day we'd go on to Florianópolis.
Thus, we had a break from our involvement in Lajes, as well
as adapting to sea level.

When we traveled from home to São Paulo by bus, we noticed
the warmth when we descended to the tea and pineapple fields.
The bus driver usually stopped at a certain house where he
shed his long underwear.

The Paraná Pine

Traveling from tropical climate south into the state of São
Paulo, one begins to see the Paraná pine tree, acclimated to
a cooler climate. The branches grow at different levels, at
each level extending from the central trunk like spokes of
an umbrella.

As the tree ages the lower branches fall off so the profile
looks like an umbrella. The whole tree turns and groans in
the strong wind. When one of them falls and lays rotting for
years, you can dig out the knots. They make good fuel for
fireplace and stove since they are so rich in resin. A bowl
fashioned from the trunk shows small knots extending symmet-
rically from the center. I loved the majesty and permanency
of the pines. Their strength and endurance inspired me.

141.

A Rural Church Called Taquaral

Taquaral means "bamboo thicket," while **taquara** is defined as one of the varieties of small bamboos. The Taquaral Church stands at the side of Highway 116 passing north/south through Santa Catarina. The members are all farm folk.

This is how Taquaral Church came into being. Wilma knew David Gomes as a fellow student at Southwestern Seminary. When he returned to his native Brazil he lived in Rio de Janeiro where he started a radio program "Bible School of the Air," beaming Bible studies throughout the country.

Dona Ana Frederico lived on a farm in Santa Catarina, and the radio broadcast captured her attention. Dona Ana was an invalid, and her devoted husband Carlos kept her radio powered, using a car battery. He charged the battery by attaching a generator to his sawmill run by a water wheel.

The whole family listened to the radio program and they became curious about the book called the Bible, which David Gomes was teaching. Senhor Carlos sent his youngest son José to the nearest town to buy a Bible, but he couldn't find one. He sought a Bible in four towns and finally he went to Mafra, about forty-five miles away.

In Mafra he made inquiries and learned there was a Baptist church there where, he was told, he could get a Bible. The sympathetic pastor gave him one and promised to visit the Fredericos a month later. He told José he would bring the missionary Adrian Blankenship who lived on the coast.

True to the promise, the two men arrived on the given date, and they found that the farm neighbors from all around had gathered at the Fredericos. Rev. Blankenship played hymns on a phonograph, amplifying the music by a loudspeaker on top of his car. We are told that the farm animals were attracted by the music and ambled near, standing at the edge of the group gathered in the pasture.

The missionary preached, and about thirty people were converted, including Carlos and Ana Frederico and their sons João and José. Senhor Carlos spoke to the people, telling how Dona Ana had envisioned a church on the mount north of their house. He told them he would start sawing lumber the next day for the church, and invited his neighbors to help. So they built a simple, wood structure.

The enthusiasm of the new converts grew until that building was too small - the flourishing new church required more space. So they built a larger one of brick, plastered inside and out. It is the only permanent structure in the community - that is, built of brick. All the homes are of wood. When we first visited Taquaral Church they did not have electricity so they installed butane lights.

142.

JLK
A young preacher, Renato Salles, with his wife Dona Sodie
came from the city of São Paulo to be the pastor. The church
gave them three acres of land across the road and the men
helped build a house. The Salleses shepherded the church
many years, leading in establishing many missions and preaching points, as well as other churches.

The church loved to evangelize. After planting crops they
had evangelistic services in communities around, until harvest
time. Some prosperous members had Jeep station wagons called
the Rural Willys. That way they could have services at regular times where the response was good. Several of the men
were capable preachers. They built a tabernacle by the church
in the early seventies, where they could have large gatherings.

Hercílio, a young man from the Taquaral community, studied
at great sacrifice until he qualified as an elementary teacher. So the church leaders established the elementary school,
meeting a pressing need. It met in the original building.

A severe car accident left Dona Sodie with health problems,
and the doctors prescribed that they live in a warmer climate
on the coast. Also because of the economic situation they
needed to earn a living. For some time Renato taught at the
Bible Institute in Ijuí, Rio Grande do sul.

WAK   **A Woman's View of Taquaral**

Elisa, João Frederico's wife, greeted us cheerily. (João
is the son of Carlos and Ana Frederico). Elisa was coming out
of their bake-house with a large, oval, wood bowl slung on her
shoulder, filled with huge loaves of freshly baked, cracked-
wheat bread. She set her burden down on the brick surface of
the farmyard, closed the door of the bake-house, and came toward us. Elisa was always cordially genuine in her pleasure
in greeting us; we knew we were welcome at the farmhouse.

Managing her family was a full-time job. Her husband João
walked on one crutch to accommodate a lame leg. Jeremias, the
youngest, was in grade school. Maria was studying teacher
training in the town of Mafra. "Zeca" worked with his dad.
Rosa was in Curitiba studying at the Deter Bible Institute.
Teresa lived at Monte Castelo, near enough to bring her boys
home for grandma and grandpa to love.

Here on the farm they used a water wheel for powering the
handmade, wooden corn grinder. They also raised mate. The
house had hot water from an ingenious system of pipes in the
kitchen cookstove. Hogs were cared for meticulously - their
raised pens were carefully washed. The farmyard was "clean
as a whistle" because it was covered with inlaid bricks so
it could be cleaned often.

143.

WAK

But Elisa and João had more than farm work on their agenda
for up the road was their beloved Taquaral Church. As leaders
they helped to care for Sunday School and preaching on Sunday;
prayer meeting Wednesday nights; and Woman's Missionary Union
meetings. Once when we approached the church for an evening
service it was dark and we assumed there was no one there.
When someone opened the front door and lit the butane lamp,
the circle of light revealed a number of people, waiting outside in the dark!

The ministry of Taquaral has gone to far-flung shores.
Pastor Renato and Dona Sodie were gifted soul winners. They
won the youth José Calixto to Christ, already with enough
schooling so he soon went to Rio to attend the South Brazil
Seminary. He became engaged to the beautiful, talented, Jap-
anese-Brazilian named Suely, studying Theology at the Rio Seminary. They delayed their marriage a year so she could graduate. The couple was appointed to Venezuela by the Brazilian
Baptist Foreign Mission Board, where they became leaders in
pioneer evangelism.

At Christmas December 1974 the children of Taquaral sang
the cantata "Eis, A Estrela!" (Lo, A Star!). The women scheduled the rehearsals so I could get there by bus, rehearse,
and return to Lajes the following day. They supervised the
children so there was 100% attendance. Some of the kids were
used to singing with gusto so we worked hard to sing melodi-
cally, not like yelling at a soccer game.

The Taquaral people have a corner of my heart. They sang
the hymns with conviction. They believed fervently that
Jesus' salvation was for their neighbors. They gave themselves in physical labor and materials, as well as prayers
for the evangelization of Santa Catarina and the world.
There must be a special golden bowl in Heaven where God
collects the prayers of these saints. It is, indeed, a fact
that the Holy Spirit hovered over the area known as Taquaral
- even though much of it was pasture or corrals or hog pens
or bean fields.

JLK   **Taquaral** **and** **Curitibanos**

Curitibanos was at the geographic center of Santa Catarina,
a location which had escalated in importance since it was at
the crossroads of a federal and an east/west highway. Our
missionary colleague Marshall Flournoy had been there and conducted evangelistic services before our coming onto the scene
February, 1970. At those services people were converted, and
consequently the Foreign Mission Board sent funds for a lot
and chapel. The lot had been purchased.

Early on, Marshall as state Executive Secretary asked that
I make Curitibanos a priority, then his dream of penetrating
the state could be realized even though he lived in Florianópolis on the coast.

144.

JLK

When I saw the lot I soon concluded that a drainage system
would need to be installed, and it needed to be leveled; this
required a permit from City Hall. I traveled the thirty miles
on the primitive, gravel road, appearing before the authorities
with my request.

"Come back next week."

Again and again:

"Come back next week."

One day I told Wilma,

"Today I get the permit."

I put a folding chair, thermos of coffee, sandwiches, and
books in the car before driving to Curitibanos. I set up all
my paraphernalia across the hall from the Mayor's office. Every time anyone opened His Honor's door, he had a view of me.
Before noon he sent the permit out to me by his secretary!

I knew that after grading and draining the lot, the money
sent by the Foreign Mission Board wouldn't suffice to buy the
nails for a chapel since inflation had eaten away the value.
So I drove directly to Taquaral, arriving at João Frederico's
house at sunset. A crowd of people was there, and as I parked
the car someone came to tell me that Dona Ana had died and
the wake was there at the house.

After I greeted the people and spoke to Senhor João he
queried,

"What brings you to Taquaral at just this time?"

I was embarrassad to speak of the purpose of my trip at
such an hour, but being a very perceptive man, he urged me to
tell him. So I explained about the situation in Curitibanos;
that there was only a little money for building the chapel.
João listened attentively, then said quietly and emphatically,

"Leave it to me!"

Pastor Renato of the Taquaral church was at the coast in
a meeting, so I asked one of the young men to go with me to
bring him. As Dona Ana's pastor, he could be there for the
funeral. We went immediately, returning with Renato early
next morning. They were already proceeding to the cemetery
a few miles east of Monte Castelo, the neighboring town. I
was so thankful that Dona Ana's own pastor was there to conduct the graveside service. Afterward, we returned to João's
house.

145.

JLK

There, João spoke to me,

"Pastor Jesse, after you left last night we had a business session as we sat around Mother's casket. All the church members were here so I presented the problem of Curitibanos. The church voted to help."

A little money was given. Several farmers donated trees from their land, and some offered their horses to pull logs to the sawmill. All offered their time. I was so amazed. João concluded,

"Now pastor, you go home and as soon as we're ready to move the material to Curitibanos I'll send you a message."

About ten days later word came that everything was ready. When I drove up to João's house, there stood the framework of the church that was to be built eighty miles away! All the pieces had been identified by Roman numerals chiseled into the wood.

As we drove the seven miles to Monte Castelo to hire a truck, I said to João,

"I'll go to the tax office to pay the transportation tax."

Patiently he explained that since the lumber was cut to specifications it was considered used, and would not be taxed.

When the lumber was delivered in Curitibanos, nine men came from Taquaral. They set up a tent and started work on a Tuesday morning. One man cooked and the others set about fitting the pieces together, and erecting the chapel, with very little sawing.

Saturday night they conducted the first service in that beautiful place of worship; José Frederico preached. We recall that he was Senhor Carlos's son who had set out to find a Bible.

How can I possibly recount the blessings shining out from the place called Taquaral? In 1971 we reported:

Taquaral is the largest church in the Planalto.
Taquaral is too poor to support a pastor.
Taquaral is the mother of five churches, as well as some
    mission points, whose combined membership comprises
    50% of the state Baptist Convention.

This church has built six places of worship without petitioning outside sources. They were to help me build another chapel in Correia Pinto just before we left the state in 1976.

146.

The text of the song "O Could I Speak" says that to sound
forth the glories of my Saviour, I'd soar, touching heavenly
strings - in notes almost divine. My years in Santa Catarina
may be evaluated as preparation for "soaring." I had always
had support for singing or playing. Now I found that I was
the planter and planner, accompanist and singer, teacher and
learner, as well as librarian, gathering music materials.

Lajes

In the church in Lajes I was the only one to play the portable pump organ. It soon was self evident that I needed more
keyboard training, although I had taken piano lessons at Ouachita University a semester in 1968. A Presbyterian lady who
had taught many years, consented to teach me.

The pastor of the church, Miguel Rocha Campos, had learned
the hymns by rote and Dona Marta Johnson, a member with Latvian
roots, had learned by rote; I tried to play the music as written
in the hymnal "Cantor Cristão." So sometimes we were in three
different melodies and time. When Jesse directed the music it
was better, for he set out the rhythm very well. It was a
difficult situation - but good training.

A church in Advance, Missouri near the Norrises, had given
me an Autoharp, then I began to build a repertoire of solos.
It was a blessing to be with Jesse when he preached, and to
sing solos with Autoharp accompaniment. God honored that music for I always sensed it was a ministry to the people, and
I knew it helped Jesse.

Jesse carried all the music paraphernalia: electric Autoharp, regular Autoharp, music stand, bags of music, hymnals,
and teaching materials; and the guitar. Sometimes he would
manage the heavy, portable organ and the sturdy wooden bench
and load them in the car.

In Lajes we looked forward to having the Christmas program
in the new church, only partially completed. I chose the cantata "Eis, A Estrela!" (Lo, A Star!) and all the children and
youth of the church worked very hard. The children were accustomed to singing choruses lustily; they loved to perform
in the closing assembly of Sunday School. To develop a cantata
was a learning time for all of us; and several who sang mono-
tone were simply part of it.

My letter of February 6, 1971:

"We moved on to costumes for wise men, angels, Mary and Joseph; bags of candy for the children, and deciding to go
to Curitibanos to sing the cantata there. It rained hard
that night, but we had a wonderful time and our people felt
they were ministering."

147.

WAK

I must write of one of the families of the church, although each family had many needs - economic and spiritual. The four Oliboni boys sang in "Eis, A Estrela!" - Roc, Luiz, Vitor, and Airton. Roc, the oldest, walked with difficulty for he had a bone deficiency. His uncle Waldir Schreiber and his wife Clara had sought medical help but it was discouraging. They were rearing Airton, the youngest, so he might have a well balanced diet.

Valéria the mother was widowed and struggled to make a living. She cooked bananas (there are many varieties) and sold bananada. The hot, cooked fruit is poured into a mold and when it's set it can be cut into slices. She made pasteis, tasty meat filling inside flaky crust and cooked in hot oil (like fried pies). She made other snacks which the boys sold on the street.

We learn that Werner, oldest of Waldir and Clara's children, grew up to be a doctor. I have trusted the Lord for the destiny of the other children.

Taquaral

The Taquaral Church was quite aggressive in promoting music. They had Clint Kimbrough, music missionary living in Niteroi, for a week of training. Clint had a magic method using blackboard and flash cards, and the people participated happily. When they invited me to come to teach keyboard on their pump organ, it meant that they sacrifically kept me in their homes, with hospitality fit for a queen!

Once when Jesse and I arrived at João Frederico's house at Taquaral we encountered despair. Their cows had apparently been vaccinated with contaminated serum, and several were down, unable to get up. Others were sick. As Jesse visited with João, I slipped into a bedroom, knelt and talked to God, pleading that the cows would be healed; that since João and Elisa were His faithful servants, they needed their livelihood. It was a simple prayer, and later we learned that the cattle got well.

"The Barrier"

On furlough we were at Southwestern Seminary in Fort Worth 1973-74. One of my courses was the piano "barrier," taught by Jesse's Ouachita College mate, Dr. T.W. Hunt. Dr. Hunt's marvelous teaching methods helped me to get through the course: all keys, major and minor: 1. Scale and reverse scale (2 octaves) 2. Arpeggio and inverted arpeggio (2 octaves) 3. Cadence. Also hymn memorization and sight reading. So when we returned to Brazil I felt more at ease at the keyboard.

Urubici
(U - oo as in rooster) Oo - roo - bee - SEE

Following World War II Latvia was ruled by Russia, bringing persecution on Baptist people. Thousands left and immigrated to Brazil where they established churches and propagated their faith.

A group of these immigrants had settled in the town called Urubici, in the mountain area four hours' drive from Lajes. They had built a Baptist church there and had received into the fellowship others who were not of their ancestry. When the others achieved slightly over 50% voting power, they sent the Latvians out. That building still stood and was used.

So the immigrants and their children and grandchildren built another Baptist church - the building where they were meeting. They did not shirk in evangelistic fervor as they followed the teaching of the Bible, desiring to see the people of the community won to Christ. Strangely, in the community they were called "Those Russians." We rejoiced with them when a Brazilian pastor and his family came to shepherd them.

We listened as they told of their persecution in Latvia; of how they determined to come to Brazil; of their suffering in an unknown culture and language. In Europe they had been doctors, musicians, engineers, and teachers; in a strange tongue some of them were reduced to day laborers. Urubici was an agricultural area.

These heroic people brought music with them. Some played the mandolin to accompany the hymns, and they loved to sing. In Latvia they had great church choirs. When Jesse was at the church for a week of preaching, the ladies scheduled the children to have music lessons throughout the day, using the pump organ.

I loved those kids - they were punctual for lessons, enthusiastic, and made progress that week. Their parents sacrificed to send them to lessons because the children worked in raising the crops and household chores.

The women served lunch for us two every day. Once we counted fourteen different foods on the table! Besides the joy of seeing the children learn, my reward was knowing that one of the girls became a church pianist. Later, when I could work a few days into our schedule, I traveled to Urubici by bus, to continue the lessons.

The winter cold in Urubici dictated that sweaters, coats, and other outer garments be made of wool. The women carded their own wool, spun it into thread, and knitted garments. But the warmth of their zeal for Christ - for Christian homes, and to evangelize - stays in my heart and memory.

149.

WAK   ## Papanduva and Correia Pinto

Pastor Walfrido and Juraci were very interested in music
training, for they wanted their children Sandra, Elisete, and
Eliel to know music. They invited me to the church in Papanduva,
and scheduled their people to study basic theory with me.

I will never really know the sacrifice the family made to
have Jesse and me in their home. I sensed that they ate a lot
of corn meal mush, but when we were there, they served chicken
and traditional dessert - a slice of guava jelly (firm) with
a slice of cheese. We knew that the pastor's salary was mea-
ger; we also knew that we were to accept their hospitality
lovingly, in the same way they offered it.

When the family moved to Correia Pinto, nearer to Lajes,
we could go there to help in their evangelistic campaigns,
and return at night. Elisete was a little girl then, and
when she grew older she became a church pianist.

Latin America Music Conference

In 1976 I attended the music conference for Southern Baptist missionaries in Latin America. We met at the Seminary
in Rio de Janeiro. Countries which didn't have personnel
specializing in music sent other missionaries.

The conference was a highlight for me, inspiring further
energy in helping people in music. The delegates exchanged
ideas and materials, shared plans and hopes for the future,
and fellowshiped together.

We studied the history and outlook for sacred music; we
sang for and with each other. Dr. T.W. Hunt was a conference
leader, and he gave organ concerts. One performing group was
from Venezuela, dressed in costumes, singing and playing indig-
enous music.

The Adult Choir of First Church, Rio, gave a concert. My
friend Anna Campello Egger was director. Anna's parents had
worked among native Indians, and she had not seen a piano
until she was a teenager. Then she became a pianist, and
trained in music in São Paulo and America. As her choir sang
advanced, intricate choral music, we were amazed, for we knew
that only a few of the choristers read music!

I believe this gathering presaged the organizing of Baptist
musicians in Brazil some years later. Thus the Brazilians
and missionaries were together in one entity.

150.

Therefore, since we are surrounded by such a great cloud of witnesses,

Hebrews 12:1a NIV

There are some people who should be listed in this category; not because they achieved fame, wealth, or prominence, but that our lives are intertwined with theirs. The following cameos are written simply to try to share something of these "witnesses."

A Baby

Nair knocked hurriedly on the door to our fourth-floor apartment in downtown Lajes. Tearfully she explained that her three-month-old son was near death. He and his twin were her ninth and tenth children.

We had known Nair and her husband Orlando in the Baptist Church at Correia Pinto, 14 miles away. Orlando was a shift worker in the paper mill, and they lived on a limited income. The parents had decided to try to get the baby to a second doctor at Campos Novos, so I consented to drive them there.

The parents seemed inconsolable when the child died. Walfrido de Sousa Luz had moved to Correia Pinto, where he was pastor. He bought the casket, a simple wooden box stapled with white plastic and a narrow silver trim. He placed the body in the casket and we covered it with white netting.

The members from the Lajes church came to the home for the Sunday afternoon funeral. Some of us slipped out of the overcrowded living room, to make room. Jesse read Scripture and spoke words of condolence, explaining that Jesus had received the little one, and that God's love was present with us.

The parents and eight children were disconsolate, never stopping their weeping. The neighbors and friends stood in the house and yard, silent and mute. Jesse and Walfrido carried the casket to the cemetery for burial.

February 6, 1971, I had written of the burial of another baby, daughter of Adão and Hilga of the Lajes church:

"The grave was roughly dug in the hard, rocky soil, and there was neither artificial grass, nor canopy, nor chair, nor hearse, nor shade tree, and no undertaker. No supporting hardware for the casket - it was lowered by hand."

Let us fix our eyes on Jesus, the author and perfecter of our faith,

Hebrews 12:2a NIV

<u>Sandra</u> <u>Amara</u> <u>Luz</u>

Sandra was about ten when we met her. The oldest child of Walfrido, pastor at that time of the Papanduva Church, she was a bundle of energy, and amazingly intelligent. She was a champion Bible reader - as a teenager she had read it seven times. Sunday and Wednesday evenings when the hour for church approached she took to the streets of Papanduva, knocking on doors and inviting the people. In winter she got up early and started the cookstove fire.

Papanduva was made up mainly of people of Polish background, also Latvians, Germans, Ukrainians, and Brazilians. Búguri Indians came annually, camping at the edge of town. They sold baskets and other wares. While Poles held strongly to the Catholic faith, mainly Brazilians and Latvians comprised the Papanduva Church.

<u>The</u> <u>Itch</u>
One winter Walfrido invited me to conduct special services on a weekend - Friday, Saturday, and Sunday nights. It was cold, and there was no heat in the church.

Friday night after service Jurací, Walfrido's wife, had a tub of hot water for feet. We were to sit in a small circle so everyone could put their feet in the tub. She also had one pan of hot water for everyone's hands. It was a wonderful solution except I had learned that many in the community had the itch.

I didn't join the group Friday and went to bed where I lay for hours before warming enough to get to sleep. Saturday night, realizing I was exposed to the itch already, I warmed in the community pans.

Sunday afternoon at the drugstore I asked the clerk what he had for the itch. He responded by placing a bottle on the counter.

"What else?"

He placed another bottle there. I bought three medicines.

It was 1:00 A.M. Monday before I arrived home. From the garage I stepped into the utility room and shed all my clothes. I ran upstairs, filled the bathtub with hot water, and poured in all the medicines. In the upstairs bedroom Wilma heard me come in the house and was curious about the delay.

"Wilma, stay out; I've got the itch!"

To conclude, one or all of the three medicines worked and I did not contract that dread disease.

152.

JLK
<u>Sandra is Persecuted</u>
The next time I was in Papanduva Sandra had lost that bouncing exuberance I loved to see - she was dejected and depressed.
Sandra was gifted in memorization and recitation of dramatic
poetry, a highly respected art. She had been popular in school
because of her performing skill. Her dad told me that all
that had stopped and she was no longer called upon. She was
being persecuted because of her faith, and the ostracism had
a dreadful effect.

    I suggested to Walfrido that he and I go to the school and
talk with the director. He declined, seeming to think it was
Sandra's christian duty to submit to the suffering. There
seemed to be nothing else I could do, so I started home.

    As I drove I remembered a lawyer whom I met the day before
in Canoinhas, a neighboring town, so I drove back there. His
name was Nicéfero, and he was big and burly, giving the impression that he was very tough. We talked about Sandra's
problem, and he was sympathetic.

    "Give me a couple of days and then come back. We'll see
    what we can do."

    When I returned he showed me a beautifully typed, two-page
document. It explained that the Constitution of the United
States of Brazil guarantees freedom of religion. It elabo-
rated on the consequences of violating that freedom.

    With the document in hand we drove to Sandra's school in
Papanduva, where we asked to speak to the director (principal).
When he came, Nicéfero announced,

    "I want a word with all your teachers."

    "Why would you want to speak to all the teachers?"

    "The Constitution of the United States of Brazil is being
    violated in this school. You need some clarification."

The director paled, and he assembled his teachers. Nicéfero
read his carefully prepared document to them, and they listened attentively. When he asked if there were any questions
there were none.

    Apparently Sandra's problem was solved and her life took
on a new direction. The next year the family moved to Correia
Pinto near Lajes, where she graduated from high school with
honors. Since Walfrido and Juraci were traveling, it was our
privilege to be with Sandra at the graduation ceremony. We
sat with her through the Catholic mass which is the custom,
followed by the awarding of certificates and honors. Sandra
and one young man were the only evangelical Christians in the
class.

153.

JLK

Sandra continued studying, then she attended the Woman's Missionary Union Training School in Rio de Janeiro. Her father had the best personal library of any pastor in our state, and Sandra read voraciously. We believe that she was the best read student in her class in Rio.

By now she had matured into a trained, sophisticated, qualified Christian worker. Upon graduation she returned to Santa Catarina and worked in the state Baptist Convention headquarters in Florianópolis. She married the state Executive Secretary, but the wedding came at a time when we just weren't able to attend.

WAK   **Helena Engel**

Clara Schreiber answered the insistent clapping at their second floor apartment door. Without the customary greetings Jesse exclaimed abruptly,

  "I want to see Helena."

Clara's eyes widened in surprise and she hurriedly called her sister to the door. Without waiting to be invited in, Jesse addressed Helena,

  "Helena, go and pack your suitcase. You're going to be on
  the 4:00 o'clock bus to Curitiba today. When you arrive
  at the Institute you're going to enroll in the advanced
  course."

Helena was surprised, yet said obediently, "Yes, sir!"

  "I'll be here early to carry you to the bus, so have everything ready."

  "Yes, sir."

Helena had her suitcase packed and Jesse, true to his admonition, carried her to the 4:00 P.M. bus.

Whatever precipitated such abrupt breach of etiquette? Why would Jesse, usually so gracious and thoughtful, intimidate a young woman, member of the Lajes church?

Helena had been a teenager when she and her sister Clara trusted Christ as Savior in a revival in Lajes, led by Altair Prevedillo. They were in the first group to be baptized. The German parents were strongly opposed and put Helena out of their home; so she was living with her married sister. She had completed the basic course at Deter Bible Institute in Curitiba, and now she was in Lajes studying teacher training, making straights A's

154.

Helena worked in her brother-in-law's electric shop located at street level below their apartment. A young "Latino" employed there began to court her. Although she had testified to being called of God to serve Him in a special way, she was in a courtship with a Catholic youth who was not a Christian, and with very little schooling.

At church the love stricken young lady moved from leadership place in the front, to the first pew, and back; then out the door as we stood by helplessly. We felt that since she had committed herself to special service, a marriage to the young man would be a tragic mistake.

This is the explanation for Jesse's most unusual treatment of Helena. At Deter Institute she cried four months for her boy friend while making straight A's in Hebrew and Greek.

In time the broken heart healed and Antônio, a student in the Theology course started to date her. The fourth time he proposed Helena accepted, and now we in the Lajes Church were happily making wedding preparations.

The Bride In White Satin
Jesse and I had received a pair of white satin sheets when we married, but they just weren't practical - we kept sliding out of bed. Also I had my niece Sharon's beautiful white satin wedding dress which she sent to me for possible use when I married, but it was too small in the waist.

Helena chose a seamstress in Lajes and a wedding dress pattern. This fine artesan crafted a gorgeous gown, layering chiffon over the satin to create a glowing, pearl finish. The women of the church sewed for her trousseau and we had the bride's shower at my house.

Antônio was employed by First Church of São Paulo so a men's Sunday School class there would furnish their first home. Helena's church in Curitiba gave them a refrigerator.

The Parents
When Helena was leaving Lajes to be married in Curitiba she went to her parents' home, hoping for reconciliation. A factor in this marriage was that Antônio was of African-Portuguese descent. The mother was seated at the kitchen table sorting rice and she did not raise her eyes or say a word in response to her daughter's greeting.

Later, however, there was a reconciliation when the mother gave Helena a crocheted bedspread, a beautiful, sacrificial gift.

WAK
The Wedding
At the wedding in the Deter Institute chapel I escorted the groom and Jesse escorted the bride. There were about two hundred fifty guests, for both Helena and Antônio were gifted in developing relationships. Helena was glowing with happiness as she greeted the guests and visited with them.

. . . There is no man that hath left house, or brethren, or sisters, or father, or mother, or wife, or children, or lands, for my sake, and the gospel's, But he shall receive an hundredfold now in this time, houses, and brethren, and sisters, and mothers, and children, and lands, with persecutions; and in the world to come eternal life.
Mark 10:29, 30 KJ

JLK
Adão Ramp

Adão was about thirty when we came to know him. The family lived in the community Morro Grande (Great Mount) on the edge of town where the wooden houses were small and crude. Both he and his wife Hilga were of German descent; Hilga was blond with blue eyes and Adão, though light in complexion, had black hair and smoldering black eyes.

He had been a Baptist in Rio Grande do Sul but was excluded because of drinking. He came into the Lajes church by reconciliation and later Hilga was converted. Adão was an excellent builder and helped in our construction projects. As his spiritual life was rekindled he became an excellent preacher. (Many laymen in Brazil develop skills for preaching, and it never ceases to amaze me). Adão was growing into a dependable person.

Time was approaching for a year's furlough so we moved from our large house into a downtown apartment for security. We were exhausted from moving, storing, hauling, and packing; it was hard to think of actually closing the apartment and driving to Florianópolis. Adão stopped on his way from work, and realizing our predicament, he took charge. By nine o'clock that evening he put us in our car along with baggage, and sent us on the first leg to the States.

July 25, 1974 when we returned, Adão met us at Florianópolis. We stayed there several days because of document work, so Adão went on to Lajes and took responsibility for our trunks and bags. When we unlocked our apartment door they were sitting in the living room.

As we started to work again, Adão gave total support. However I developed health problems and the Board's medical consultant Dr. Franklin Fowler recommended a more moderate climate. The decision to move was traumatic for us as well as for Adão. I doubt he slept the night after we told him. The next morning he was at our house early, and told me his story:

156.

"I was about five years old when we lived in Rio Grande
do Sul. My father had a shotgun and warned me never to
touch it. One evening while he and Mother were in the
next room I decided to examine it and it discharged,
killing my father. My mother was so bitter toward me
that she gave me away. I suppose she thought the worst
thing she could do to me was to give me to a family of
black people."

Adão shared nothing of his life in that home. He simply said,

"You are the only father I have ever known."

As we prepared to move to the state of Minas Gerais I was
handicapped because I was recovering from surgery on my vocal
cords. Adão arranged the moving van and persuaded the manager
of the company to give his employee a vacation so he could
ride in the truck to Belo Horizonte on its several-day trip.
I remonstrated,

"Adão, we're glad that you want to go and help; but you
must go with us in the car, not in the truck."

"But you never know where the trucks go, nor where they
stop. I'll go with the truck to see that it goes directly
to Belo Horizonte."

When the movers arrived at our rented house in Belo, Adão
stayed to help set up the furniture. When we took him to the
airport to return to Lajes, we three sensed the pain of separation. As he turned to board his plane, tears were stream-
ing down his face.

Hilga told us later that Adão lived with the thought of
moving to Minas Gerais to work with us. May 24, 1978, we
learned of his death. He was on a ranch where his father-in-
law was building a house. Adão was in the pasture where a
vicious bull attacked, and he was killed instantly. We traveled back to Lajes to be with Hilga, Daniel, David, and Deborah for a few hours, and to see Adão's grave.

We know what it is to love a son.

We know what it is to lose a son.

Miguel Rocha Campos

If I were to introduce you to Miguel he would politely shake your hand then duck in embarrassment because he was so timid. He wasn't tall or handsome and spoke with a country accent, carried over from his youth in Espírito Santo state. The story of how the Gospel called him from a desperate, lowly situation, is multiplied in many, many lives.

Miguel was a hired man working in the field in Espírito Santo, without hope of continuing his education. When he was eighteen he went to hear missionary Harrison Pike preach. He responded to the call of Jesus Christ and was converted. He felt the Lord leading him to preach, so he needed to further his education beyond the elementary level. He finally qualified to enroll in the Theology course at Deter Bible Institute in Curitiba, Paraná. It gets cold there - an extreme contrast to Espírito Santo's heat.

Miguel was pastor of First Church in Lajes when we moved there February, 1970. His beautiful wife Teresa had just given birth to their second son. Teresa was the daughter of João Frederico in Taquaral and was a marvelous complement for Miguel's ministry.

Jesse cared for the Wednesday night prayer meeting, enabling Miguel to attend night school. Miguel was a plodder; faithful to the philosophy and program of the Santa Catarina Baptist Convention. He was faithful in his pastoral ministries; many of the thirty-nine church members were untrained, and some had unreasonable expectations of a pastor.

When Miguel became certified to teach he moved his family to the town of Monte Castelo where he taught Portuguese in grade school. This was near to Teresa's family at Taquaral, so grandparents Frederico helped care for the boys.

NOTE: Monte Castelo is named for a battlefield in Italy where Brazilian soldiers valiantly fought in World War II.

There were three sons by the time the family moved to an apartment of the South Brazil Seminary in Rio de Janeiro, where Miguel would study. They carried sacks of rice, beans, and other products on the bus from Taquaral, for their pantry.

Then the twins were born. In spite of the crowded living situation Miguel's grades at the Seminary won highest regard and appreciation; almost perfect grades in Hebrew and Greek!

After graduation Miguel and Teresa endeared their friends and family in Santa Catarina, for they returned to that home state to take up a pastorate.

Heronete Brum and his young wife were missionaries of the
Brazilian Baptist Home Mission Board, arriving in Santa Catarina to establish new work in the West. On their way to
Chapecó they spent the night at our house. Their baggage was
light: several suitcases, some heavy denim sacks, and hand
baggage to carry on the bus. They would buy furniture and
appliances at their destination.

The young missionaries worked zealously in Chapecó. They
rented a small dwelling in the public housing development
(called Popular Housing). Then they rented the adjacent house
where they began children's Bible clubs and evangelistic preaching. The work flourished and a day in December 1972 was set
for the formal organization of this mission, under auspices
of the Taquaral Church.

First, I needed to go to the coast to Florianópolis. Then
I drove west to Taquaral where I picked up five men: Renato
Salles the pastor, José Frederico the evangelist, Hercílio
the teacher, and two laymen - "Zeca" Frederico and Euclides.
Wilma came to meet me there, since it would have been out of
the way for me to go to Lajes.

The journey to Chapecó was hot, dusty, and long. Bottled
drinks didn't begin to assuage our thirst, but in spite of
the heat the men joked and sang all the way. When they began swapping plays on words (endless, in Portuguese), Wilma
and I were well entertained by the frivolity.

When we arrived at the meeting place Renato called the business session to order and it was declared that the mission
of the Taquaral Church was established formally.

Renato questioned the twelve candidates for baptism, and
the youth and two adults responded to the doctrinal questions
satisfactorily. We then went to the river where Renato baptized them. According to custom, after each one is baptized
we sang a stanza of a hymn. I thank the Lord for this custom,
for I love the hymns used for baptism from the "Cantor Cristão."

   "Côro Santo" - page 274 (Ring The Bells of Heaven)
   "Batismo" - page 145
   "Ditoso O Dia" - page 407 (Happy Day)

The missionaries had prepared a simple lunch. We understood
that finances were limited, so we ate the dessert as if it
were a rich pudding: thin tapioca, colored pink and faintly
sweetened. Computing the mileage from leaving Lajes until
arriving at home, it came to over 1,000 miles. We were exhausted, but we thanked God "from whom all blessings flow."

JLK

The presence of the Brums in Santa Catarina helped all of us missionaries since it meant the realization of the dream of establishing congregations and churches in the extreme West of our state. Now the Brazilian Baptist Convention was having more input about this pioneer state, where European culture was so prominent. Heronete's wife was from the city of Petrópolis in Rio de Janeiro (state). Once when they were at our house she cried, lamenting that she couldn't understand Portuguese spoken at Chapecó, since so many Italian expressions were commonly used.

THIS EPOCH CLOSES

In Santa Catarina we devoted six years of hard work in very harsh circumstances, and we wanted to count the score and see the results. But this was not God's will. I had surgery on my vocal cord to remove a polyp, and although recovery was going well Dr. Franklin Fowler of the Board encouraged us to move to a more moderate climate. The State Baptist Convention of Minas Gerais invited me to lead their Missions Department as we lived in Belo Horizonte. I learned there was a voice therapist there who had been trained in the United States. I hoped that he could direct the therapy of retraining my voice.

Evaluating our work as field missionaries, we could say:

Seed had been sown up and down the Planalto and out to the west end of the state. We conducted revivals, stewardship studies, Bible courses, music events and study, and I had given pastoral supply. We helped build two chapels, and finished a church building.

The new chapel in Curitibanos stood with its doors locked, and there was no hope they would be opened and that there would begin to be a ministry to the people's spiritual needs.

We left Santa Catarina April, 1976. In January, 1978, I traveled to Curitiba, Paraná, (the state just north of Santa Catarina) to attend the annual National Baptist Convention. The Home Mission Board report highlighted the exciting work in our state of Santa Catarina in January and February, 1977.

Baptist young people from schools, alongside Home Mission Board personnel, had done a "highway and by-way" evangelistic thrust, in house-to-house visitation and evangelistic services. The results were phenomenal. Never in the history of the work in Santa Catarina had there been such sweeping victories. The doors of the Curitibanos chapel re-opened, and a church was organized in it. New churches and missions were established.

A new day had dawned for Santa Catarina, and we realized that God gives the harvest in His time and in His way!

VII.

UNTIL A YOUNGER MISSIONARY COMES?

"And Until A Younger Missionary Comes Along?"

Belo Horizonte had been our home for nearly two years. I worked with the Missions Department of the Minas Gerais state Baptist Convention which had a number of men employed throughout the state. The Executive Secretary of the state work, José Alves Bittencourt, talked to me about North Minas: the developing churches, enthusiasm of the leaders, need for leadership, and for someone to baptize and disciple new believers; someone with a pioneer spirit.

Periodically I enthusiastically mentioned the challenge to Wilma. She reasoned the negative factors why we should not consider moving to Montes Claros. After all, hadn't we just come from over six years of isolation? There was talk about the bad water - that it contained minerals. People there got amoeba, schistoza, and Chagas. Chagas is the dread heart disease contracted from the insect called barbeiro. Also, the North was famous for the unmerciful heat.

I was pastor of Parque Durval de Barros church in the industrial suburb of that name, in Belo Horizonte. I did not mention North Minas to Wilma again, providing the time she needed to seek God's will. Then, together we considered the challenge and the invitation.

In 1977 under the leadership of Pastor Levy Penido the North Minas Baptist Association appealed to the state Executive Committee to locate a missionary in Montes Claros. The Association is about one-fifth the size of Texas, or about 52,403 square miles (almost the size of Arkansas). There were eighteen churches, nine pastors, and total church membership of around 2,000. Although we considered the vastness of the North, the great need, and the fact that we were beginning the last decade of our career, we decided to make a field trip.

Levy Penido, president of the Association and pastor of First Church, was our host when we arrived in Montes Claros. Arrangements had been made for me to preach in his church on this, Wednesday night. Our hotel was downtown and we stood in the lobby and watched the people as a hard rain fell. They deliberately went into the streets and "ran in circles," dancing in the downfall, celebrating the first rain after the dry season. The intense heat in spring and summer brings the rain.

Levy did an excellent job of showing us the field, and we were thoroughly convinced of the need on every hand. Montes Claros was the economic center for about 1,500,000 people. The municipality had 300,000 and was growing; and in that city there were only four Baptist churches.

JLK
   We were convinced of the need and overwhelmed by the stag-
gering task that any missionary would face. We remembered
that health problems had led us from Santa Catarina to Belo.
As we prepared to return home I said,

   "Pastor Levy, this field has large possibilities, but it
   is a field for younger missionaries, not for a couple
   coming into their last decade of service."

"And until a younger missionary comes along?"

He did not say any more.

   Back in Belo we struggled with his response for several
weeks until we finally determined, "This is our open door."

> A door seldom used
> To a place long neglected;
> The door - the city of Montes Claros
> The place - North Minas Gerais.
> The door, at first glance rough and uninviting;
> The place, hot and dusty in the dry season,
>   hot and humid in the wet season;
> Whether dusty or muddy - always hot.
> The door opened to us, and we would enter,
>   to spend over ten years!

". . . See, I have set before you an open door, . . .
**   Revelation 3:8 NKJ**

The Beginnings of Baptist Work in North Minas

   In 1914 a layman named Domingos de Novais Neves started
a work in the communities Juramento, Buritizal, and Malhada
Grande; this was in the municipality of Montes Claros (corres-
ponds to the term "county").

   The next year, 1915, a schoolteacher named Joaquim Coelho
dos Santos came to the same area and baptized some believers.
He had come from the state of Bahia.

   In 1918 First Baptist Church of Belo Horizonte (state capital of Minas Gerais) organized two churches in the area known
as North Minas. One was at Juramento; the other was in the
rural community Boa Vista dos Matos. Due to a shift in population the church in Juramento moved to Montes Claros and became the First Baptist Church of that city, a church which
always had a powerful witness. She is the second largest in
the state and has produced a number of churches through her
missions and evangelism program.

Note: The first Baptist church to be organized on Brazilian soil was in 1882 at Salvador, Bahia. It was just thirty-six years later, 1918, that these first two churches came into being in North Minas. It was not until 1939, or twenty-one years later, that another church was organized in vast North Minas.

Poor traveling and economic conditions and persecution were enemies to the struggling new Baptist witness in the harsh and hostile land. When the state Baptist Convention met at the Montes Claros church in 1954, the messengers were warned that when they walked on the streets they should go in groups since Baptists there had suffered persecution.

In 1949 the Association of Baptist Churches of North Minas Gerais was organized with three churches: Boa Vista dos Matos, Primeira de Bocaiuva, and Primeira de Montes Claros.

After 1959 there was a dramatic increase in the growth rate of new churches in North Minas mainly because that year the national Brazilian Baptist Convention adopted the Cooperative Program for financing and promoting Baptist work. An element of cooperation was added to the union of churches, strengthening all areas of development.

The Southern Baptist Foreign Mission Board sends missionaries to the three geographical divisions in Brazil: South, North, and Equatorial Brazil Missions. They are supported by the Southern Baptist Convention; however all this is done in cooperation with the Brazilian Baptist Convention. The Brazilian Baptist Conventions of various states may invite Southern Baptist missionaries to work in their areas; they actually govern to a great extent where the missionaries will live and work.

Renting A House And Moving

If the possibility of finding a rent house were as remote as in other cities, it would be a long time before we found a place to live. When we returned to Montes Claros to rent a house, we spent three fruitless days. Pastor Levy, familiar with the city, appealed to people in his church and to businessmen who might know of leads. Now we were driving up and down the streets, inquiring. Our conversation was rather glum but I observed,

"God is never early, neither is he ever late."

On the street Olímpio Dias de Abreu, Levy stopped to ask some small boys if they knew of a rent house. A lady, overhearing, approached.

"My son's house right here is for rent."

She said she would arrange a meeting with her son, Antônio Luiz Amaral Figueredo, his wife, and herself. Later we all gathered at house number 329, and sat at the Figueredo's table. Antônio explained he had already promised the house to a doctor. But his mother, Dona Angelita, argued that when they lived in the state of Bahia the other son attended the Baptist agricultural school in Jaguaquara. She insisted with Antônio that since we were Baptists we merited the house, and finally he acceded.

The amount of rent was decided and Wilma suggested to Antônio that when we returned to Belo we could send him an advance for the first month. Antônio drew himself erect, looked at her sternly, and said,

"Está falado!" It is spoken!

This was the beginning of a fine relationship between landlord and renter until October 1988. Antônio was fair, honest, and considerate. Dona Angelita who lived next door, cared for us as if we were her own family.

It was March 1, 1978 when we left Belo Horizonte at 9:00 P.M. to move to our new home in Montes Claros. On the highway beyond the city lights a full moon illuminated the way, brightening our spirits. New opportunity, new friends, experiences and victories, and an excitement about trying to serve our Lord. We arrived at 2:10 A.M. and slept a few hours at the hotel before meeting the moving truck at Olímpio Dias de Abreu 329, to supervise the unloading of our furniture.

Health And Living Conditions

There were always health threats; either because of the nature of our work or our geographical location. Amoeba, an intestinal parasite, was the most common debilitating condition which reduced energy and vitality. We were often subject to amoeba because of the travel and hygiene conditions. After the laboratory analysis the doctor would recommend the dosage of medicine - always a harsh one. Many times we needed to travel to Rio de Janeiro where the laboratory was considered dependable.

The parasite giardia is more difficult to treat. Then there are worms. No matter how meticulous our care of food, we became subject. We desisted eating uncooked or unpealed food, and lettuce.

Schistosa (colloquial for schistosomiasis) is contracted in lakes and rivers where the current is sluggish. Antônio our landlord had it, and he attributed it to his being around cattle. Schistosa attacks the intestines, urinary bladder, liver and spleen, and is difficult to treat.

166.

JLK

In North Minas we faced the reality of <u>Chagas</u> (a disease of the heart) on every hand. I was in the Francisco Sá Church one Sunday evening when a woman among the worshipers, pointing to a roach-size bug crawling up the wall, screamed,

"<u>Barbeiro</u>!"

Immediately everyone ran outside. The insect causing <u>Chagas</u>, <u>barbeiro</u>, is commonly found in adobe buildings, or mud and thatched shelters. The disease is found mainly in central Brazil: in Mato Grosso, Goiás, and Minas Gerais states; also in southwestern Mexico.

If a small child is infected, it is almost always fatal. An adult may live a normal lifespan with a damaged heart, or die suddenly. The threat of <u>Chagas</u> is dreaded more than snakebite, because snakebite has an anecdote; <u>Chagas</u> has none. Infected people who can afford it might have a pacemaker implanted. During our period in the North, Pastor Joaquim of Grão Mogol died of it, also Pastor Geraldo Nunes of Montes Claros. Pastor Benjamim Soares da Cruz lived with it. In the town Butumirim a doctor told me that ninety per cent of the people buried there died of <u>Chagas</u>.

Survey of Basic Needs

When we arrived in 1978 Montes Claros was at the end of the pavement. Anywhere one went except to Belo Horizonte was on dirt roads. In the rainy season the vehicles made deep ruts. In the dry season the ruts filled with dust, permeating ones clothing and hair, even the nostrils.

Half of the eighteen churches were near enough to visit and return home the same day but the others required an overnight trip or longer. I had a Mission car; however if I lacked funds or if the way were precarious, I used bus, slow-moving train, pulpwood truck, rented pickup, my two feet, or a horse. I made it a question to be available to the churches and I had the joy of baptizing believers in most of the rivers of North Minas.

Economic conditions were very poor for there was little industry aside from agriculture or ranching. Smaller, more remote churches being cared for by willing but untrained laymen rarely saw a visiting pastor to baptize new converts and serve the Lord's Supper.

My job as Co-ordinator of the Association could mean almost anything I determined. Since no one had given me a job description I made up one as I went along. The Association was loosely structured although it had its Constitution and By-laws. We lived too far from the state headquarters to daily receive orientation from there.

167.

JLK

With a wide range of freedom to proceed as I felt best, I set out to determine the basic needs of the churches and how to meet them. My survey revealed:

1. Very limited number of pastors: only nine for eighteen churches scattered over an area 1/5 the size of Texas
2. Few trained leaders in the churches
3. Lack of Bibles and literature
4. Lack of training in personal evangelism
5. Critical lack of finances
6. Several long established congregations needed to become fully organized churches. One of these was Riacho dos Machados, having existed for forty-seven years. They had a complete record of Sunday School attendance for their entire history.

We Start Together

We started quarterly meetings with the pastors and leaders of the churches who helped to formulate what we needed to accomplish. I thought it necessary to visit the churches for a hands-on relationship with the people. The leadership of the Association had determined that since I had a car I should shepherd all pastorless churches. Having this care gave me a freedom of movement and very helpful access to the people. Since they thought of me as their pastor they were ready to listen. The churches were open to my leadership and the homes extended a welcome.

We started out with the objective of strengthening the existing churches and establishing new congregations. I was always teaching and witnessing - in small gatherings of pastors and leaders, in services in the churches or visiting in the homes. Paul was my example when he said in Acts 20:31 KJ

. . . I ceased not . . . night and day . . .
No opportunity was lost.

Therefore they that were scattered abroad went every where preaching the word.   Acts 8:4 KJ

Baptists love goals. We are very aware that
Where there is no vision, the people perish . . .
**   Proverbs 29:18 KJ**

God gave Wilma and me a vision of doubling the number of churches during our last decade in Brazil. If I considered the health, travel, and economic conditions I would wonder about this. But after I had visited all the churches the vision remained fiercely fixed. Like Peter, if I took my eyes off the Lord of the harvest for one moment, I would sink.

But when he saw that the wind was boisterous, he was afraid; and beginning to sink he cried out, saying, "Lord, save me!"   Matthew 14:30 NKJ

JLK

With no more than a few small pebbles did I dare confront
the giant? Who was I to think of trying to devise a plan to
reach 1,500,000 people? Once I was sure the vision was from
God, I determined the place to start was in each of the churches, who must be led to take a positive role in the spiritual
conquest of North Minas. They must learn to pray to the Lord
of the harvest - that He would send the leadership needed.

Matthew 9:36-38 became the text of all my sermons for the
next several months. I still believe this is the most neglected of all the commands of our Lord. Everywhere I went I preached that sermon.

Don't call Him Jesus, Lord, Christ, or God.
Call Him by the name he gives us here,
   "Lord of the harvest."
O Lord of the harvest, send us workers.

In the Brasília de Minas church I preached the same sermon
three times until I heard them pray in that manner.

In the Association there were more than a dozen towns each
with population of at least 40,000 - with no churches, not
even preaching points. There were four young people expressing God's call to give their lives in Christian service; they
had gone away to distant seminaries to study. Terezinha was
the only one of these four to come back to work in our area.

As the churches began to realize they had not really prayed
as the Lord had commanded, we saw a wonderful change. Young
people started to respond to God's calling. Mature men with
families realized that God was speaking to them too. I had
come to believe that except in rare cases, only people who
had grown up in the North and understood the culture, could
really adjust to the conditions and have a ministry.

The Church Named Croslândia

The drive from Montes Claros to Croslândia took more than three hours on rough, dirt road. Within two months of our arrival in the North I made my first visit to the Croslândia Church and I was overwhelmed with the terrible needs of the people. The church had almost 200 members, making it the third largest in the Association.

It was three years since the last pastoral visit; no one to baptize or serve the Lord's Supper. Young couples wishing to marry simply joined together or were married by a public official without the benefit of a church ceremony. Families buried their dead without even a pastoral prayer. There was no one to guide them to a deeper knowledge of the Bible.

"Therefore take heed to yourselves and to all the flock, among which the Holy Spirit has made you overseers, to shepherd the church of God which He purchased with His own blood.
"For I know this, that after my departure savage wolves will come in among you, not sparing the flock.
Acts 20:28,29 NKJ

I promised the church I would come the first Sunday of every month, leaving home Saturday and returning Monday. This was the beginning of a wonderful and fruitful relationship.

How did Croslândia Church come into being? A man named João Branco was converted and baptized in the city of São Paulo, then he moved to this remote part of Minas Gerais. He was a garimpeiro, a diamond miner. As he searched for diamonds he preached the Gospel. As he evangelized he baptized, being unaware that as a layman he did not have that authority.

Word of a growing number of converts at Cristália reached Feliciano Amaral, pastor of First Church of Montes Claros. He determined to resign and move with his family to Cristália. Then the Christians were severely persecuted. (In our time João Branco lived at Alegre, where he died.)

A rancher who owned some land about three miles west of Cristália offered to give his land to the Baptists, where they could live. Pastor Amaral wisely offered to buy the seventy acres in order to have a legal deed. The pastor and his flock built temporary shelters and set about to build a community of their own. They named the community and church Croslândia, after Southern Baptist missionary Daniel Crosland who was a pioneer in Minas Gerais.

Feliciano Amaral was known throughout Brazil as <u>O Sabiá do Sertão</u> - The Songbird of the Wilderness. He traveled Brazil conducting meetings, giving concerts (he had a marvelous tenor voice), and raising support for Croslândia. His records, produced by the Baptist Publishing House in Rio de Janeiro, sold prolifically. He captured the imagination of the people.

The idea of a community of Christian people free from persecution, bars selling alcoholic beverages, and other distractions, was appealing and people were generous.

The Croslândia community developed a brick and tile factory, the only industry in an agricultural community dependent upon a precarious climate. They built a gothic type church building on a two-acre plot circled by the believers' homes and they had their own grade school. The place known as Croslândia prospered for several years.

But the pressures of responsibility and hard work took their toll and Pastor Feliciano Amaral with his family and adopted children moved to Rio de Janeiro. Now the Croslândia church was in a state of decline. Many members had moved away; the brick and tile factory had been sold and moved. But hope sprang up in the people with the possibility that the missionary would come monthly.

On my third visit I was met by a group who, having heard that I would be there, had walked eleven hours through the heat of the wilderness. They were believers who wanted to be baptized. It was very humbling to realize that God gave me the privilege of baptizing those precious, determined people.

A <u>Great</u> <u>Revival</u> <u>In</u> <u>Cristália</u>

As the attendance in Croslândia increased and the people became more courageous Senhor Pedro, the layman leader, talked about a service in Cristália. I questioned the wisdom of such a meeting, because of the persecution and bitterness of the past. Since I could be there only on the weekend I didn't want to promote a meeting that would cause conflict, without being there to help with any problems.

Senhor Pedro insisted and wanted to have the meeting in his yard. He reasoned that if the people came on his private property to attend the gathering they should not object to the preaching of the Gospel.

On the night of the meeting over 150 people crowded into the yard, standing closely to each other. The moonlight was bright and we scarcely needed any other light. The church people sang with joy and I preached a simple evangelistic sermon on the need for salvation.

JLK
As I was nearing the close of the sermon Senhor Pedro whispered to me,

   "Pastor, you must give an invitation."

I did and over thirty people came forward confessing their need of the Savior. The church members were ecstatic and it was after midnight before everyone left. I was a guest in Senhor Pedro's home. When everyone had left he said,

   "Pastor, do you have any idea what happened here tonight?
   The couple who led in the persecution that drove us out
   of Cristália almost twenty years ago, was converted tonight!"

   Victory at last! Baptists had suffered long years. They had been patient and faithful. On this wonderful night they had been wonderfully rewarded. This was the beginning of a new chapter in their lives.

EQUIPPING THE CALLED
A Bible Institute Is Founded

   God was answering prayers by calling young people, men, and women - prompting them to offer themselves in Christian service. The leaders of the Association realized they needed to provide study opportunities. Those who had the necessary preparation and could go away to study in seminaries, were encouraged to do that. Young people without educational back-ground to do seminary level studies needed the opportunity of growth.

   Then there were some mature family men who were already into correspondence and other study plans. These men had to think of caring for their families, and most had already es-tablished their business and professions.

   The Bible Institute opened September 1979 in First Church of Montes Claros with fifty students. Courses that first se-mester were Introduction to The Bible, Personal Evangelism, and Introduction to The Life of Jesus. Class met one night a week, with the qualified local pastors teaching:
   Jacinto Pereira Faustino
   Salmon Alencar de Souza
   Dionísio A. Martins
I also taught, plus traveling weekly to Capitão Eneas to teach ten people there.

   Wilma's letter of April 1, 1980:

   "Jesse is happily laboring in his Institute course. He has a large class at First Church, and fourteen students at Fourth Church. The pastor at Curvelo (halfway to Belo) has eighteen students, studying the same book."

172.

The greatest problem was textbooks. The best available on the Institute level was a three-year programmed course published in São Paulo by the Regular Baptists. Our students moved at such a rapid pace they got ahead of available textbooks so two years into the course we had to switch.

Since we were on a local plan we gave the students credit for completed studies and moved on to our own curriculum. Finally the Minas Gerais State Convention seminary in Belo Horizonte took us under their Institute curriculum, resulting in a stronger, more stable plan. I was honored when the Institute was named "Jesse L. Kidd Bible Institute." After 1988 the plan of studies was upgraded to seminary level, offering Greek and Hebrew.

There were some men in the Association who were already studying in either of two plans.

1. The Ravena Course. For many years the annual, one-month study was done at the city of Governador Valadares, then it was moved to the State Convention encampment near the small town of Ravena, out from Belo Horizonte.

   The students studied eleven months at home and at the annual month at Ravena they took examinations and received study materials for the next year. That way, men with families and professions could embark on a four-year study plan.

2. Theological education by correspondence offered by the North Brazil Seminary in Recife, Pernambuco.

THE BEAST

Rubelita

We planned to leave from Montes Claros at 4:00 A.M., going to Rubelita. There were eight of us in the First Church Volkswagen van, with Pastor Levy in charge. Day was just dawning when we reached the high plateau above Francisco Sá, the first town. Further on we came to a hitchhiker and stopped for him. We had been singing as we traveled, so after the stop we continued. Our new passenger was seated next to me so I sensed it when his body began to shake with sobs.

"Friend, is there something wrong?"

"On the contrary, it is wonderful! I know who you people are and I belong to you. But in my community they call me 'Beast' because I believe like you do."

**Because zeal for Your house has eaten me up,
And the reproaches of those who reproach You
have fallen on me.**
Psalm 69:9 NKJ

I asked our friend where he lived.

"I live in Barrocão, just off the road where you picked
me up."

He rode with us for the next three hours, leaving us at
the town Fruta de Leite. It was a very happy journey for
him. I was never to see him again, but I would hear of this
man several times. We traveled on, passing through the thriv-
ing town of Salinas which was destined to become a very important focal point for the Baptist witness.

We reached Rubelita late in the afternoon, where Pastor
Levy inquired on the street about Paulo Machado, with whom we
were to meet. We stopped two or three times but no one knew
him. A young man in our group remembered,

"Pastor, ask for him by the name Paulo <u>Crente</u> (Believer)."

Soon we found someone who knew him and directed us to his
home. Our man was known by his faith and not by his real name.

"Therefore by their fruits you will know them.
Matthew 7:20 NKJ

At Paulo's home we were met by his wife and family who directed us to the ranch about seven miles out, and a young boy
accompanied us. It was a typical Brazilian ranch - a large
corral with high fences built of heavy wooden planks. The
caretaker's house stood to one side.

Paulo <u>Crente</u> was delighted when we introduced ourselves.
He said it had been over thirty years since receiving a visit
from a pastor or a church. Yet he was known in his town by
his faith - not by his real name!

The sun set and evening shadows gathered. It seemed perfectly natural to gather around this man in the corral where most
of the ranch work took place. A full moon rose and bathed
everything in tropical radiance. No one was hurried and we
listened while Paulo talked at length about his life and witness as a believer.

A great white cow, drawn by the voice of her master, joined
the circle, chewing placidly on her cud as the moonlight reflected on her massive horns. No one disputed her right to
be there!

It was after 9:00 P.M. when we returned to town where Paulo's
wife served a delicious meal. After we ate, Pastor Levy led
in a worship service. Several neighbors had come in and though
it was late it was a time of rejoicing and worship.

JLK   **The <u>Bus</u> <u>Driver</u> <u>and</u> <u>the</u> <u>Beast</u>**

I chose to travel to the more remote churches by bus rather than using the Mission car since the roads were so rough. The car was bought by Lottie Moon Christmas Offering money and I knew there wouldn't be a replacement soon.

Leaving Montes Claros on Saturday morning, I visited First Church in Januária that night and Sião Church in the same city on Sunday morning. Leaving Januária Sunday noon, the bus followed the São Francisco River to Manga so I could be in that church Sunday night.

Monday morning I'd cross the river by boat and take a bus to Jaiba for service in the Fonte Viva Church. Jaiba was a new town where everything was very rustic and frontier.

All of this travel was by very dusty roads. Sometimes I stayed in Brazilian homes and sometimes in the simple, rustic hotels, and food was very limited. Hopefully there would be bottled drinks for sale.

In Jaiba I recognized my bus driver, who seemed worried. When I indicated an interest, he said,

"I usually stay at Riacho dos Machados for the night and return to Montes Claros the next day. But they've extended my route to that desolate place, Barrocão. It doesn't even have a hotel, and I don't know anyone."

I thought,

"Poor soul. I know the feeling."

Tuesday morning I traveled by bus to Riacho dos Machados where everything went well at the church; the service that evening was excellent. Wednesday morning early I was at the bus stop to return to Montes Claros. Boarding, I noticed the driver was in a jovial mood.

"How did the night in Barrocão go?"

"I had a wonderful time. I spent the night in the home of a man with a very strange name. They call him 'Beast.' We had a wonderful visit."

> **How beautiful upon the mountains**
> **Are the feet of him who brings good news,**
> **Who proclaims peace,**
> **Who brings glad tidings of good things,**
> **Who proclaims salvation,**
> **Who says to Zion,**
> **"Your God reigns!"**
> **Isaiah 52:7 NKJ**

I traveled to Hemphill, Texas June 9, 1979 to be with Willie Mae's husband Rex Mathews, who was terminally ill. I returned to Brazil June 29. Rex died January 5, 1980.

DISASTER RELIEF
Espinosa

In December 1979 (these dates are unverified) the spring rains started on schedule in North Minas. The further north one goes the more dependent the people are upon farming, so rain is a necessity. Everywhere the farmers were planting cotton, corn, and beans, the staples of the area. The outlook was good and expectations were high.

Then the rains stopped. The hot sun scorched the tender plants and pastures dried up; within weeks a dusty pall covered the land. Farmers and field hands were driven from the land to hunt the shade. If the six-month rain doesn't come it can mean eighteen months without moisture. The dry season never fails to arrive on schedule; only the rainy season forgets its turn.

This was the situation in January/February, 1980, when word came of food riots in Espinosa. There was a Baptist church there so I traveled eight hours by bus to investigate the plight of our people.

After leaving Janauba the land looked more desolate with each mile. Leaving Porteirinha, we never got away from the stench of rotting farm animals which had starved to death. Government trucks passed each day to fill the barrels set in front of every farmhouse. I had not witnessed such devastation since walking through bombed-out towns and countryside in China during World War II.

In Espinosa I hurried to the home of Senhor Lourival, deacon who cared for the church, maintaining the services since there was no pastor. Lourival said there had been a riot in which one man died. However he assured me that none of the church people had participated.

We decided to go to a friendly merchant who knew the church people, asking that he let the people buy on credit if we guaranteed the payment. I caught the next bus to Montes Claros and called Fred Hawkins, chairman of Disaster Relief for the South Brazil Mission.

With his authorization I called the Foreign Mission Board in Richmond describing the situation, and the response was immediate. I returned to Espinosa with funds in hand. We couldn't hope to meet every need, but we encouraged the people to be ready to plant their crops again.

176.

JLK
    That night heavy rainclouds moved in - the rain fell in
sheets and the following day there were flood conditions.
Having done what I could to administer aid to the people of
the church, I caught the bus to go home. (Months later when
I visited the Espinosa church I enjoyed fresh vegetables that
were grown from seed from this Disaster Relief aid.)

    Two hours down the road we stopped where floods had washed
out the bridge. There was only a huge log across the swollen
stream. We got off the bus and gingerly crossed on the log.
On the other side we learned that a relief bus was on its way
from Montes Claros.

    Knowing that it would be hours before it arrived, I spied
a stack of wood under a large, spreading mango tree. I decided to take a nap there, since I'd not had much sleep the
last three days.

    I was almost asleep when several calves came to stand in
the shade of the tree - Brahmas with long ears hanging down
like shopping bags. Just outside the circle of Big Ears was
a colt that was anything but "all things bright and beautiful" for the poor thing didn't have one hair on its miserable
body.

    Even that didn't disturb my sleep. When the relief bus
arrived and blasted its horn I joined the other passengers
in boarding. I heard someone comment,

    "That American knows how to take care of himself."

I awaken groggily about 3:00 A.M. and wonder,

"What is it?"

"It" is music - rather a lament - a dirge. People have gathered and the group passes slowly in the streets, wailing to honor some pagan god. The sad lament is in the minor key - joyless and hopeless. Perhaps they have come from a nocturnal visit to a cemetery where they obtained some bones.

The sound diminishes as the procession moves past our house and down the street past Dona Angelita's house, then around the corner. I hope to drift back to sleep, wishing that it will be some time before the procession repeats their nocturnal lament, leaving me sad and disturbed - and sleepless!

                    ****

I awaken groggily about 3:00 A.M. and wonder,

"What is it?"

"It" is music - youthful voices singing their joyous praise to God. We arise, dress, and invite the young people in. They are from the Boas Novas Church, and they have come to serenade us.

This is the delightful custom of the youth of the Baptist churches. Dressed in jeans, slacks, shirts, blouses, and sweaters, they don't look at all sleepy. They sing their greeting accompanied by guitar, then someone reads a passage of Bible scripture and has prayer.

I will drift back to sleep as the joyful tunes reverberate through my being; I have been many times blessed and I will peacefully capture several more hours' sleep.

William Barnes of New York City

Januária is an old city, population about 70,000 located on the São Francisco River - accessible only by riverboats until the road from Montes Claros was cut through the wilderness, sometime before 1978. I was there making plans for the annual meeting of the Association, staying in Hotel Minas because it had screens.

This two-story hotel had a bathroom for each floor. Breakfast was typical: strong, black coffee, a small loaf of French bread, butter, and fruit (bananas, oranges, papaya). The hotel owner introduced me to the other American there. William Barnes was from New York City: tall, rather thin, blond, with sunburned nose, probably under thirty. He said he lived west of Januária several hours by bus, and he came to town monthly for supplies and mail.

William's nearest town was Serra das Araras, about halfway between Januária and Brasília, the national capital. A rickety bus traveled weekly from Januária to Brasília and back on the winding dirt road.

William explained that he had been working in a night club in New York City and became addicted to drugs. A Brazilian suggested that he go to Brazil so a change of scene would help him break the habit, but in Rio de Janeiro he found drugs were easily available. Someone suggested the far interior; hence he came to Serra das Araras.

He bought land five miles out, built a modest adobe house, and learned to raise vegetables. He owned some cows and chickens, and several cats. Cats were to keep snakes away. He had tried dogs but the boa constrictors got them. He married a Brazilian girl and they had a child. I queried if he missed New York.

"I don't miss New York but I miss a Bible. When I was
   little I went to Sunday School, and I miss that."

I promised a Bible to him on my next trip, and we agreed I would leave it with the hotel owner. Two weeks later I brought a Bible in English and several more in Portuguese.

Months later we met at the same hotel, and William thanked me profusely for the Bibles. **There had never been a Bible in his rural community;** three generations of people there had never seen one.

**So shall My word be that goes forth from My mouth;
It shall not return to Me void,
But it shall accomplish what I please,
And it shall prosper in the thing for which I sent it.**
                              Isaiah 55:11   NKJ

Alegre was beyond Grão Mogol. From home to Grão Mogol it took at least three hours by Mission car, then I usually hired an old pickup (pronounced peek-ahhp) to travel thirty-five miles on an overgrown trail. When aspiring political candidates campaigned they favored the citizens by such amenities as grading this trail.

The death of Pastor Vicente left the church at Grão Mogol in my care, for as missionary of North Minas I tried to care for all pastorless churches. When I visited Grão Mogol the church members frequently spoke of Alegre, their mission point. Since I was caring for several churches on a once-a-month basis the mission points just came up short. But during one visit to Grão Mogol Maria Nazaré, the widow of Pastor Vicente, urged me,

   "Pastor Jesse, there are several people in Alegre awaiting baptism!"

That got my attention! João Branco from Alegre had ridden horseback to the worship service so I spoke to him about arranging for me to be at Alegre on my next trip. I hoped he would be the spokesman for spreading the word to the candidates for baptism. He started making excuses, explaining that all the visitors to Alegre stayed at his house; that now at harvest time his house would be full of corn, beans, and other crops.

   "Sir, I will not be there to be entertained. I do not require the services of your house. I spent several months sleeping in the jungles in Burma and I know how to take care of myself."

(Senhor João was noted for being complicated, and I had dealt with him before.) When we were out of earshot Maria Nazaré reassured me that she would take care of everything.

When I returned to Grão Mogol the next month a man named Alfredo was there to guide me to Alegre, and I would stay in his home. The trail had recently been graded so I could drive. When we came to the end of the trail I stopped and looked to Alfredo questioningly for there was not a house in sight.

   "Drive the car into that open space in the bamboo."

I did and he quickly hacked down some of the tall bamboo to hide the car. Three of his children appeared over the rim of the canyon. They hoisted my pack upon their backs along with Alfredo's purchases and we hiked down the canyon to his home. There, my room was freshly plastered with a thin layer of clay mud - walls and floors, to seal all places where the deadly <u>barbeiro</u> (insect) might lurk. A bunk bed, the only piece of furniture, was built of fresh bamboo strips.

That evening the worship service was in Alfredo's yard, by a campfire. I judged from the singing that a large number had come walking over the wooded trails (I couldn't see beyond the light of the fire). The next day we went to the adobe-block chapel for the service. Doors and windows were simple wooden shutters. Pews were split logs resting on flat rocks. The chapel was packed and people stood at every window and at the doors so they could see and hear.

I had misgivings about how much the people would understand for I was a foreigner and they were not accustomed to my accent. As we sang I decided I would speak very slowly and distinctly. I started preaching and occasionally stopped to ask,

"Do you understand?"

After I did this several times my hostess threw up both hands,

"Yes, we understand! Preach!!!"

I preached and afterward we went to a stream where several youth and adults were baptized.

After the service, again Alfredo's children carried my pack as we ascended to the car. A man came galloping up on his horse,

"Pastor, I was trying to get to the service; I so wanted to be baptized!"

I assured him I would return in a month and when I did return he was baptized, along with others who had come a great distance.

Geraldo Nunes was with me that time. Geraldo was from Montes Claros, and I cherished his unselfish support and companionship. We were in the hired pickup driving on the rough trail from Grão Mogol when the motor began to sputter. Worriedly, I inquired,

"Senhor Pedro, are we going to have engine trouble?"

"This truck has never once left me on the road. But I have left it a few times."

I had learned that most of the members of this mission had never partaken of the Lord's Supper, so I had come prepared to serve it. First, we had the baptismal service, then I administered the Lord's Supper. Later, some pastors of the Association remonstrated with me for having done this. They felt the Lord's Supper could be observed only in the church building.

JLK
    We left June 15, 1980 for our six-month furlough, and a
whole year passed before I returned to Alegre. Two young men,
brothers, met me as I approached the chapel.

    "You may not remember us, but you baptized us on your last
    visit a year ago."

Milton Gonçalves Moreira and Ermino Gonçalves Moreira were
eighteen and twenty years old. They continued,

    "We thought you would like to know we are preaching the
    Gospel now."

I noticed only one had a Bible, and I knew the nearest school
was thirty-five miles away - in fact most of the people were
illiterate.

    "Have you gone away to school?"

    "We've learned to read on our own. But we have a problem -
    we just have one Bible."

The youth with the Bible clarified,

    "This week I do the preaching and get to use the Bible.
    Next week it will be his turn."

When I left Alegre I left without a Bible! How many times
have I seen people lifted from illiteracy and darkness to
renewing light in Christ, when they hear the Good News!

    The word "Alegre" means happy - cheerful. Could there be
any place more beautiful? Even palaces, fine buildings, roads,
and Cadillacs could not make any place happy - cheerful.

Bus Trip on Carnaval Weekend
or The Dog Was A Gentleman

    Grão Mogol is a very old town, located in some of the wild-
est country I have ever seen. Very early in Brazil's history
explorers found diamonds there; hence the town is named "Grão
Mogol" for the name of one of the largest diamonds found in
Brazil.

    The town is perched between the mountains and a river. The
main street is narrow and follows the contour of the river.
The houses are built of stone, brick, and adobe blocks.

    I visited the Baptist church in Grão Mogol whenever possi-
ble. This visit coincided with the Carnaval season. Carnaval
means "feast of the flesh," the time of year to throw off all
restraints. Carnaval precedes Ash Wednesday, and it is, indeed, the "festival of the flesh."

JLK

Travel to Grão Mogol took three hours by auto but I chose
to travel by bus this time, since the road was so rough. The
bus made many stops for passengers, extending the tiresome
trip. Nonetheless, I always met many people and there was
a lot of friendly conversation among the passengers.

This time, I should have gone by car, for the passengers
were ready to celebrate. As soon as we left the city limits
bottles of cachaça began to appear. (Cachaça is brandy made
from fermented cane juice.) It is amazing how, after a few
drinks, everyone becomes an opera star, belting out the ri-
bald songs of Carnaval.

As we made our tedious way along there were frequent stops
to let off passengers and take on others. The stars of the
West would change, but the unfolding drama was the same.

Two hours into the trip a man at the side of the road sig-
nalled for the bus to stop. The driver acquiesced, then there
was a lengthy exchange between the two men. The would-be passenger had a large, handsome dog. The driver argued that it
was against regulations to let the dog board, and its owner
insisted that the dog was very obedient and wouldn't cause
any trouble.

The driver finally looked back at his passengers thoughtfully. He shrugged his shoulders as if to say,

"All other rules are being broken - why hold out for this
one?"

He granted the man permission to board with his dog, and he
took his seat, instructing the dog to sit in the aisle by him.

Afterward, every time we made a stop for other passengers
the dog would get off the bus and stand patiently by the door
until all movement was over. Then he returned to his place.

It was pleasant to observe the behavior of the dog. Actually, one can find more companionship with a well behaved ca-
nine than you can with the drunken, disorderly sons of darkness. In a busload of people who were dog drunk, the dog
was the only gentleman!

A Brazil Nut

Christmas would be here in a few days and I am getting frantic. What would one buy for an American husband, in the city of Montes Claros? Wistful dreaming of stateside laden stores and specialty catalogues availed nothing.

Jesse did not wear the Brazilian ready-made suits, shirts, shorts, undershirts or shoes because they didn't fit, and he preferred American ties. He loved Brazilian socks, but a package of socks for a Christmas present? A book was not possible since there wasn't a Christian bookstore in the city.

In desperation I walked the main streets of Montes Claros. The beautiful lengths of fabric for men's trousers were enticing, but then we would have to engage a tailor. Drugstores had attractive toiletry sets, but certain allergies discouraged this. Book ends? There didn't seem to be a book-end store!

I looked in one store which sold dishes, kitchen ware, silverware, etc., but there was nothing in silver, crystal, stainless steel or porcelain suitable for a man. Then I went to another store of household items. Surely among all the unusual things for Christmas there was something. And there, among the stainless steel ice tongs, sugar/creamer sets, pitchers, silverplated silverware and tea sets - there it was -

A GOLD NUT

About the size of a baseball. The two halves were joined by a gold spring and opened to reveal a blue velvet lining. What could be more delightful than a gold nut for tie tacks, seminary class ring, and keepsakes?

On Christmas day the gold nut was received with delight and pleasure. It is still in use today, a cherished jewelry box.

What kind of a nut? Not a black walnut, nor an English walnut, nor a cashew nut etc. etc.

Just a Brazil nut!

To get to Mato Virgem I rode a bus to Butumirim where I caught a truck hauling wood. At the end of the road I walked three miles down the canyon trail. One time when I arrived all the houses in the little community were closed tightly. I clapped and clapped (the proper way to seek entrance) until someone fearfully peaked out the door.

"Pastor, there has been a prison break at Grão Mogol and the woods are full of escaped criminals. How did you manage to get here?"

In spite of the jail break I was able to continue with my ministry. I preached Friday night, Saturday morning and night, and Sunday morning. I left at noon by horseback to catch a bus in Butumirim. We'd been riding about three hours when my guide/companion said without explanation,

"This is as far as I'm going."

I got off and the guide with his two horses turned back to Mato Virgem. As I walked the last mile, I puzzled over the unexpected departure.

You see, my guide did me a favor. He understood that if I had continued riding I might not be able to walk the next day!

His skin was reddish brown; he had a round face; reddish brown eyes and dark reddish brown hair. I thought he might be eight years old. He looked dusty, but that is questionable, depending upon the eyes of the beholder. He seemed to know me and was clapping at my door asking for - what - I do not remember.

I thought that the little boy at my door was from a family of Third Church. One of the ladies there had been widowed when her husband died suddenly of Chagas. She had three children. She was an earnest seeker and learner, often amazing us by her faith and spiritual perception.

There was a widower of the same church who had several children. The two married, and they had two children. I knew that this happy home didn't have food or clothing to spare. I remembered that one of the little boys was about eight years old, with reddish brown complexion, a round face, and reddish brown hair.

WAK
   I gave the young lad some food and we sat in the door of
our house chatting about this and that. Since I thought he
was from the family at the church I presumed I had the liberty
to comment that perhaps he would like to wash himself, since
he appeared dusty.

   He seemed to consent so we went to the back yard where
the tanque (outdoor sink) was. I methodically helped him
wash. All the time he kept looking at me with his brown
eyes, and he didn't show any fear.

   When he was dried off he didn't seem to look any less dusty,
but he must have been refreshed by the cool water and the food.
But to this day, I wonder if I had identified the child correct-
ly, and if I really washed the boy I thought I washed.

JLK   JOSENÓPOLIS, A CENTENNIAL CHURCH
        The Church That Would Not Meet In A Rented Sanctuary

   Josenópolis was over fifty miles from Grão Mogol by primitive roads through a reforested area. Pine seeds were imported
from the United States; eucalyptus seeds from Australia. This
reforestation was to supply badly needed lumber, charcoal, and
pulp for paper.

   Josenopólis, population about 5,000 was well laid out but
the houses were very humble, being made of adobe blocks with
dirt floor, and simple tile roof with no ceiling. There was
no water or sewer system and they had electricity only during
limited hours.

   Faithful laymen from Grão Mogol had established a congregation there which simply kept on from year to year. With
the advent of the missionary in the North to give encouragement and support, the possibility of organizing into a church
took hold and this was one of three Centennial churches organized in the Association in 1982.

   The others were Boas Novas in Montes Claros and Centenário
of Marcela. 1982 was the centennial year marking the organization of the first Baptist church on Brazilian soil at Salvador, Bahia.

   A year had passed since my last visit here. From the home
of my host, Antônio, we started walking to the church. At
the corner to turn left to go down the hill Antônio directed,

   "No, we go right. We built a new place of worship while
   you were away."

I thought that was interesting, since the church had never
asked for aid for a building project.

186.

JLK
   Antônio explained,

      "In 1982 the first time the newly organized church met we
      decided we had to build a place of worship. As a fully
      organized church we could not go on meeting in a rented
      place."

   Although they were very humble people and there was no
pastor or missionary to guide them, they faced the challenge:

      "How are we to accomplish this?"

Someone said,

      "I have a lot I will give."

Men, women, and children offered to do the work. A little
money came in.

   On the back of the new lot they scraped back the top soil,
making a ring of dirt about twelve feet in diameter. They
loosened the soil with spades and carried water from the river
about one-fourth mile away.

   They poured the water into the ring and barefooted, they
stomped in the mud until it was well mixed. They poured the
mud into wooden molds and set them in the sun to dry, repeating this until they had enough building blocks; this left a
hole about six feet deep.

   They chopped down trees in the forest to make framing for
the roof. For roofing they put clay mud in molds and baked
the tiles in a homemade kiln. With the gifts of money they
bought cement for mortar to hold the blocks together, and to
plaster the walls inside and out. Then they whitewashed
the building.

   We walked up to that place of worship standing on the highest point in Josenópolis, gleaming white in the sun. I thought,

      "This is surely a miracle."

There it was - the cleanest, whitest building in a town of
shabby little houses - no Mission funds, no outside aid. The
people had a mind to work.

   **So we built the wall, and the entire wall was joined
      together up to half its height,
   for the people had a mind to work.**
                                    Nehemiah 4:6   NKJ

An Evangelistic Trip To The Havoline Ranch (Caititú)

Domingos, a layman who had visited in one of the ranching communities, asked me to conduct baptismal service for several people whom he had won to Christ. Senhor Hortensia, now deceased, had witnessed in this area; it might be considered a preaching point of the Francisco Sá Church; it was an hour's drive from that city. Six of us arrived at the Caititú ranch Saturday afternoon.

The large ranch house was made of adobe blocks. For the evening service almost 100 people gathered in the large room at the center of the house. A man in charge led the song service, then introduced me as the preacher. I preached, then returned "the word" to him. He led in another song service and said,

"The missionary will preach."

After the third sermon, having determined the protocol, I said firmly that we would close the service with prayer.

It was midnight and even so the people seemed reluctant to leave. An elderly woman remained and apologetically spoke to me,

"Pastor, I walked all day to get here. I have some questions and I must have the answers."

This was Maria Tereza, a rural school teacher. The only people in her area who could read and write had been taught by this woman who had dedicated her life to teaching. I invited her to sit down.

She started asking deep, probing questions, and forgetting about being tired, I dealt with her questions about salvation. After a while she smiled, and as she stood to leave she said,

"Pastor, I have my answers now."

Months later I was called to conduct Maria Tereza's funeral. I drove to the town of Catuní where she was to be buried, arriving just as they were bringing her body from her rural community about seven miles away.

They had wrapped her body in a sheet and tied the ends to a bamboo pole. The men of the community had carried their beloved teacher into town on their shoulders. They placed the body in a casket and we went to the cemetery for the graveside service. As I preached the sermon I was comforted as I remembered her words,

"Pastor, I have my answers now."

Francisco Sá is about thirty miles from Montes Claros. I
went with some of the church members there to two of their
remote preaching points. I had baptized one of them two years
previously - a young man who was an excellent guitarist. Another of the group was a young man who obviously had the gift
of wisdom because he seemed to know the right thing to say
at the right time; otherwise he was quiet. A married couple
who had relatives where we were going, served as guide.

Leaving Francisco Sá we drove along a newly built dirt
highway then we turned off for another five miles through a
reforestation area. American pines grew on one side and eucalyptus trees on the other. Then several miles through rough,
hilly country.

A seriema challenged us for a race, stretching its long
legs and only rising to fly when it decided it might not win
the race. A seriema is a long-legged bird about 39 inches
long and 34 inches high. Its habitat is open, wooded terrain
covered with trees, thickets of shrubbery, cacti, and tall
sedge.

We paused only briefly in the little village of Catuní to
make plans for our activities there the next day. Then we
went seven miles to the farming community of Jambreiro. I
was anxious to make this visit, for I had baptized several
there who became members of the Francisco Sá Church.

Jambreiro was a typical farm setting in the interior of
the North of Minas. The people cordially welcomed us, and
we went to the Ribeiro home - set about half a mile from
other residences.

The large, rambling structure of adobe blocks had a tile
roof, and the floor was hard-packed earth. It appeared the
house had been enlarged as need arose. At one end the Ribeiro
family had built a one-room school where Dona Maria Tereza
(the rural teacher of this remote area) had taught. The school
was also the place of worship.

People gathered from miles around for the Saturday night
service which lasted until 10:00 P.M. Afterward we were
served cake and coffee, and everyone participated in the
fellowship. It was a wonderful time to be together.

When everyone had gone the lady of the house set about
getting us guests situated for the night. Going through a
large living room, I noticed six 100 lb. sacks of beans, the
family's store until next harvest. I shared a room with
Odilon, a deacon from Francisco Sá, a leather hat maker
by trade. Four sacks of corn in the room would be pounded
into meal as the need arose. Over my bunk bed hung a new,
beautifully hand-tooled saddle.

The night was pleasant. Guineas chanted softly from the orange tree outside our wood-shuttered window. After midnight the proud rooster faithfully reported the passing hours. At dawn everyone was up, for farm chores had to be attended. The farmer milked the cows and cared for the pigs and chickens.

While the family scurried about their work we guests gathered in the farmyard in the shade of a large mango tree. We were served black, sweetened coffee with bread. A kingly turkey gobbler strutted pompously up and down, making solemn pronouncements.

The family's pet parrot called out greetings from the living room window. About mid-morning a quartet of fat, fluffy puppies formed a circle and facing each other howled out their little hearts, proclaiming their disappointment because mother was late with their juice-and-cookie break.

There was a handmade, wooden sugar cane press, including rollers. The farmer hitched two fine oxen into their yokes and put them to work showing how the press functioned. I marveled at this engineering fete of a man devoting untold hours to its construction.

This was rural life in Brazil. Some of the most able leaders came from rural communities. José Cordeiro, native of this community, was a seminary student in Belo. His father Domingos Cordeiro, deacon of Esplanada Church in Montes Claros, cared for this congregation.

We had Sunday morning service at 11:00 o'clock, with Sunday School scheduled for 12:00 noon. Many had walked long distances and there was good attendance.

Afterward we returned to Catuní. They were just finishing 2:00 o'clock Sunday School in a home when we drove up for the preaching service. There were decisions for Christ which caused great rejoicing among the Christians.

This community was receiving electricity for the first time. The shiny new posts stood out against the background of ancient adobe-block houses. There was only one other automobile on the street beside the Mission auto. There were several ox-drawn, two-wheel carts. Up and down the street there were at least fifty saddled horses at the hitching rail.

Deborah gave her heart away because she never held anything
in reserve for herself. When my relationships with others
ebbed and flowed, I could count on Deborah even though we
might be absent from each other for days - months - years.
She is a true friend.

Deborah had some health problems, and her parents ministered to her with herbal medicine. Deborah's father, Jacinto
Faustino, was a highly respected pioneer pastor of our area,
and her mother Eugênia had great joy in personal, one-on-one
evangelism. I think Deborah's main qualification is, "She
has a loving heart."

When I undertook to produce a drama with the youth of Third
Church in Montes Claros, Deborah enlisted, cajoled, begged,
persuaded and promoted, until each youth was in his/her place
at rehearsals. The drama "came off" not because of my dili-
gence or knowledge - although I did desire that the Gospel
be given through drama; but because of Deborah. She loved
the Lord and had a conviction that God's Word should be en-
hanced through the drama.

Deborah became engaged and I refrained from providing the
trousseau because I thought her mother needed to do this. I
thought it was such a privilege to buy the grinalda (head
piece) and the veil.

Deborah wore my cameo necklace for her wedding. She dressed
at our house, and her sister Julimar helped with her makeup.
The photographer was there and made a beautiful picture of
her with our samambaia (cascading fern) in the background.
The bridegroom's sister and others completed the trousseau.

Deborah's first baby was born by Caesarean section. After
the birth she was groggy from the anesthetic when the nurse
brought the baby, David, to her. He was not dark, but naturally light in complexion. Deborah told the nurse,

"This is not my baby; my baby should be dark."

The nurse assured Deborah it was the right infant; that he
would assume his natural complexion later.

When David was several months old his mother brought him
to spend some hours at my house. He was vigorous, and Deborah had to watch that he did not roll off the bed. We were
watching him and discussing his healthy progress when Deborah
said that she felt his color was a little odd - sort of purple.

I agreed that his skin seemed to have an unusual tint. We
hurried to consult with her pediatrician. As we sat in the
small waiting room at the doctor's office, those passing
through did a "double-take." Dark Deborah was at my side, and
I was holding little David, who had dark hair.

191.

WAK

The lady pediatrician expertly examined David, turning and positioning him as if he were a little insect. Then she started to giggle softly and turned to the mother,

"Deborah, my dear, there is nothing wrong with this baby. He is simply beginning to assume his natural color."

Nonplused, Deborah picked up her son and we went home quietly, occasionally breaking out in delicious laughter, embracing and explaining to David as if he, too, understood!

JLK
MONTES CLAROS EXPANDS

Montes Claros had four Baptist churches when we arrived there in 1978, Fourth Church being the last one organized. March 22, 1980 Esplanada Church was organized. The city was expanding unbelievably; new communities were springing up. A custom for building a home was to secure a lot and build the shell. Rather than waiting until the house was finished, the family moved into the shell and the refinements were added when possible.

I tried to keep a challenge before the churches for keeping pace with the population growth by opening preaching points and missions. The general attitude for this was optimistic, and some churches had several preaching points.

There was the possibility of appealing to the fund handled by the state Baptist Convention for buildings and lots, called COBAM (Convênio Brasileiro-Americano). The money came from the Lottie Moon Christmas Offering.

The COBAM committee was composed of three Brazilians, three Southern Baptist missionaries, and the state Executive Secretary - ex officio. They met regularly and studied numerous requests from the churches for grants. To be eligible, the church must be cooperating with the State Convention, and contributing to the state Cooperative Program. The grants seldom covered the price of a lot or a chapel (small church building) so the church always had to do something on its own.

Nova Canaã Church

As the number of churches in Montes Claros increased, in our time there were no divisions of churches through strife except the founding of Nova Canaã Church. Before 1978 Second Church had split from First Church, but the result seemed like Siamese twins; within Second there were two strong groups.

192.

As the stress in that church mounted, a business meeting was called and the president of the Association, Jacinto Faustino, and I were invited. There was an attempt by the members to come to terms with their differences. We listened quietly to all the arguments, and gave attention to all the suggestions until it grew late. At 1:30 A.M. the president of the church council and all those elected to responsibilities, except the treasurer, voted to leave Second Church and form a new nucleus.

The following Sunday this nucleus met in a member's home and elected a treasurer. Three months later, September 12, 1984 they organized as the Nova Canaã Baptist Church. The story of their phenomenal growth is tied in with the account of the ordination of Francisco Ferreira, their pastor.

They built one of the largest church buildings in the state. They started two missions in new communities, building places of worship for them. At least one has been organized into a church. Early, they received recognition as second highest in the state, for annual baptisms.

Third Church

Jacinto Pereira Faustino was the pastor. This man was a great warrior, a pioneer for the Gospel. He with his wife Eugênia have started many new churches in the North.

Third Church had suffered long with a family of squatters living next door. They occupied the lot illegally, but there was no way the owner could evict them. (Countless valuable properties in Brazil have been taken over by squatters, never to be reclaimed by the rightful owners.)

These neighbors turned up their radio and the woman did her wash during church time. Having wet and soaped the clothes, she put them on a board and beat them with a paddle, making "Whomps" that jarred our ears and consciousness. There was no solution since the windows on that side needed to be open for circulation.

The people of the church kept praying about that property next door - valuable because it was a corner lot. The city of Montes Claros determined that it would be sold for delinquent taxes. The legal owner spoke to Pastor Jacinto about it, but the church was already struggling financially.

Some money had come our way for mission work, and we wanted to help. Every church in the Association needed help, but we decided to respond to this need, as long as the gift were considered anonymous. Pastor Jacinto agreed he would never divulge the source of the money.

JLK

We went to the bank to sell dollars and deposit the Cruzeiros
(Brazilian currency) in the church's bank account. We sold
$727.00, enough to buy the lot and help build the wall. A
guard there, Hezequias, who was a member of Third Church, wanted
to chat. So I spoke to Wilma in English,

"You take care of the deposit and I'll visit with our friend."

I felt like we were holding up the bank while making this
deposit!

What joy and excitement to see the church go to work, once
the squatters had left! Men, women, and children worked in the
heat to clear the rubble. Then the lot was carefully surveyed
to determine where the protecting wall would be built. The
addition helped the church plan for expansion, and the worship services were conducted in peace!

Jardim Palmeiras Church

This church, Fourth, was organized under a mango tree on
December 4, 1977. The name was later changed to Jardim Palmeiras (Palm Gardens), for the suburb where it was located.
It was said the suburb had a population of 10,000 - being
one of the main ones of the city of Montes Claros. It was
divided by a wide avenue named Avenida Jardim Palmeiras.

A corner lot became available on that avenue, mid-point in
the community. The church was awarded some funds from the
Lottie Moon Christmas Offering - enough to pay down on the
lot. This lot was purchased for its location, not for its
beauty; it was covered with water. The church appealed to
the city government and they installed some of the drainage
system. The rest of the drainage was completed by deacons
who labored day after day in the mud.

It took at least another year to complete paying for the
lot, then we launched a building program. The people were
very poor, and their contributions were made at personal sacrifice. We knew, however, that we had to construct a building adequate enough for a growing church in a prominent community.

The men and boys contributed their labor. My sister's husband died in 1980 and Willie Mae gave a tithe of the insurance.
This was the largest gift for the entire building project.
Now we were able to lay the foundation for a two-story building and put up the walls of the first floor. When we got
half the floor covered with a concrete slab we moved in.

JLK

What a day that was! We met in the rented space which had long been too small. We had a brief worship time for declaring that using that part of the residence for worship had ended. One boy carried the pulpit Bible, and two men picked up the pulpit. Others carried benches. We marched the four blocks, singing songs of praise.

We set up in the new space and thanked God. We were so happy in the shell of only one-fourth of the structure, with blocks stacked checkerboard in the windows, for glass. And we thanked God!

A spacious, comfortable, two-story church stands where once there was nothing but a mudhole. December 4, 1979 when Jardim Palmeiras celebrated its second anniversary, the church had 101 members.

WAK   **THE BIRTHDAY PARTY**

On Sunday night in January I am driving, alone, from Esperança (Hope) Church after the Sunday evening worship. As I descend the street to our driveway, a figure appears from the side street, pauses, then retreats as my little white 1977 Corcel chugs alongside. (Corcel is a small, stick-shift, four-cylinder Ford.) I pause, recognizing that it is Pastor Francisco of Nova Canaã Church, and call to him jokingly,

"Francisco, are you lost?"

I puzzle about this as I turn into our garage and enter our house, carrying the portable Casio keyboard, Bible, and hymn-book. Then reality dawns - this is January 27! My birthday was yesterday and the church people will be here for a surprise birthday party. I greet Jesse, not revealing I have guessed, and we carry on as usual. Surely enough, here they come, singing.

We welcome our guests into the dining room and adjoining, small living room. They are crowded as they stand for the singing of hymns, Bible reading, prayer, and greetings.

Jesse has slipped into the kitchen and brings out the traditional lunch: bottled soft drinks and a beautiful birthday cake. Also pasteis (small squares of flaky, salty crust enclosing succulent ground meat), and varied crackers.

Pastor Francisco was nonplused that he had spoiled the surprise, and I had reason to tease him. The people have joy in the birthday gatherings, even though the gifts and refreshments are most humble. The love is complete.

I said the birthday party guests in our home were crowded, as they stood in our dining and living rooms. Was there ever a situation wherein they were not crowded?

Usually when one is born there is not ample room in the crowded home for a bassinet or baby bed, unless one is born into the home of more financial security than many homes of our church people.

Brother or sister will carry the new baby, so there is no urgent need for a baby buggy. After the baby is weaned, brother or sister will feed it. It is hard for a mother to gather the family for a joint meal because the children may be on different school schedules and the father works on shifts.

Transportation is by foot, bicycle, or public bus. Buses are usually overloaded and seats are at a premium. The families with finances enough to have an auto were few and far between among our church people.

What was the space situation in the churches of the North Association? Not enough room. Only the larger churches had special rooms for the small babies. Otherwise, Mother might spread a blanket on the floor and place the sleeping baby there during the worship service and Sunday School.

When the baby grows to be a toddler it might wander from its mother to the children sitting on benches, so high that their feet don't touch the floor. In one church, when visitors came, children were asked to give up the benches - some of them went outside to play.

The children's workers in the churches were always trying to find space and seating for the little ones. I tried to help with this in Montes Claros at Esplanada, Third, Esperança, and Jardim Palmeiras Churches. The valiant workers - men and women - were remarkable in their dedication to teaching and providing for the children.

CAREER MISSIONARIES

We were encouraged when we received a letter from Thelma Bryant, Administrative Assistant, Eastern South America. She advised us that December 8, 1981, the Foreign Mission Board was to change our category of service from Missionary Associate to Career.

"A NEW SONG"

> Sing joyfully to the Lord, you righteous;
> it is fitting for the upright to praise him.
> Praise the Lord with the harp;
> make music to him on the ten-stringed lyre.
> Sing to him a new song;
> play skillfully, and shout for joy.
> **Psalm 33:1-3 NIV**

Since my early days in Rio de Janeiro I wanted to teach music to those who had never studied it. I wanted people in the church to know that they could be "literate" in music and could use it to glorify God. I knew the Lord had implanted this desire and that He had a purpose for me in the North Association.

What Was Happening In Church Music?
(When We Arrived in 1978)

The children loved to sing solos or in groups, in the closing assemblies of Sunday School. Whenever the people got together, they sang with enthusiasm and freedom that was inspiring. I felt the sincerity and devotion of the music.

Soloists, quartets, double quartets, small ensembles or large choirs - they lovingly sounded out their worship of God. In many churches the hymns were sung in four-part harmony.

Pastor Isaias Alves Martins knew the tenor and soprano of just about all the songs in the hymnal. He was in the quartet from this pioneer family.

First Church of Montes Claros had an ancient piano and Second and Third Churches had pump organs. There seemed to be no other keyboards in the Association.

The bateria (drum set) would become a common part of the church's furnishings, along with the electric guitar and keyboard. Those who had guitars seemed to naturally move into tantalizing rhythms and intricate chording.

The "Cantor Cristão" was the hymnal in use; some people had one with music, but most had only the small book with text. They carried their music book with a Bible since the churches did not furnish hymnals in the pews.

The Período de Louvor (Period of Praise) was to become longer and louder. This was the part of a worship service when the people sang choruses gustily as they clapped.

There was vocal music at weddings, retreats, encampments, and Woman's Missionary Union gatherings. Small children, juniors, adolescents, young people and adults were all part of it.

WAK

I was thrilled and excited about the timbre and range of the voices. At Esperança Church in MOC (Montes Claros) a young man sang solos. Accompanying himself on the guitar, he belted it out and it actually sounded like a calf bawling for its mother. I loved it, for I knew his witness for the Lord. I remembered the man in Cambuí Church in Santa Catarina. He announced he would play all three stanzas of the hymn on his harmonica; he was worshipping.

I learned there were generations involved in the teaching of music. March 1987 we traveled back to Santa Catarina and worshiped in the beloved Taquaral Church. That Sunday morning I had trouble sorting out the new generations. I thought Zeca's daughter was his wife's sister. A grandchild of the pioneer Frederico family said,

"Dona Wilma, remember how you tried to teach me to play guitar and I couldn't learn? Now all my children are studying music in the town of Mafra."

Choruses "floated" among the youth. A meaningful, enchanting chorus would be sung at some gathering, then the youth returned to their own churches and taught it to their companions. Music cassettes also "floated" around; the original probably bought at a religious book store. Guitar was the going accompaniment.

There was a federal government music conservatory in MOC where people of all ages studied. They were required to study manual arts also.

I did not investigate the music curriculum of public and private schools of our city, but there seemed to be no symphonic or marching bands and I never heard of a school choir or vocal ensemble. The school children were trained to march and play in drum and bugle corps to celebrate the national Independence Day, September 7. We usually attended the annual parade, trying to encourage the children of our churches.

The Beginning Music Reader

"Beginning Music Reader" was the book I used for basic music theory. Pastor Levy of First Church MOC thoughtfully consented for the class by that name to convene weekly at his church. We studied at night in September, October, and November that year, 1978. Students ranged in age from ten to fifty years; eleven completed the course. By reducing the course to six evenings it could be taught in other chrches.

There was a programmed text for beginner Music Theory, written by a missionary of our state. When we were in Belo, Pastor Evaristas's wife studied and worked through the book alone; to my immense pleasure she made perfect scores. When there was a cry for help from Diva, Pastor Demas' wife in Grão Mogol, she accepted the challenge to study through the book and she completed it, alone, with near perfection.

198.

WAK

Jesse and I co-ordinated our transportation since we had only one car. Then in 1984 we bought a 1977, 4-cylinder stick-shift Ford Corcel for me. My husband kept it running by his continually taking it to the mechanic for upkeep. I say the word "co-ordinated." There was more! My husband was encourager, supporter, right hand, and adviser, often adapting his schedule so I could fulfill some engagement.

Besides caring for the briefcases heavy with music and hymnals, he carried the instruments: Autoharp, electric Autoharp, folding pump organ, its bench, the guitar and the music stand. Later my nephew Charles Norris II helped us buy a portable electric Casio keyboard.

The Music Clinic

June 14, 1979 I wrote about the music clinic led by Clint Kimbrough, fellow music missionary living in Niteroi (across the bay from Rio de Janeiro). Morning and evening classes were in First Church MOC, and counting both sessions the average attendance for the five days was 118! Clint had all ages together, and the people loved his wit and the "fun" way he taught music theory. His philosophy was that he would work in any church, anywhere, regardless of "status" or "prominence." The people sensed that he loved them.

Diva And The Keyboard

In the late 80's Diva, pastor's wife at Grão Mogol, wanted to study keyboard. She came to Montes Claros periodically and had a woman stay with her two small girls. We spent hours at the piano. She was so intelligent and eager that we advanced through some of the piano "Barrier" course I had studied at Southwestern Seminary in 1974 (although at home she had only a tiny keyboard for practice).

The University Students

Sometimes Montes Claros seemed to be swarming with students. To matriculate in a university, one had to first pass the stringent entrance exams. Our city had several universities. Young people came from rural areas to take courses which were not available at home; or to prepare for the university exams.

Some youth would get together and rent joint rooms; this was called a república. Also private homes hosted the youth.

When the universities gave the entrance exams, the prospective students had to go to the school of their major study: medicine, dentistry, geography, letters, science, agriculture, etc. Passing a university entrance exam was a major milestone.

199.

David Gomes Evangelistic Crusade

Singers from the four churches in Montes Claros rehearsed together for weeks, enthusiastically perfecting music in four-part harmony. The evangelistic crusade was October 26, 27, and 28, 1979. David Gomes, the preacher, was known in all Brazil through his radio program "Bible School of the Air."

Since the crusade was in the sports arena "Darcy Ribeiro" people did not seem to be inhibited about coming. This was an exciting undertaking, so there were many helpers to carry benches from the four churches. (After the services the benches had to be carried outside and stacked.)

The outstanding result was that the people worked together with a will. They invited neighbors, friends, relatives, and people from neighboring towns. They distributed invitations. They prayed; and they filled that vast arena. We were so elated with the preaching and the singing! For those days and after-ward, Baptists seemed to rise to a new identity!

North Association Woman's Missionary Society

The W.M.S. women of different churches liked to get together. Sometimes women of several churches came together; or all the churches of our city. They made the gatherings festive occa-sions. They might charter a bus and travel to a country church for a prayer retreat. Intercâmbios (interchange - groups fel-lowshipping together) were part of Baptist life.

Yearly when the time came to plan for the annual Association-al meeting, music was part of the challenge. The women usually convened prior to the general Association. The women planned their agenda, reports, election of officers, and special pre-sentations. In 1978, our first year, the annual meeting was in the Pirapora Church.

Pirapora, Curvelo, and Buenopólis were on the edge of our Association geographically. Later they became part of the neighboring Association, Central. When we visited the pastor and his wife at Buenópolis April 1980, they had a new baby - their fourteenth child.

The women of the four Baptist churches in Montes Claros gathered to form a chorus, practicing music "in two voices" as the W.M.S. president requested. Some choristers were nat-ural altos, which was good, for we didn't have a lot of time to rehearse for the annual meeting.

WAK
   We developed this repertoire so the women could be somewhat
prepared each year (sung in Portuguese):

   Beneath the Cross of Jesus, music by Frederick C. Maker
   One Day, music by Charles H. Marsh
   Victory In Jesus, music by E.M. Bartlett
   Follow Me, harmonized by Herbert G. Tovey
   Seguir A Cristo Não É Sacrifício (It Is No Sacrifice To
      Follow Jesus), composed by fellow missionary Joan Sutton
   Alleluia, Music by W.A. Mozart
   It Pays to Serve Jesus, music by Franck C. Huston
   We've A Story to Tell to The Nations, by Henry Ernest Nichol
   I Stand Amazed in The Presence, Charles H. Gabriel
   On Jordan's Stormy Banks, Negro Spiritual
   Let Us Sing Together, Anonymous
   Nothing is Impossible, by Eugene L. Clark
   O Sons and Daughters, Let Us Sing, music by Thomas Tallis
   Agora É Meu! by John W. Peterson and Alfred B. Smith
   My Lord, What A Morning, Negro Spiritual
   There's Room At The Cross For You, Ira F. Stamphill
   If Jesus Goes With Me, C.A. Miles

   Once the women had an evangelistic service at Second Church
MOC as part of their annual meeting. The teen-age girls sang
with the women, and we practiced the music assiduously.

   That evening when I arrived at the church there were so
many people inside I didn't know how I could get in, but I
finally did by elbowing and pushing. When it came time for
the chorus to sing they had to struggle to move to the platform.

   They sang with conviction and beautiful harmony. I noticed
there was one extra in the group. Afterward we decided she
was of the host church, and she just wanted to be with us!

   At the annual meeting June 14, 1979 the women highlighted
the eleven countries where Brazilian foreign missionaries
served. Eleven women dressed in the national costumes.

   Once I had the bright idea for the children to sing at
the annual meeting. I industriously practiced with the children in their churches. The afternoon of the meeting there
was a horde of children, and they sang with abandon. Then
their mothers took them home - leaving only a few women to
carry on the business meeting. So much for the missionary's
bright ideas!

First Mission Friends Day Camp

Dona Eugênia, pastor's wife at Third Church MOC had the first "Day Camp" of our area for Mission Friends. This is the missions education organization for children. As early as 8:30 A.M. the children came in large groups from the area churches.

There were so many we thought they would overflow the church! Dona Eugênia had a heart for telling children about Jesus, and she handled the crowd with loving care and compassion. She led them in reciting Bible verses then another leader told a missionary story. When we sang together, the children "raised the roof," for they were accustomed to "sing louder."

When we went into the yard for the mid-morning lunch, I was to take pictures. Spotting a camera, all the children moved toward me, and I couldn't back up to make space because my back was against the wall. I was hemmed in by Mission Friends!

All those children - needing a ministry in the churches. As I write I can see them - happy, and looking to us for comfort and teaching.

The Camp was dismissed about 12:00 noon. When I arrived home, imagine my surprise and pleasure to find that Jesse had cooked a special lunch: roast chicken and dressing with gravy, fresh string beans and collard greens!

Girls' Auxiliary and Young Women's Auxiliary

The women's group nurtured these missions education organizations, which were really mission minded. With their leaders they visited homes of prospective church members, or where there was an invalid. The young girls testified of their faith in the Lord. They sang choruses and led in Bible reading and prayer. They gave programs in the churches and highlighted needs for the annual offerings for State, Home and Foreign Missions offerings.

Minas Gerais Baptist Convention Annual Meeting

August 4, 1983 I wrote about this state meeting in Montes Claros. Also, the state Woman's Missionary Society met. It was the seventy-fifth anniversary of the women's organization, and they presented a pageant one night citing every state in Brazil, represented by young women.

Also, First Church MOC presented a pageant about the North Association, written and directed by Dona Herlinda Silveira. As she cited the date of organization of each of our twenty-four churches, a young woman took her place and the pastor stood by her.

Jesse's name was cited thirteen times as pastor. He had talked to Dona Herlinda, explaining that was in excess. But she didn't acquiesce; she said the people needed to know about the need for pastors to come and work in the Association. The impressive pageant closed with the twenty-four girls reciting a choral reading by memory and singing about doing God's will.

Time Off

I sometimes took time off and explored the shops in town. We realized that by the time we arrived in the North, 1978, some of the early pioneer spirit of the people had changed, for modernization had arrived. Some family-owned businesses had been displaced by chain stores in the principal cities and the managers were brought in from other areas; they were not natives.

There was a super market in our city, with one branch. I enjoyed exploring the old, established cereal stores with open gunny sacks (burlap) of many qualities of rice and beans. There were cereal bowls on the counter with samples.

The veterinarian supply store was crowded with open gunny sacks of cereals and seeds. Sometimes I wandered in the stores that sold saddles, rope, and farm and ranch equipment.

We were accustomed to shops being completely open to the sidewalk but when new stores were built they were closed in, to accommodate air conditioning. Electronic equipment and communication in the banks would replace other systems.

At the tailor shop you purchased a length of cloth from the attractive fabric displayed. The tailor took the man's measurements and then proceeded to sew the suit or pants. Tergal, name of one quality of synthetic fabric, was good for ladies' skirts.

Some women sewed for the public in their homes. Some specialized in shirts; some in pants. The ready-made clothing did not fit the larger man.

I recall my early days in Brazil when the well dressed man wore a white linen suit with white shirt and simple, dark tie. Now the fashion was well pressed jeans and a silk shirt, or a suit of the exquisite fabric using a blend of silk or cotton, and conventional shirt. Of course, fashion changed daily!

Joan and Boyd Sutton came from Rio de Janeiro for Christmas 1981. I was helping with the program at Jardim Palmeiras Church MOC. Joan played the pump organ for the adolescents and juniors as they sang. Corresponding Christmas scenes were shown by flannelgraph pictures.

Boyd sang two solos and Joan played her arrangement of "Silent Night" on her violin.

We had good times together, and we were so happy to have "family" for Christmas.

Third Church MOC
The youth and adolescents of Third Church gave a Christmas drama. We used the very legible music in Faustini's book "Hinos Tradicionais de Natal". Most of the youth were new converts except for Pastor Jacinto's family Julimar, Deborah, Paulo, and Jonatas.

The drama developed through live scenes onstage. We used the idea of astronauts who go back in time and history and interpret all the Christmas scenes. The choir and soloists in their eighteen numbers, and readers - accompanied the scenes onstage.

I wrote January 3, 1983:

"The Christmas program went well. Baby Jesus put up a howl even before he made his debut onstage. I was merrily pumping on the organ, meticulously following the program, when I heard the baby crying. When the curtains parted for Mary, Joseph, and the baby, he was doing the best with his lung power. Everyone was enchanted.

"The soprano section of the choir was weak, then we had to tell one soprano she couldn't sing because she insisted on being involved with a young man with an arrest record who was dabbling in drugs.

"This was summer vacation time and most of the choir members had failed their school courses and had to be in recuperation, or cram courses. However we kept plugging away. The choir had one soprano, three altos, three tenors and two basses, all young people.

"They came through with an A-Plus in interpretation, expression, and tuning."

We used the same program in Esperança Church MOC in 1987 - and then we presented it twice in the El Dorado community. A church member had gotten the use of the Catholic church's social hall and both times it was full; many people there were not Christians.

The Easter season in Brazil is so different from my recollection of the stateside celebration of new birth and Christ's resurrection. The dry season was just commencing and spring, or planting time, would come in November. In the Baptist churches this season was the opportune time to have revivals.

My letter of April 1, 1980:

"At home I was listening to the playback of 'Celebrate Life'
when Julimar, pastor's daughter at Third Church, came to
our door pleading for help with the youth of the church.
Together we started to plan a pageant for Passion Week."

We didn't have a machine to create mist or thunder and lightning, but we had twenty-two youth who vigorously entered into rehearsing - singing, reading, and acting. One young man, Gilberto, had recently been baptized. He was lead cashier and head of personnel at Bradesco, the city's largest bank.

The scenes were:

Entrance into Jerusalem
Who Is Jesus?
The First Lord's Supper
Gethsemane
The Disciples Flee
Who Judged Whom?
The Crucifixion (A few men and women looking to the cross,
    shown as a shadow)
The Disciples After the Crucifixion
The Women Discover the Open Tomb
Song of Victory
Closing Prayer

The young people who had worked so diligently on the drama produced a moving, exciting Easter story in their own church, Third, then Pastor Jacinto requested that we present it at Second Church MOC. Jesse was pastor of Jardim Palmeiras Church and since it was near to Second, both congregations could attend. The youth were so co-operative so we repeated the performance.

(Gilberto had sought Jesse's counsel and help when his father died. Then he asked that we serve as legal <u>testemunhos</u> in his wedding; that is, along with others we signed the civil marriage document. We saw Gilberto grow as a Christian.)

Sacred Music Recital

Charlotte Hallock Greenhaw came from São Paulo to accompany
me in my music program April 23, 1983 at First Church MOC.

Charlotte was living with her parents in Rio de Janeiro
when I worked there, then she left for college and marriage
to Houston Greenhaw. Now she was our fellow missionary, teaching music at the São Paulo seminary.

Dona Talitha, teacher at the music conservatory, helped
me to rehearse; without this I could not have been prepared.

People from the city's Baptist churches, the music conservatory, and nearby towns comprised the audience. I felt they
participated in exalting the Lord through the music. It was
an exhilarating time.

PROGRAMA

OS SALMOS

Quão Lindas as Moradas..Samuel Liddle
Salmo 84 (How Lovely Are Thy Dwellings)

Salmo Primeiro (First Psalm)........Gene Bone e Howard Fenton
Adaptação por Joan Sutton, Serra Negra, SP 3 de Julho, 1981

Graças a Ti (Thanks Be To Thee)........Georg Friedrich Handel

NATAL

Prepara-te O Sião (Prepare Thyself, Zion)............J.S. Bach

Que Infante É Este?...Greensleeves, Melodia Tradicional Inglesa
Guilherme Chatterton Dix (1837-1898)
Tradução por Adelina Cerqueira Leite, 1946

Se Eu Fosse Ver Jesus (If I Had Seen Baby Jesus)....Almir Rosa
Almir Rosa

A VIDA CRISTÃ

Pastor Amavel É Jesus............................Virgil Thomson
Salmo 23 por Isaac Watts
Tradução por J W Faustini, 1960

Em Jesus Amigo Temos..............................Janet Sanborn
(What A Friend We Have In Jesus) Joseph Scriven
Tradução por Catarina K Taylor

Meu Mestre (My Master).......................Frances Macphail
Harry Lee (1874-1942)
Tradução: Joan Sutton para Wilma Alice Kidd,
Serra Negra, SP 14 de Julho, 1975

Deus Cuidará de Ti (God Will Take Care of You).....W. S. Martin
Solo por Charlotte Greenhaw, Pianista

A CRUZ

Morreu na Cruz........Melodia do David's Psalmen, Amsterdã 1965
(I Gave My Life for Thee) Estribilho por J W Faustini

Perto da Cruz (Near The Cross)......................Letha Cole
Fanny Crosby   Adaptação por Joan Sutton

CONTEMPORÂNEA

Jesus Is Coming Again! (Jesus Voltará!)..........John Peterson
Solo por Charlotte Greenhaw, Pianista
Alleluia!..............................Ferdinand Hummel Op 78
Frederick H Martens - Salmo 63 e 23
Tradução por Joan Sutton, Caxambú, MG 7 de Julho, 1968

Ride On, King Jesus! (Espiritual Negro)...Arranjo, Hall Johnson

O Senhor É Minha Luz (The Lord Is My Light)....Frances Allitsen
Salmo 27 Adaptação por João Barbosa Batista 1977

At home I was into the work of the whole Association as I
answered the telephone, cared for correspondence and bookkeeping, and received guests and visitors. It was my joy to make
an attractive, orderly home with carefully prepared, healthful
meals.

The Association did not have an office so Jesse worked
out of our home. He pastored Third, Jardim Palmeiras, and
Nova Canaã Churches MOC at different times - besides caring
for pastorless churches in the Association.

In the church where I was a member the people shared their
lives and I found companionship, inspiration, and comfort.
The people may not have had many material comforts, but they
were committed to the Lord's work and to His church.

At first I was in First Church MOC but when the need for
an organist was evident at Third, I changed. Many of the
people there were recent converts, and some were illiterate.

There was a need which inspired my moving to Esplanada
Church MOC. By then I had the portable keyboard which was
perfect for the auditorium. It seemed that the volume was
equal to that large space. The building was not protected
by a surrounding wall, so I gave my tithe for bricks and cement. The men donated their labor until the wall was complete, which meant the property would be protected.

My letter of November 28, 1984

"I have found in the people of Esplanada a lifting up and
encouraging. I 'preached' yesterday afternoon. This was
in a new section laid out for lots where the people are
building lovely little homes. A lady there asked for a
worship service in her home. She is young, with husband
and two children. Someone else led the songs, then I
talked about the friendship of David and Jonathan; then
about the love and caring that Jesus offers."

At Esperança we labored with the need for space for children. Again, I gave my tithe for building a wall, so there
was space outside for the teachers to spread a large sheet
of plastic so the smaller children had a place.

There had been an interim when I was at Jardim Palmeiras
and they were in process of building a church building. How
I was challenged by the people who donated their labor. When
we moved to the new construction, only half of the floor was
covered by rough cement; the other half would be completed as
money became available.

208.

The Kimbroughs Come Back

Clint and Dolores came to Montes Claros with their daughter and son-in-law, Leigh and John Blizzard. (They studied at Southwestern Seminary, where Clint and Dolores had studied.) They graciously scheduled a concert in First Church MOC the night of June 26, 1985, having given seventeen concerts in Rio de Janeiro, Recife, Vitória, and Brasília.

Publicity posters had been displayed in places of business, and announcements had been sent to the churches of the Association.

Clint accompanied on the piano as Leigh and John sang to a filled auditorium.

John

Arrangements by missionary Ralph Manuel, (in Portuguese)
    Ask Ye What Great Thing I know, by Johann C. Schwedler
    Glorious Is Thy Name, by B.B. McKinney
    What Wondrous Love Is This, American Folk hymn
Largo Al Factotum, from "The Barber of Seville" by Rossini

Leigh
(In Portuguese)

I Am His and He Is Mine, by George W. Robinson, arranged by
    Ralph Manuel
Amazing Grace, Virginia Harmony 1831
Rejoice Greatly, O Daughter of Zion, "The Messiah" by G.F.
    Handel

Duet

One of the duets was: Now Sing We Joyfully Unto God, by Gordon
    Young, arranged by Ovid Young

****

Although the family was road-weary they sang with conviction and persuasion, and the audience was very responsive and appreciative. We were proud of the Missionary Kid - now grown up, and singing convincingly about God's love.

As Americans we endeavored not to speak of Brazilians as "they," and ourselves as "we." We practiced several philosophies for strengthening relationships:

1. When someone was in our home they were to enjoy the protective "umbrella" of our fellowship - that is, we did not discuss others with our visitors. As the people came to understand this, our fellowship was strengthened.

2. We did not loan money. If undesignated funds came to us and we sensed a need, we gave it as a gift, with no conditions.

3. We started a revolving fund for selling Bibles at a reduced rate, for many in the churches did not have personal Bibles. Sometimes gifts from stateside friends were added to the fund. (I had heard a veteran missionary explain that when needy people requested a Bible it was more meaningful if it cost only a few coins.)

4. It was common knowledge that we did not possess a firearm or a short-wave radio. We did not even have an American flag! This came up when a group of young people came to our house on a scavenger hunt, seeking our flag.

Jeans and Sweats
Fifteen students from Southwest Baptist University, Bolivar, Missouri, came to Brazil for evangelistic work. They had been in the country some days with no opportunity to catch up on their laundry. They came to our city in August, 1988, on the way to Porteirinha, the cotton capital of our state.

We were in the rainy season; we didn't have a clothes dryer; and there were just several days to handle the youths' laundry - mostly jeans and sweat shirts. A washer lady took care of the jeans and I washed the rest in our automatic washer. The sun shone just enough to dry everything! We folded those wonderful, clean clothes and took them to the hotel. What a pleasure to see those young people claim their laundry! They were so grateful.

Blonds Were In The Majority
Jesse and I both noticed that many of these Americans were very, very blond. We were with them in Porteirinha as they walked door-to-door, witnessing about Jesus. That night we were dead tired, and went to our hotel room early. As we were getting ready to retire, Jesse said thoughtfully,

"They're all so light!" Thoughtfully, seriously, I replied,

"Well, Jesse, we're light, too!" And we giggled and laughed!

<u>The <u>Women</u></u>

For the Lord gives wisdom;
    From His mouth come knowledge and understanding;
He stores up sound wisdom for the upright;
    He is a shield to those who walk uprightly;
He guards the paths of justice,
    And preserves the way of His saints.
                                Proverbs 2:6-8 NKJ

There had been something going on in the hearts of the
women of the North for many years. They comprised an inte-
gral part of the advancement of God's kingdom; as one considered the history of Baptist work, the spirit and dedication
of women were interwoven there.

The women were **generous**. They shared food with those who
walked distances to the church services. They were sensitive
to needs for clothing, money, food, employment, medicine, bus
fare, and school supplies.

The women had been granted a portion of **God's spirit**. Their
prayers opened doors. They were burdened for unevangelized
cities of Minas Gerais as well as the suburbs of their own
villages and cities. Their prayers and mission offerings
encompassed Brazil and the whole world.

The women did **mission work** and they nurtured missionary
education for young women, girls, boys, and smaller children.

When a new church was under construction the women **worked**;
they carried cement, brick, and water and helped to clear land.
They swept the church, dusted, arranged furniture; they placed
linen cloths on the Lord's Supper table and the pulpit. They
arranged flowers.

The women prepared the **weddings**. They cleaned and dusted
the church and decorated with beautiful, original arrangements of ribbon and tropical flowers. They planned and made
refreshments for the reception.

When someone of the church died women prepared the body for
burial and brought natural flowers for the **funeral**.

How **gracious, energetic**, and **dedicated** were the women of
the North! In the culture in which they lived and witnessed
<u>Crentes</u> (non-Catholic Christians) were considered as a sect
on the fringe of society. (Albeit, more than one of Brazil's
presidents were educated in Baptist schools.) As the women
witnessed to people about Jesus, they might be dealing with
someone involved in paganism, witchcraft, idol worship, athe-
ism, or spiritism. Hence the strong resistance.

Following are sketches of four of the standard-bearers.

MARIA BITTENCOURT

Maria Dutra G. Bittencourt is wife of José Alves da Silva Bittencourt, executive secretary of Baptist work in Minas Gerais (emeritus). She retired as mathematics teacher in junior high school, but has continued as state Executive Secretary of Woman's Missionary Union.

She is a graduate of Woman's Missionary Union Training School in Rio de Janeiro. The Bittencourts have four adult children.

Dona Maria is in leadership training for missions education, all ages:
Woman's Missionary Society for women
Young Women's Auxiliary for young women
Girls' Auxiliary for girls
Royal Ambassadors for boys
Mission Friends for children

She often traveled over the state; sometimes with her husband or to encampments, retreats, or other activities of missions education. Considering the primitive road conditions and transportation, this was a valiant accomplishment.

Dona Maria executes the work of Woman's Missionary Union with astuteness and vision; she is part of the national W.M.U. leadership; she nurtures annual offerings in the churches for State, Home, and Foreign Missions. She just has a heart to love the people.

Her influence has flowered in the lives of many women who have developed in serving the Lord with zeal.

JOAQUINA DIAS DO CARMO
Joaquina's story illuminates the lovingkindness of the Lord. She told me that once when she was young her family got into financial problems until they didn't have much food in the house, and no fat or lard for cooking. They were walking along a country road when a horseback rider galloped rapidly by them.

As he passed, a package wrapped in paper fell to the ground. The rider was soon beyond shouting distance, so they picked up the strange oddity and unwrapped it. It was pork fat which they could use in cooking! There was no way they could return it to the rider, so after discussing it a long time they took it home and relished its wonderful succulence. They'd been so hungry for some fat.

Joaquina thought there must be some divine being who felt pity and helped them by the strange appearance of the mysterious package. When she became a young woman someone witnessed to her about Jesus, and she eagerly embraced Him as Savior and Lord of her life.

212.

WAK

Joaquina's name is the feminine of "Jehoiakim" in II Kings 24:5,6. She married Joaquim (masculine form). When Joaquim felt God was calling him to preach the family moved so he could study at a Bible Institute called Peniel (SEE Genesis 32:30).

When we met the couple in their home in Bocaiuva Joaquim was a practical dentist. He was pastoring Boa Vista dos Matos Church, and they had eight children.

They invited us to their home for a noon meal, and we accepted happily for we loved being with those bright, attractive children. Joaquina served the rice and beans, potato salad, and tomato and lettuce salad.

Then she served a roasted, stuffed turkey! We had forgotten it was Thanksgiving Day. (Joaquina had learned about our holidays from Americans at Peniel.) She had killed, plucked, dressed, stuffed and baked the turkey, herself!

Joaquina was absolutely faithful in her service to the Lord. It was not easy to be known as a Crente (Christian). The children faced derision in their school. But Joaquina never wavered, and her loving devotion to her Lord is a lighthouse .

HERLINDA SILVEIRA DE SOUZA
Herlinda de Souza is one of the thirteen children of Senhor Herlindo Rodrigues da Silveira and his wife Maria. Considered a pioneer, she attended dentistry school and set up her own practice when women rarely entered this field. In Montes Claros she specialized in treating women and children.

Herlinda is quiet-spoken, never wasting time in unnecessary talk. Her late husband Joel Guimarães de Souza was head of a department of our city. Their children have now grown to young adulthood.

An ardent leader in First Church MOC, Herlinda's quiet efficiency is forceful. Her very presence brings out the best in people so they want to work harmoniously with others. Those of the large Silveira family respect her.

Herlinda was active in missions education in her own church and in the Association. Her ardent support of the offerings - State, Home, and Foreign Missions, influenced the giving.

As a Sunday School teacher she was on the cutting edge of Bible teaching. When her church established its own school system she was active in that. She loves music and is in the music ministry in her church.

Herlinda exemplifies how an educated, professional woman can enter into the Kingdom work and have measureless influence. And she is our trusted friend!

213.

EUGÊNIA PEREIRA FAUSTINO
There are so many facets to Eugênia's personality. To explain them is like trying to capture the right light when
painting a picture - or taking hold of the rainbow! She had
joys and sadness.

Eugênia grew up in a family that had not loved the Lord,
and as an adult she yearned for the training and support she
had missed. But she had a boundless burden for "the untouched"
- people who did not know Jesus Christ as Savior; people in
the suburbs of our city; or in neighboring towns, counties,
states - until the people of the world.

She and her husband Jacinto are known as pioneer church
planters, having devoted over a quarter of a century in the
North Association. They have seven children. Ezinete is
married and lives in Belo Horizonte. Paulo is a businessman
in Montes Claros. Jonatas is a pastor in São Paulo state.
Julimar and Deborah are pastors' wives.

When we arrived in the North in 1978 Eujácio, the youngest,
was four. His sister Eujácia was five. Eugênia urged those
precious youngsters to recite poems, Bible verses, and to sing
in church. Now Eujácia is married and Eujácio is in the
States studying English. Each of the seven children is gifted.

Eugênia trained her children to care for the housework.
Since she was away from the home so much in personal evangelism, she planned the meals and cleaning with her family,
and sometimes a maid.

Eugênia always needed shoes for she walked so much. I
gave her some of mine, and she would soon wear them out. She
might walk in a neighborhood and strike up a conversation
with a strange woman, who would soon be telling her about her
husband, children, and her health. As a friendship developed
they might set a day when they would invite the neighbors there
and Eugênia would talk to them about Jesus.

She had several mission points going. A "mission" is a
group meeting regularly for Bible study or Woman's Missionary
Union, or Bible stories for the children. It might be meeting in someone's house or back yard - or even in a rented
room. On special occasions the people from the missions came
to the "mother" church - Third - for worship. Hopefully,
the mission points would develop so as to organize into
churches.

Eugênia was an "all age" person; she entranced the women
of the church, young people responded to her, and children
loved her. She was a genius in planning fun times.

WAK
Our lives were intertwined. I was a member of Third MOC
when Jacinto pastored there. She could mother and guide me
and by her wisdom our chatter never took on gossip or slander.

We could talk about our personal prayer time. We agreed
that we'd get everything straightened out with the Lord, and
find that the next day we'd again have to put our tendencies
to sin before Him.

We might disagree, then the trait of patience shone out
in Eugênia.

When sorrows came to me, she was there. When the going
was tough, she was there. We shared new insights and joys.
I tried to be the same confidant that my friend was to me.

To sum up Eugênia: she loved the Lord!

A FAMILY DEATH

We mourned the death of my brother-in-law Charles Leonard
Norris who died November 16, 1984. We could not be at his
funeral in Fredericktown, Missouri. But in our reminiscing
we recalled his unfailing love for missions; his prayers in
our behalf; and his caring for us. He was part of our mission
service.

**But you be watchful in all things, endure afflictions,
do the work of an evangelist, fulfill your ministry.**
2 Timothy 4:5 NKJ

Soon after we arrived in North Minas I determined that one
of the basic needs of the churches was training in personal
evangelism. Fellow missionary Jack Young had translated and
adapted the evangelism course WIN (Win People To Christ).

The Association was awarded $5,000.00 by the Foreign Mis-
sion Board in 1982 for this course in the churches. Everyone
who would agree to do the course and engage in a week of evangelism was enlisted. The people were enthusiastic, especially
the youth.

A nucleus of workers took the course at First Church in
Montes Claros, and the next week they divided into teams and
went to participating churches. The teams taught evangelism
then led the participants to go into the communities, actually
doing personal soul winning. I visited every church where a
team would work to determine living and working conditions.
Insofar as possible I took the workers in the Mission car
with me.

The town Butumirim was a preaching point of Second Church,
Montes Claros, where Jessé Toledo was pastor. I took a group
there where we planned to work Saturday night and Sunday doing
door-to-door evangelism.

There was no hotel so we stayed with the one family of
believers, a police sergeant with his wife and little girl.
We men slept on the floor in one room and the women in the
kitchen. José Pinto, an active deacon in his church, was
next to me. He was so excited about this new venture he
talked most of the night.

A few weeks later I met him by chance and he brusquely remonstrated with me for not speaking to him on the street the
day before.

"After our trip to Butumirim together I am surprised that
you would slight me."

"José, I am terribly sorry, but if I didn't speak to you
it was because I didn't see you. I wouldn't meet the
devil without speaking to him."

He laughed and gave me the Brazilian <u>abraço</u> (hug). We
became better friends than ever, and he never once failed to
respond to any request I made of him. Understanding the psy-
chology of the people of the North was God's gift to me.

JLK

Our evaluation of the WIN evangelism project rated it a complete success. In the few months that followed, the number of baptisms in the churches rose steadily. Many of the team members said they felt called to dedicate their lives to Christian service. Never in Baptist work in North Minas had so many people become involved in personal evangelism; never had there been so many answering God's call to full-time Christian service.

JLK   **SPECIAL PROJECT II - 1984**

There were towns and communities in the North Association with no Baptist witness, mainly three areas - each having at least three towns over 40,000 population each:

    Eastern Section   - focal town being Salinas
    Northern Section   - focal town being Porteirinha
    Western Section   - focal town being São Francisco

In 1983 I made a survey and wrote a proposal for buying lots and building chapels, requesting $30,000.00 of the Foreign Mission Board. According to protocol of the South Brazil Mission and the Board, I would present the proposal several times until hopefully it would be approved.

When our fellow missionaries of Minas Gerais were in their regular meeting I asked that my item be placed on the agenda. There were fourteen of us in the state - six couples and two single women. The proposal was approved.

I then requested that my item be placed on the agenda of the regular meeting of the Executive Board of the State Convention of Minas Gerais. In that meeting the Executive Secretary of the Convention fought furiously against the proposal.

His opposition was understandable, for he had been hailed as "The Man With the Plan" for leading the national Brazilian Baptist Convention in the financial plan called the Cooperative Program. He had valiantly led the Minas Gerais State Convention in financial planning wherein the state was self-supporting. He felt my request for outside funds to open new work threw his accomplishments into reverse.

I argued that the vast North Minas had never been a recipient of funds from the Board - there had not even been a missionary to work in the area. The work we were trying to open up would be in cities which were also targeted by the State Convention's Missions Department. The Executive Board approved the proposal in spite of the Secretary's opposition.

JLK

I now had two letters of approval which I joined with my proposal and mailed to the Finance Committee of the South Brazil Mission. (They routinely studied all requests in order to make recommendations to the South Brazil Mission in annual session.)

At the next annual meeting of the South Brazil Mission the Finance Committee was given several times on the agenda. The first time they reported on their work, no mention was made of my proposal, so I talked to some committee members.

"We did not receive your proposal in the mail."

I furnished photocopies to every member of the Finance Committee. The second time their report came to the general business session, my proposal was not mentioned. Again I talked to some committee members.

"Your proposal was misplaced."

The same thing happened again.

"Your proposal is not being treated."

When the whole Mission was in business session and it was evident that the Finance Committee would make no recommendation on my proposal, Jack Young, my fellow missionary, spoke.

He made the motion that my proposal be approved even though it had not been treated by the Finance Committee. The motion passed.

God teaches my hands to war.

> **Blessed be the Lord my Rock,**
> **Who trains my hands for war,**
> **And my fingers for battle -**
> **Psalm 144:1 NKJ**

Having received the funds from the Foreign Mission Board, we were able to start the project in 1984. By then the Executive Secretary had come to terms with the undertaking. He transferred Pastor Sinésio Vilaça da Silva of the state Missions Department to Salinas. He was very capable of implementing the project.

JLK

   Who would be able to adequately evaluate the benefits and
blessings of this special project? Some of the places where
we worked have established missions in other towns. In Rubelita Mr. Paulo <u>Crente</u> had been at work over thirty years,
alone and praying that one day help would come. His prayers
were answered; this is but one example of God's glorious works.

<u>Results</u> <u>of</u> <u>Project</u> <u>II</u>

<u>Eastern</u> <u>Section</u>

1. **Salinas.** Two lots were purchased and Pastor Sinésio supervised construction of an attractive chapel. The congregation <u>became</u> <u>a</u> <u>church</u> <u>in</u> <u>1984</u>.
2. **Taiobeiras.** A large house was purchased and renovated, to
   become a chapel. A congregation was established.
3. **Fruta de Leite.** A chapel was constructed on land bought by
   First Church of Montes Claros. The congregation <u>became</u> <u>a</u>
   <u>church</u> <u>in</u> <u>1985</u>.
4. **Rio Pardo de Minas.** We rented and renovated a house for a
   chapel. A congregation was established and a couple was
   located there as leaders.
5. **Rubelita.** We rented and renovated a house for a chapel.
   A congregation was established.

<u>Northern</u> <u>Section</u>

   The state Missions Department employed Pastor Jacinto, a
veteran, experienced pioneer, to live in Porteirinha.

1. **Porteirinha.** Bought land and built a chapel. The congre-
   gation there <u>became</u> <u>a</u> <u>church</u> <u>in</u> <u>1988</u>. Living in Porteirinha, Pastor Jacinto gave leadership to the Riacho dos
   Machados Church. They built a new church building.
2. **Mato Verde.** Bought land.
3. **Monte Azul.** Bought land and built a chapel. Established
   a congregation.
4. **Pai Pedro.** This railroad community was not part of the
   project. However Pastor Jacinto gave assistance, result-
   ing in <u>formation</u> <u>of</u> <u>a</u> <u>church</u> <u>in</u> <u>November,</u> <u>1988</u>.

<u>Western</u> <u>Section</u>

   In the western section no suitable person was found to
place there. Time was running out and we were coming up to
our final furlough in October, 1988.

The churches had prayed to the Lord of the Harvest that He
send forth workers. Now we took seriously the responsibility
of equipping the called ones to do their work. We no longer
expected to see pastors leave the great cities of Rio de Janeiro, Recife, and São Paulo to come to our economically depressed North. Now the question of ordaining the workers God
had called, had to be handled.

There is a strong sentiment all across Brazil that a man
should not be ordained until he has graduated from a seminary,
a persuasion maintained by pastors of the two largest churches
of our Association. It didn't seem to matter that there were
many churches in the area without pastors. I was caring for
ten churches, trying to visit them once every two months. A
pastor supported by the State Convention was dismissed. He
was caring for three churches: Manga, Espinosa, and Sião in
Januária. I added that responsibility, making thirteen.

The load became too much and I developed a severe ear problem. Dr. Linhares, ear specialist in Rio de Janeiro, could
not pinpoint the problem, but he thought I had a tumor between
the inner ear and brain. He recommended surgery, warning of
the possibility of paralysis to the face. Our family doctor
in Rio, Dr. Henrique Mayr, told us in confidence,

"For such a serious problem, you need to go back to the
States."

Dr. Mayr and Dr. Franklin Fowler, the Board doctor, con-
ferred and Dr. Fowler recommended that I see Dr. Jack Hough,
ear specialist in Oklahoma City. The Board arranged the mission residence of Putnam City Baptist Church and we departed
Brazil June 16, 1982. We were royally entertained at Putnam
City Baptist Church in Oklahoma City.

Dr. Hough ran many tests. He finally stated his conclusion:

"I have seen all kinds of red flags indicating that you
have had a problem. But you don't have a problem now."

He dismissed me and we returned to Brazil August 31, 1982.

There was a lot of divine help those eleven weeks. Dr.
Fowler and people at the Board headquarters in Richmond, Virginia were praying. The Board left nothing undone in caring
for me. Putnam City Church had a prayer room which they
staffed with pray-ers twenty-four hours daily. When I was
able, we became pray-ers. Max Alexander, associate pastor of
Putnam City, brought three prayer warriors to our residence
and they devotedly, quietly, ministered to me. The Charles
Suttons furnished a car. Charles' wife, Neva, was W.M.U.
president, and that group ministered.

JLK
During those eleven weeks in Oklahoma City I came to terms
with God's will concerning the ordination of the workers He
had called for North Minas, and I felt I had to proceed as He
led. There were some good men who had been sacrificially diligent in preparing for their calling. Three were university
graduates but they had not graduated from a seminary:

Francisco Ferreira
Geraldo Batista Nunes
João Dutra

Facing The Conflict - Ordaining Pastors

I list the ten men who were ordained, in date order. They
were committed to what they believed to be God's will for them.
I was convinced they would, in the words of Paul,

**. . . take heed to yourselves and to all the flock,
among which the Holy Spirit has made you overseers,
to shepherd the church of God which He purchased with
His own blood.**

Acts 20:28 NKJ

I was convinced they had the same dedication that Paul had
when he said,

**. . . nor do I count my life dear to myself, so that I
may finish my race with joy, and the ministry which I
received from the Lord Jesus, to testify to the gospel
of the grace of God.**

Acts 20:24 NKJ

All the men understood that they would support themselves
- that the financial remuneration for their services would
be "zero." Only two owned automobiles. During the first
five years in the North we ordained three men for the ministry.

JOÃO ARAÚJO
João Araújo had moved from São Paulo. He had almost com-
pleted an Institute program similar to ours, in São Paulo.
His pastor Levy Penido and I helped him finish his course.
He was ordained and became pastor of the Grão Mogol church.

****

ISAÍAS MARTINS
Isaías Martins was son of the first convert in North Minas;
the fourth son of his family to be ordained. He had completed the Ravena Institute course offered by the State Convention Seminary of Belo Horizonte. The Manga Church requested
his ordination; he was ordained and became pastor of that
church.

****

222.

DEMAS VIERA SOBRINHO

Demas Viera Sobrinho was a special gift from God. He, his wife Diva and their two little girls came to live and work in Grão Mogol. Demas was an interior decorator in São Paulo but he decided to move because of the violence. At Grão Mogol he would attend one of the most difficult areas of the Association from the standpoint of physical stress. Demas had studied in a seminary in São Paulo, and was well qualified for his ordination.

Later he influenced another worker to move to his area - José Marcos Silva who had been with the Brazilian Baptist Home Mission Board. They lived in Cristália and cared for the Croslândia church and its mission points.

****

December 31, 1981 Levy Penido, pastor of First Church of Montes Claros, left. He and his wife Leia were appointed by the Brazilian Baptist Foreign Mission Board to serve in Ecuador. Then Pastor Josias and Dona Ruth of First Church in Janauba retired. These two men were strong supporters in the matter of ordination.

The two new pastors in these churches were the opposite of their predecessors. It seemed that they had no interest in the field beyond their own churches; in fact, they resisted much of what the churches of the Association were striving to accomplish. They both held the philosophy that ordination was only for the seminary graduate.

DÉCIO ATADEU DA SILVA

Décio Atadeu da Silva, a young man, had just graduated from the seminary in Belo Horizonte and his parents moved to Montes Claros. Nova Jerusalém Church of this city called him as pastor and requested his ordination.

****

GERALDO BATISTA NUNES

The beloved **Geraldo Batista Nunes** had been a deacon of First Church of Montes Claros. When he served as president of the Association for one year he endeared himself to the entire membership. He was still studying in the seminary in Belo Horizonte when Boas Novas Church of Montes Claros called him as pastor and requested his ordination.

****

Now, despite very strong opposition from men in prestigious positions we proceeded with ordaining five more good men to lead needy churches. This was not accomplished without a struggle.

JLK   **BENJAMIM SOARES DA CRUZ**
     Benjamim Soares da Cruz had lived all his life in North
Minas and was a very capable man. He had led in the founding
of Fourth Church in Montes Claros (Jardim Palmeiras). Soon
after we moved to North Minas José Alves Bittencourt, state
Executive Secretary, suggested that Benjamim be ordained, although some of the pastors had serious doubts.

     However after years of waiting he was ordained and assumed
leadership of two churches: Engenheiro Navarro, about thirty-
four miles from Montes Claros, and Jardim Alvorado in our city.

                    ****

                   FRANCISCO DOS REIS
     Francisco dos Reis was a building contractor. As a member
of First Church of Montes Claros he was well respected but he
was not so well known outside of his home church. The fact
that he lacked adequate schooling for enrollment in a seminary
was discouraging to him.

     He had a deep conviction of his calling to the ministry,
so I encouraged him to study in the Ravena course. He made
excellent grades. When the Mt. Sinai Church of Montes Claros
requested his ordination, some of the pastors were not enthusiastic.

     The president of the State Convention, Pastor Oiracú, was
one of Francisco's teachers in the Ravena course and was impressed with him as a student. We invited him to come and
help with the ordination ceremony. His position as Convention
president and professor of the candidate was very helpful in
Francisco's ordination service. Francisco was called as pastor of Mt. Sinai Church.

                    ****

                       JOÃO DIAS
     João Dias, middle-age, lived in Jaiba. He studied the In-
stitute course, spending a month each year in Governador Valadares, about five hundred miles from his home. (Later the
course was administered from the state encampment near Ravena.)
João was a quiet, dedicated man, having finished his theological course before I got to know him well.

     When I visited the Jaiba Church where he was a member I
learned that the church had written several times to the North
Association requesting his ordination but had no reply. Jacinto Pereira Faustino, president of the Association, traveled
with me to Jaiba where we went to the houses of church members,
inquiring about the life and witness of João. Everyone gave
a good report.

                          224.

Next day we drove the twenty miles to Janauba to talk with the pastor there. As secretary of the Association, after receiving the letters, he would have passed them on to the Association officers. He said he had gotten the letters, but since João was not a seminary graduate he didn't think he should be ordained.

Before returning home we requested the Jaiba Church to send their request to Jacinto. They did, so we had authority to proceed. I took five pastors with me to Jaiba for the doctrinal examination of the candidate. Three other pastors arrived by bus, including the one from Janauba. All these men comprised the examination council.

Soon after we started it was clear the Janauba man intended to block the ordination. The council spent almost as much time dealing with his objections as they did in examining the candidate. Finally I spoke,

"How long have you been pastor of the Janauba church?"

"Three years."

"How many times have you come to Jaiba to lend assistance to the church here?" (I knew they had asked him for assistance.)

"Today is the first day I have been here."

"You have lived just twenty miles away. You have been invited several times to help, but you have not responded. How is it you can object to ordaining a man who has made so much effort to prepare himself for service and is willing to spend his life here with this church?"

The council voted immediately to approve the ordination, and set the date for the ceremony.

That service was one of the most impressive ordinations I have attended. João's friends and family traveled more than twenty-four hours by bus from São Paulo. The mayor of Jaiba, a Catholic, was there and asked permission to speak. Very unusually, this was granted. He spoke congratulatory and appreciative words.

João became pastor of the Jaiba church as well as the Manga Church on the São Francisco River. This was one of my most difficult churches to care for, considering physical effort and travel expense. João Dias was a blessing to me!

****

FRANCISCO FERREIRA GONÇALVES

Francisco Ferreira Gonçalves, a university graduate, was a history teacher in high school and junior college. He was a deacon of Second Church of Montes Claros. His wife Flor de Nice was a school teacher and devoted church worker. Their three sons were active in the church. When Second Church was without a pastor, Francisco was often elected to the leadership.

There came a time when a strong group in the church (including Francisco) decided to form a new church. They started the Nova Canaã Church. The site they chose was the confluence of three suburbs, none of which had any church. They purchased five lots; it is almost unheard of in Brazil for a new church to start in this way.

It seemed obvious from the beginning that Francisco should be the pastor of the group, although he himself never presumed to make the suggestion. He and Flor de Nice were people of remarkable leadership and dedication. Francisco had felt God's call to preach when he was single. When he was preparing to enroll in seminary his father died and he had to support his mother and siblings.

He and Flor de Nice married and they studied at the university in Montes Claros. Francisco had a deep regard for the office of pastor and didn't think he was worthy of the ministry; nevertheless he was a very positive leader.

The Nova Canaã Church made a request of the Pastors' Order (organization of pastors) for Francisco's ordination. The Ordination Council was convened to examine the candidate; four of the members strongly objected to the ordination.

They vociferously cited that the candidate was not a seminary graduate. They were very, very vocal. Francisco answered all the doctrinal questions posed to him, but the opposition prolonged the questioning to six hours. Francisco never grew impatient, and was very courteous. Finally, as president of the Council I suspended the procedure until a future, undesignated date (I didn't disband the Council).

Soon we traveled to the annual Mission meeting, where I had time to think it through. I had a growing conviction that the four who objected should not have the power to prevent a new and rapidly growing church from having the pastor they felt God wanted them to have.

When we got home I talked with Jacinto, president of the Association. We decided to reconvene the Ordination Council (this was July, month of school vacation). We decided the examination was to be in the presence of the requesting church, Nova Canaã, so the church people could witness the questioning. They had been deeply grieved the last time; now they were delighted, since their confidence would be restored.

The church was meeting in a rented, former machine shop, and was packed at the appointed time. The two strongest opponents were absent. Each member of the Council had opportunity to ask questions. Then Francisco was asked to speak on one church doctrine of his own choosing, for fifteen minutes. The entire Council approved the candidate and we proceeded with the laying on of hands and the prayer which concluded the ceremony. Then the Nova Canaã Church convened in business session and officially declared Francisco its pastor.

* * * * * * * * * * * * * * * *

But the opposition was not through yet. At the next annual meeting of the state Baptist Convention, July 1987, two dissatisfied pastors demanded that a committee be appointed to question Pastor Jacinto and me about unethical conduct. While the convention was in session we met two times with that committee, with the accusers present. We were, of course, exonerated of any unethical conduct.

The Nova Canaã Church went from victory to victory under the able leadership of Pastor Francisco. They built a fine, adequate place of worship, established missions (at least one became a church), and set a record in number of baptisms.

* * * * * * * * * * * * * * * *

JOÃO DUTRA

João Dutra, middle age, had an attractive family - his wife, two sons and a daughter. A university graduate, he had been on the city council of Montes Claros for over fifteen years. He was a spiritist. Talking was João's gift. He had a radio program which broadcast over North Minas Gerais. He advertised, made announcements, and promoted spiritism. It was known about that he performed surgical operations while in a trance, though he had never studied medicine.

Early morning we could hear his talk show from the radio in the convenience store across the street from our house. He started with spiritist music, a thought on spiritism, then moved to the business of the day.

One Sunday his fifteen-year-old son attended services at First Church, Montes Claros, at the invitation of the young people there. He was wonderfully converted. He rushed home, bounded into the living room to his father, and enthusiastically - joyfully - told him that he had found Jesus as Savior. Nonplused, João remonstrated,

"In that case you can pack your things and leave this house."

227.

The son went to his room, grabbed a pillowcase from his bed, stuffed some clothing in it, and started from the house. In shock, João exclaimed,

"Wait, son. If you are that sure about your decision I will go to that church and see what this is all about!"

He fulfilled his word, going to First Church the following Sunday where he, too, was converted. In time he and his family were baptized into the fellowship of that church.

This was a potent blow to the spiritist movement, one to which a large percentage of the population of our city belonged. When João was converted, so was his radio program. Instead of spiritist music in early morning, we heard João talking about Jesus as he witnessed, unashamed. He gave quizzes on the Bible, offering a Bible itself to the winners.

João warmly offered to help me. He would ask about my itinerary as I visited churches and missions in the North. He then announced my travel plans, advertising where the missionary would be. It was a pleasure to arrive at a church filled with those who learned of my arrival via the radio.

João was a large man, overweight from a sedentary life. When he had a heart attack he was taken to Belo Horizonte for care, where he had surgery. When recovering, the surgeon said to João when he realized he could talk,

"All right, João, you can go back to your politics."

"No, doctor, not to politics. God wants me to be a minister."

News of João's surrender to preach met with mixed reactions. Those in spiritism realized there was no hope of his return to them. People in the churches were elated. As soon as João recovered he addressed the responsibility of his calling with extraordinary vigor. His educational background and innate intelligence lent to rapid development in an understanding of his newfound faith.

His inquiring mind was ever expanding. His pastor thoroughly taught him doctrines of the Bible, and he invested in good reading material. He studied in the North Association Bible Institute and enrolled in the correspondence course of the North Brazil Seminary in Recife. Soon he was invited by the churches to preach.

Esplanada Church of Montes Claros had gotten off to a good
start after its organization. There were active deacons of
firm and mature doctrine. The neighborhood was responding to
the ministry and the church was growing. This church requested João's ordination and extended a call for him to be their
minister.

Some of the pastors were suspicious. One spent a lot of
time and energy going to the pastors' homes, trying to cut off
João's ordination. But three of the more stable pastors, a-
long with the men who had passed through the fire, were strong
in their affirmation.

The pastors met at the appointed time and the Ordaining
Council was formed. The opposition argued loud and long to
prevent the process and it seemed that the examination would
degenerate into a shouting match. When the opposers realized
they could not prevail they walked out. The ordaining ceremony was administered, and João became pastor of Esplanada
Church.

The church was in a bogged-down building program that took
on new vigor. Evangelism came alive. Young people of the
Association cherished him for his vital ministry to them.
God gave João a brief but rewarding ministry.

Many times he said that if his life and ministry were brief
he could die a very happy man. Actually he had little more
than three years before his death, but they were so fruitful
that Heaven is blessed by them.

This was the last ordination ceremony in which I participated, on Brazilian soil.

                    ****

Geraldo was orphaned as a child so he was placed with relatives who lived near the town Coração de Jesus (Heart of Jesus). He was neglected and mistreated and when he grew to teenage years he was already an alcoholic. His adoptive family and their friends lived from drunken orgy to drunken binge.

One day Geraldo was lying on his back under a palm tree, gazing up into the fronds against the sky. He thought,

> "I wonder who made those fronds. Someday I shall find out who made the leaves - and the tree - and the sky."

When the youth needed medical attention he was sent to someone in Montes Claros, riding there in the back of a truck with the pigs being taken to market. A doctor who treated him mercifully befriended him, so he could start studying.

His inquiring mind led him on a search for answers to spiritual questions. He went to several churches; at one of the Catholic churches he met a priest named - Geraldo. His quest led him to an encounter with Jesus Christ as personal Savior. But when he went to his friends at a Catholic church to share his salvation they told him to leave and never come back.

Geraldo was married to beautiful Minervina and they had three children: Charles Wesley, Shirley Mary and Sheila Cristina. They were attracted by an announcement of a revival at First Church, Montes Claros, and one night when the invitation was given Geraldo and Minervina raised their hands.

Geraldo - declaring that he had been saved and wanted to be a part of the church; Minervina - indicating she received Jesus as Savior. When they were baptized into the fellowship of the church they began a pilgrimage of faithful attendance, stewardship and spiritual growth.

The three children followed their parents' example and were baptized and integrated into the church life. Geraldo said that Charles was so devoted in his love for Jesus that he preached at an open-air service when he was ten years old.

Geraldo was elected president of the North Minas Association in its annual meeting July 1984, the first layman to serve in that office. His Christian witness and integrity as a businessman were tremendously helpful as he and I started working together. Every missionary dreams of working with a man of this caliber.

We were hardly unpacked from furlough when he announced he was ready to visit each church. These travels took him away from his accounting business for many days, and the visits to the churches brought healing to the fellowship of the Association, which had been thrown into disarray.

There was a problem in Monte Siāo Church in Januária, on
the Sāo Francisco River. Immediately Geraldo and I traveled
there and stayed at a hotel; he had his typewriter. Although
the church was meeting in rented quarters, a lot had already
been purchased with Lottie Moon Christmas Offering money in a
very promising community. For some reason the documentation
was not done properly and a movement was underfoot to confis-
cate the lot.

I worked on the streets securing documents and records from
the city government offices and Geraldo worked in the hotel
room. He knew the legal requirements to get the property se-
cured.

We worked unceasingly for two days. That evening I was exhausted and while he was still working I fell asleep. Sometimes I had nightmares about combat in Burma in World War II,
if I were extremely agitated or tired. Around midnight Geraldo
awoke me from one of these nightmares and gently shaking me
he said,

  "The peace treaty was signed, but for you the war still
  goes on."

Geraldo and Minervina were earning a moderate living by
their accounting business; however God had a sacred plan and
He called Geraldo to preach the Gospel. He responded and enrolled in the seminary in Belo Horizonte. Thus, Minervina was
totally responsible for their business. Geraldo was living
with young seminary students in the men's crowded, noisy dormitory. He traveled to Montes Claros for weekends, usually
preaching in the churches there on Sundays. (The bus trip
took at least six hours.)

This young man (he was in his middle forties) had an effer-
vescent personality and an unending sense of humor. The two
of us were in the Grāo Mogol Church and Geraldo was preaching about the cleansing of the temple at Jerusalem. He always moved about when he preached. To make his point he left
the pulpit and walked down the aisle to the door. He picked
up the door mat, rolled it up, putting it under his arm.

  "Those Jews were carrying everything into the temple. Here
  comes this Jew with a pig under his arm."

He paused:

  "No, a Jew wouldn't have taken a pig into the temple - it
  must have been a turkey!"

After a year of seminary study Geraldo was ordained and became pastor of Boas Novas Church in our city. One day when Wilma returned from an errand, she found my note which I'd hurriedly posted on our door:

"Geraldo is in the morgue at Santa Casa Hospital."

She found him at the morgue - there was no attendant, and she stood quietly by him - there on a slab. He had died April 12, 1986, after only a few hours in the hospital. People said that the cause was a heart damaged by <u>Chagas</u>.

During the dignified funeral at First Church, and interment in the modest vault at the cemetery, we reflected on the miracle of God's hand in his life. We would miss his complete compliance to God's calling. We would miss his loving, caring friendship.

> I will extol You, my God, O King;
>   And I will bless Your name forever and ever.
> Every day I will bless You,
>   And I will praise Your name forever and ever.
> Great is the Lord, and greatly to be praised;
>   And His greatness is unsearchable.
>   Psalm 145:1-3 NKJ

WAK   ## The <u>Dusty</u> <u>Halo</u>

Francisco Reis, who was training to become a pastor, mentioned that he had a sister-in-law who might be interested in working for us. Thus we were introduced to our angel, sent from the Lord. Martha was sixteen when she first came. She walked from her parents' home, arriving at 7:20 A.M. In rainy or dry season, she cleaned all the hardwood and tile floors daily, Monday through Friday (she came on Saturdays if I needed her).

Martha patiently and lovingly did the peeling, paring, and cutting of fruits and vegetables, and I did the cooking and flavoring. She cooked delicious rice, a daily staple, without a glance at the clock. Her quiet spirit brought peace to our home.

Martha's conversation was very minimal; however, she did observe the many people who came to our house, and she had her own system of judgment. Sometimes she would quietly comment,

"So-and-so is exploiting you."

I did not slack in speaking to Martha about Jesus. I knew her parents and brothers were traditional Catholics. Her sister Carmen was Francisco Reis' wife, and she supported him in his calling to be a Baptist pastor. When I spoke quietly to Martha as we washed dishes together, she always said that she would think about becoming a Christian.

The dusty halo. During the dry season we and our households were dusty, as well as the garage, sidewalk, street in front of the house, back porch, and the flagstone back yard. It was then that the "angel with the dusty halo" took action. She washed everything, every morning, as well as giving the hanging ferns in the garage their morning drink. I helped her wash our side of the street by holding the hose while she swept the dirt down the gutter.

We usually traveled during January and Martha's only responsibilities were to sweep and dust a little and water the plants. One year when we returned from our travels she told me that one of the leaders in the church work had tried to get her to work for her. She explained to Martha about the wage. Martha's reply to her was,

"Dona Wilma has already paid me. It is spoken."

(There's that phrase emphasizing that one's word is completely binding).

233.

We would never be able to recompense our angel. When we dismantled our household we gave Martha a wooden five-drawer chest of drawers. (I had bought it from missionary Minnie Lou Lanier for $25.00 in 1963). It was solid wood, with carved design. In Martha's quiet way she simply said, "Thank you."

Martha loyally stayed with us until the morning in October, 1988, when we left our house for the last time. Her loyalty and faithfulness were immeasurable.

The Vegetable Lady

She brought the most beautiful vegetables to our gate, especially greens. Couve (collards) tender and fresh. Bright, fully developed carrots. Chicory and water cress. Red lettuce. New okra. Parsley and green onion.

She was so slight - a small woman. When I responded to her clapping at the gate I would help lift the heavy, round woven basket from her head. Then we would chat and she would find the choicest of her vegetables from the orderly arrangement in her basket.

She sometimes needed medicine and I shared some of what we had. I shared Jesus with her. As I paid her I tried to add something to the price she asked. Then we would arrange the towel on her head, twisting it into a ring, and lift the heavy basket, balancing it on top of the towel.

"Oh God, thank you for this precious one. Thank you for this happy, cheerful person beneath the heavy burden of that basket of vegetables. Thank you for her thoughtfulness. Thank you that she handles the vegetables tenderly, and that she takes pleasure in coming here. Thank you for letting her be a part of my life."

The dry season was merciless for the people who could not escape the terrible dust of the street. I could stay inside my clean, washed, and dusted house, but the vegetable lady had to be in the worst of it. When the lungs had so much dust the fever, chills, and flu ensued.

One day I was leaving the hospital Santa Casa in Montes
Claros, where I had visited a man dying from the dreadful
disease <u>Chagas</u>. This was during the dry season when the
city was engulfed in clouds of dust. Workmen were building
a new wing onto the hospital, and as I came out the door
I noticed they had all gathered on the second floor of the
construction, looking down at the street.

Being curious about what held their attention, I hurried
to the sidewalk. Women sweepers were customarily hired to
clean the city streets, and there was one of these women.
She was probably a widow or by the law of averages had been
abandoned by her husband and left to support her children
alone. She would be drawing the lowest possible salary.
She should have been sulking about her miserable lot in life.

As she moved along, rythmically swinging her broom and
sweeping, she was singing a great hymn of faith. Manually
she was sweeping the dusty street, but in her spirit she
was worshiping her Lord in her own language:

    My hope is built on nothing less
        than Jesus' blood and righteousness;
    I dare not trust the sweetest frame,
        But wholly lean on Jesus' name.

    On Christ, the solid Rock, I stand;
        All other ground is sinking sand,
        All other ground is sinking sand.

    I thought,

    "No wonder everyone around came to a standstill. She had
    brought the presence of God to us."

We had already stopped making commitments for out-of-town
engagements for October 1988 we would leave Brazil. But a
letter came from the First Church in Januária asking me to be
present for the twenty-eighth anniversary of their church.
Brazilian churches never fail to celebrate their founding date.

Since they had no pastor I felt that I could not refuse
their invitation. When I got to the church their song service
was already under way. The building was full and people were
crowded around the door and at each window, looking in.

The aisle was full of people in chairs so I had some difficulty getting to the front of the auditorium. When it was
time to preach I noticed that there was a family of five people who didn't seem to be local. The people of Januária tend
to be dark, and these were light. My sermon was evangelistic.
As soon as I gave the invitation all five of the visitors
stepped forward immediately.

The deacon leading the service called another deacon to
take the family into a side room for counseling, where they
remained for some time. The service continued and others
made decisions. These, being local people, were counseled
promptly.

Finally just when we had dismissed the service the family
of five was brought to me.

  "Pastor, I was out inviting people to attend the service
  when I came upon this family camped under a bamboo shelter
  down by the river. I want them to tell you their story."

They were attractive people; the man was tall, standing
like a soldier. This is his story:

  "We are from the Northeast. We had several years of drouth
  and could no longer earn a living. We sold what we could
  and paid a truck driver to let us ride on top of his load,
  hoping to get to the city of São Paulo where I could find
  a job to support my family. But the truck brought us here,
  a distance from São Paulo. It would take perhaps two days
  to get there but we have no funds.

  "Last night my wife and I agreed that we would let Sunday
  pass. Then we would drown our children and commit suicide.
  But, thank God, tonight we stepped out of the jaws of death
  into life, for we have found Jesus."

Several people had gathered around. One man offered them
the use of a vacant rent house for a few days. Some gave
them money. I later learned that the next day the man had
been given a job on a nearby ranch. He and his family had
found a new life.

ASSOCIATION OF BAPTIST CHURCHES
OF
NORTH MINAS GERAIS
(Listed by Year of Organization)

01. First (Montes Claros).......1918
02. Boa Vista dos Matos.........1918
03. First (Bocaiuva)................1939
04. Cristália - Croslândia..............1953
05. First (Janauba).....................1957
06. First (Januária).....................1959
07. Capitão Eneas.............................1963
08. Second (Montes Claros)....................1966
09. Engenheiro Navarro........................1967
10. First (Grão Mogol).............................1971
11. Francisco Sá..................................1974
12. Espinosa.......................................1975
13. Third (Montes Claros)..........................1975
14. Sião (Januária)...............................1975
15. Vila Nova de Minas.............................1976
16. Manga..1977
17. Tabuas...1977
18. Jardim Palmeiras (Montes Claros)............1977
19. Riacho dos Machados..........................1978
20. Esplanada (Montes Claros)..........................1980
21. Esperança (Montes Claros)........................1981
22. Fonte Viva (Jaiba)..............................1981
23. Boas Novas (Montes Claros).......................1982
24. Josenópolis.....................................1982
25. Centenário (Marcela)............................1982
26. Nova Jerusalém (Montes Claros)..................1983
27. Nova Canaã (Montes Claros)......................1984
28. First (Salinas).................................1984
29. Peniel (São João do Paraiso)...................1984
30. Monte Sinai (Montes Claros).....................1985
31. Fruta de Leite..................................1985
32. Jardim Alvorada (Montes Claros).................1986
33. Memorial (Janauba)..............................1987
34. Filadélfia (Bocaiuva)...........................1987
35. First (Porteirinha)............................1988
36. Monte das Oliveiras (Montes Claros).............1988
37. Getsêmane (Montes Claros).......................1989
38. Jardim Eldorado (Montes Claros)....................1990
39. Pai Pedro (Janauba)..............................1990

NOTE: The last three churches listed were organized after
we came to the States.

237.

September 21, 1988 was an historic date for Jesse, for the
city council of Montes Claros awarded him the Certificate of
Honorary Citizenship that night.

Joel Guimarães de Souza was the councilman who initiated
the process which culminated in the honor. Joel was a member
of First Church of our city.

Eleven pastors of the Association were there; also Joel
Rodrigues da Silveira, new co-ordinator of the North Minas
Gerais Association. Joe Tarry represented the South Brazil
Mission.

The youth choir of First Church sang two songs before Jesse
spoke. It was planned that he would have a prepared discourse,
and he preached about the saving grace of Jesus Christ.

In making the presentation, Joel recalled that this was
the second time in the city's history for the honor to be
granted to a pastor, and the first time to a foreigner. He
handed the certificate to me, and I had the honor of passing
it to Jesse.

An article reporting the distinguished award appeared in
the state Baptist paper "O Batista Mineiro" December 1988;
also in "O Jornal Batista," national Baptist paper.

We went to Belo Horizonte for the month of February, 1988 to escape the heat and to face the reality of leaving Brazil the following October. Joe and Leona Tarry were on furlough, and invited us to use their apartment #903 at Rua Aluminio 138.

We tried to maintain a walking schedule daily up on the hills beyond Rua Aluminio. There was a residential street above, and we drove up there where we could walk freely on the street, away from broken sidewalks and numbers of pedestrians. From that height we looked down upon the center of the city as it spread out through the valley.

We prayed about the coming separation from Brazilians, from Brazil and from missionary life. There we came to a peaceful agreement with God that it was by His grace and power that we would separate and be separated. But we did not realize that our church people were not having an opportunity to come to a like agreement.

The bestowing of honors began at the annual state Convention meeting at Carangola July 21-24, 1988. The Brazilians bestowed honors generously and lavishly, placing our photograph on the back of the Convention program book. The state Convention and the state Woman's Missionary Union presented silver plaques.

For the annual meeting of the North Association June 10, 11, and 12, the program book also bore our likeness and plaques of appreciation were presented by the Association and the Woman's Missionary Union.

The honors at the annual South Brazil Mission in July were easier. Traditionally Angie Wilson wrote a comic tribute for each retiring missionary and we were "spoofed."

We were in Belo when the state Executive Committee was in session August 30, 1988. Pastor Orivaldo Pimentel Lopes had come so as to present a plaque of appreciation given by the national Baptist Convention.

Now we were dismantling our household, libraries, and personal things: selling, giving away, or packing and crating for overseas shipment. Many items in Jesse's library were helpful to the pastors and young theology students. I distributed my music library to those finding the books and music helpful.

The principal wooden pieces of furniture would go to the States: buffet, table, piano, and nightstand. Jesse was preaching at First Church of our city on the evening when the truckers were crating furniture and packing personal items.

WAK
    Dona Joaquina, our special, special friend said,

  "You are going to come to my house before you leave, and
   you WILL sit on my sofa."

  "But Joaquina, there are no more hours left. We will close
   our house late tonight, and leave tomorrow morning."

Joaquina kept on insisting.

  "All right, Joaquina. We'll be at your house at 11:00 P.M."

When we arrived we confessed that we had not eaten, so she
set the table and served food she had cooked for her family -
rice, beans, and roast beef.

    The next morning we drove away from our home at Rua Olímpio
Dias de Abreu 329 at the promised hour of 9:00 A.M. We had
been instructed to stop at a certain point outside the city,
which we did - but there was no one there. Soon several cars
of the dear people of First Church came, and at the side of
the road they conducted their last service in our honor.

    Dona Valda, gifted in dramatic readings and poems, recited
a poem; the male quartet sang; words of endearment and parting
were exchanged and the final prayer was prayed. They instructed:

  "Now we are driving ahead. Wait a few minutes, then proceed on your journey - but don't stop as you top the hill."

So we drove up the long hill from the valley that was Montes
Claros, and as we passed the waving group at the side of the
road we tried to swallow our sobs and control our tears as
we waved,

  "Goodbye!"

EPILOGUE

We had returned to Brazil in 1991, and lastly we spent nearly all of June and July 1997 there. On this trip we were one week in Fortaleza, Ceará with a partnership group of Americans, and in Juiz de Fora, Minas Gerais one week with another group.

Also Joe and Leona received us in their home in Belo Horizonte. There we were with Luiz and Alexandre. Alexandre was in his surgery internship and Luiz was studying medicine. (He graduated in 1998.) Humberto was already practicing medicine. These three lived in our neighborhood in Montes Claros when they were kids, and were often in our home for English conversation and fun times.

Jacinto and Eugênia, and Deborah and her family received us in their homes in Marataizes (on the coast of Espírito Santo). In fact, that weekend nearly all the children and grandchildren were there. In São Paulo we were with José and Aldenice and their son Bruno. (José received the Master's degree at Angelo State University.)

In Montes Claros we were guests of Geraldo in his hotel Monte Sião (Mt. Zion). As we visited in the churches of the city, the warmth of love exchanged was overwhelming. The people just wanted to talk, and we tried to give ourselves to listening. The junior boys and girls had grown up and wanted us to see their children.

The Seminary which met in First Church had grown. Dona Herlinda Silveira's recent history giving the number of established churches lent opportunity to compute the growth since 1978. In 1997 there were:

23 Baptist churches in Montes Claros, or 475% increase
52 Baptist churches in the Association, or 188% increase

The July 2, 1997 issue of "Veja," leading weekly news magazine of Brazil, reported on pages 88-93: In the decade of the 80's the growth rate of people in evangelical denominations was about 100% while the country's population growth was 31%.

Demas and Diva carried us to their home in Grão Mogol. Jesse preached in the church there, and one night in Cristália and Croslândia. We went to Porteirinha to the annual meeting of the North Association, where Jesse preached. Many of the pastors were young and had young families.

In two months Jesse preached twenty-six times, and Wilma sang with Autoharp almost each time. It was refreshing - it was a blessing - and a wonderful closure!

241.

HOW TO BECOME A CHRISTIAN

The ABC's of Salvation

Some people think God's plan of salvation is something only Bible students can comprehend. Actually, salvation is simple enough for everyone to understand. Here are the ABC's of how to experience salvation.

A. All persons need salvation because none of us is perfect and all of us are sinners. We have rebelled against God and His laws (Romans 3:10-18). The result of sin is spiritual death (Romans 6:23). Spiritual death means eternal separation from God. Consequently, we all need the salvation God can give us.

B. Because God loves each of us, He offers us salvaton. Although we have done nothing to deserve His love and salvation, God wants to save us. In the death and resurrection of His Son Jesus, God showed the greatness of His love for each of us (John 3:16).

C. Come to Jesus. He alone is the source of forgiveness and eternal life. Admit your sins and trust Him to forgive your sins and to give you salvation, or eternal life (Romans 10:9-10). Tell your pastor or a Christian friend about your decision. Join a local church and profess your faith in Christ through baptism.

****

JLK

My mother used to sing the hymn "Never Alone!" with such expression. I could see "the lightning flashing;" and hear "the thunder roll," and feel "the breakers dashing." Then the song concluded, "He promised never to leave me, Never to leave me alone."

Back then I wasn't sure about the soul. It would be years later before I understood the meaning of "soul." You see, we usually say, "I have a soul."

That is not true. We _are_ souls. We have bodies, but we _are_ souls. One day we will lay aside our bodies. As living souls we will go on forever.

That is why we need to be properly related to Jesus the Author of Salvation. This brings real meaning and purpose to life. Until we know Him we have but an existence. With Jesus Christ as our Savior and Lord we have purpose and meaning. He gives meaning to life and a mission in life.

APPENDIX
CUDDLE DOON by Alexander Anderson

The bairnies cuddle doon at nicht
  Wi' muckle fash an' din,
"Oh, try and sleep, ye waukrife rogues;
  Your faither's comin' in."
They never heed a word I speak,
  I try to gie a froon;
But aye I hap them up, an' cry,
  "Oh, bairnies, cuddle doon!"

Wee Jamie wi' the curly heid -
  He aye sleeps next the wa' -
Bangs up an' cries, "I want a piece" -
  The rascal starts them a'.
I rin an' fetch them pieces, drinks -
  They stop awee the soun' -
Then draw the blankets up, an' cry,
  "Noo, weanies, cuddle doon!"

But ere five minutes gang, wee Rab
  Cries oot, frae 'neath the claes,
"Mither, mak' Tam gie ower at ance;
  He's kittlin' wi' his taes."
The mischief's in that Tam for tricks;
  He'd bother half the toon,
But aye I hap them up, an' cry,
  "Oh, bairnies, cuddle doon!"

At length they hear their father's fit;
  An', as he steeks the door,
They turn their faces to the wa',
  While Tam pretends to snore.
"Hae a' the weans been gude?" he asks,
  As he pits aff his shoon.
"The bairnies, John, are in their beds,
  An' lang since cuddled doon."

An' just afore we bed oorsels,
  We look at oor wee lambs.
Tam has his airm roun' wee Rab's neck,
  An' Rab his airm roun' Tam's.
I lift wee Jamie up the bed,
  An, as I straik each croon,
I whisper, till my heart fills up,
  "Oh, bairnies, cuddle doon!

The bairnies cuddle doon at nicht
  Wi' mirth that's dear to me;
But soon the big warl's cark an' care
  Will quaten doon their glee.
Yet, come what will to ilka ane,
  May He who rules aboon
Aye whisper, though their pows be bald,
  "Oh, bairnies, cuddle doon!"

      JESSE L. KIDD: Passport Record of Time in Brazil/U.S.

Arrived in Brazil   Mar 19, 1958
Departed from Brazil   Oct 17, 1958   Brother George's death

Arrived in Brazil   Mar   1959
Departed from Brazil   Apr 19, 1962   Furlough before the
                                          McNealy's furlough

Arrived in Brazil   May 30, 1962
Departed from Brazil   Dec 17, 1965   Mother's death

Arrived in Brazil   Apr 17, 1966
Departed from Brazil   Oct 09, 1967   To be married

Arrived in Brazil   Jul 08, 1969
Departed from Brazil   Jul 10, 1973   Furlough 1804 Broadus,
                                          Ft. Worth, TX
                                          Southwestern Seminary

Arrived in Brazil   Jul 25, 1974
Departed from Brazil   Feb 26, 1977   Furlough Lonoke, AR
                                          403 S. Center

Arrived in Brazil   Oct 15, 1977
Departed from Brazil   Jun 09, 1979   Terminal illness of Rex
                                          Mathews, brother-in-law

Arrived in Brazil   Jun 29, 1979
Departed from Brazil   Jun 15, 1980   Furlough Park Hill Church
                                          North Little Rock, AR

Arrived in Brazil   Nov 09, 1980
Departed from Brazil   Jun 16, 1982   Medical 5613 NW 41st St.
                                          Oklahoma City, OK
                                          Putnam City Church

Arrived in Brazil   Aug 31, 1982
Departed from Brazil   Sep 16, 1983   Furlough Camden, AR
                                          1129 Herbert St NW

Entered Quito,Ecuador   Sep 16, 1983   Visit Levy Penido Family
Left Quito, Ecuador   Sep 19, 1983   En route to the States

Arrived in Brazil   May 01, 1984
Departed from Brazil   Jul 18, 1985   Wilma's Family Reunion
                                          & Medical

Arrived in Brazil   Aug 25, 1985
Departed from Brazil   Oct 29, 1988   Furlough & Retirement
                                          Dec 01, 1989

Arrived in Brazil   Sep 20, 1991   Partnership:Campo Grande,
Departed from Brazil   Oct 05, 1991   Rio Grande do Sul

Arrived in Brazil   Jun 04, 1997   Partnership: Fortaleza,
                                          Ceará & Juiz de Fora,
                                          Minas Gerais; & visit
Departed from Brazil   Jul 28, 1997   friends

Arrived in Brazil   Sep 12, 1963

Departed from Brazil   Oct 09, 1967   To be married

Arrived in Brazil   Jul 08, 1969
Departed from Brazil   Jul 10, 1973   Furlough 1804 Broadus,
                                          Ft. Worth, TX
                                          Southwestern Seminary

Arrived in Brazil   Jul 25, 1974
Departed from Brazil   Feb 26, 1977   Furlough Lonoke, AR
                                          403 S. Center

Arrived in Brazil   Oct 15, 1977

Departed from Brazil   Jun 15, 1980   Furlough Park Hill Church
                                          North Little Rock, AR

Arrived in Brazil   Nov 09, 1980
Departed from Brazil   Jun 16, 1982   Jesse's medical, Oklahoma
                                          City, OK Putnam City
                                          Church 5613 NW 41st St.

Arrived in Brazil   Aug 31, 1982
Departed from Brazil   Sep 16, 1983   Furlough Camden, AR
                                          1129 Herbert St NW

Entered Quito,Ecuador   Sep 16, 1983   Visit Levy Penido Family
Left Quito, Ecuador   Sep 19, 1983   En route to the States

Arrived in Brazil   May 01, 1984
Departed from Brazil   Jul 18, 1985   Gemmell Family Reunion
                                          & Jesse's Medical

Arrived in Brazil   Aug 25, 1985
Departed from Brazil   Oct 29, 1988   Furlough & Retirement
                                          Dec 01, 1989

Arrived in Brazil   Sep 20, 1991   Partnership:Campo Grande,
Departed from Brazil   Oct 05, 1991   Rio Grande do Sul

Arrived in Brazil   Jun 04, 1997   Partnership: Fortaleza,
                                          Ceará & Juiz de Fora,
                                          Minas Gerais; & visit
Departed from Brazil   Jul 28, 1997   friends

BABES IN THE WOODS

My dear, did you know
How a long time ago
Two sweet little babes
Whose names I don't know
Were stolen away
On a bright summer day
And taken to the woods,
So I heard people say.

And when it was night
So sad was their plight
The sun went down
And the moon gave no light,
They sobbed and they sighed
And they bitterly cried,
Poor babes in the woods
They lay down and died.

And when they were dead,
The Robin so red
Brought strawberry leaves
And over them spread,
And all the day long
He sang them sweet songs
Poor babes in the woods,
Poor babes in the woods.

****

SWEEPING THRU THE GATE

I am now a child of God, I've been washed in Jesus' blood,
I am watching and I'm longing while I wait;
Soon on wings of love I'll fly, to a home beyond the sky,
To my welcome, as I'm sweeping thru the gate.

O the blessed Lord of light now upholds me by His might,
And His arms enfold and comfort while I wait;
I am leaning on His breast; O the sweetness of His rest!
Hallelujah! I am sweeping thru the gate.

Burst are all my prison bars, and I soar beyond the stars,
To my Father's house, the bright and blest estate;
Lo! the morn eternal breaks, and the song immortal wakes,
Washed in Jesus' blood, I'm sweeping thru the gate.

Chorus:
Sweeping thru the gate, Sweeping thru the gate;
In the blood of Calv'ry's Lamb, washed from ev'ry stain I am,
Hallelujah! I am sweeping thru the gate.

****

GLOSSARY

Association
The organization of Baptist churches of an area for the purpose of promoting their common mission and goals.

Baptism
For Baptists, this is the immersion in water of a new believer
in Jesus Christ as his/her Savior. Infant baptism is not
practiced. Baptism symbolizes beautifully the death, burial,
and resurrection of Jesus.

Bluing
Dark blue liquid to be added to rinse water when one washes
laundry. It brightens the white fabrics.

Chapel
The term in Brazil for the building which accommodates the
meeting of a small church or congregação.

Church
A body of Christian believers having common beliefs and interests, with the Bible as their guide. They meet regularly
for mutual support and inspiration.

Congregation
In reference to the church, an assembly of persons gathered
for religious worship and instruction. (In Brazil the translated word, congregação, means the assembly of Christians
not yet organized into a church.)

Convention
Organization of Baptist churches which promotes Christian
fellowship in education, evangelism, and missions. The Convention does not have authority over the local Baptist church,
which is autonomous.

A state Baptist Convention embraces the state. A national
Baptist Convention may embrace a country, as "Brazilian Baptist Convention." The Southern Baptist Convention has member
churches even beyond the United States.

Cookstove
Wood or coal-burning stove with a surface for cooking utensils
and an oven for baking. It was usually made of black cast
iron; some models were more sophisticated.

Decision for Christ
The decision made by a person who recognizes his/her need of
Jesus Christ as Savior. It generally leads to baptism and
membership in a local church.

GLOSSARY (Contunued)

Foreign Mission Board, Southern Baptist Convention
(Now International Mission Board)
Elected persons from the areas in the Southern Baptist Convention make up the Board. These men and women meet periodically to care for the business of the Board. This is the sending agency for 4,546 missionaries serving in 127 countries (as of January 26, 1999).

Gospel
Good News, or the story of the life, death and resurrection of Jesus. "Gospel" also refers to the first four books of the New Testament.

Invitation
The appeal given by the pastor (usually following the sermon) inviting those present to acknowledge their faith in Jesus Christ as Lord and Savior.

Lottie Moon Christmas Offering
Lottie Moon served as a Southern Baptist missionary in China for 39 years until her death December 24, 1912. Inspired by her sacrificial life, Southern Baptists promote an annual offering in December. This offering underwrites about 50% of the International Mission Board's annual budget.

Mission
"Mission" has several meanings:
1. The global plan of the church to win the world to Jesus Christ, according to His command.
2. A group of missionaries working together in a given area. We lived and worked in the South Brazil Mission.
3. A group of people who meet for worship and Christian fellowship; possibly coming together in a rented place, or a borrowed room. Hopefully the group will develop to be a church.

Missionary
Someone who gives his/her life to the work of encouraging others to become followers of Jesus Christ, in keeping with Christ's command in Matthew 28:19,20. It is not the purpose of missionaries to win people from other Christian denominations; rather, to tell people about Jesus Christ.

Open Air Service
A time of worship, singing of worship music, prayer and Bible study conducted on a street corner, or in a park, outside a church building.

Ordain
The solemn act of setting aside (preparing) a person for the
work of preaching the Word of God. The Ordination Council,
comprised of ordained pastors, is usually called into existence by a church in response to a certain church's requesting the ordination, so the candidate may be qualified to serve
as pastor. The Council examines the candidate, asking questions regarding his beliefs, his life, and Christian experience.
When the Council is satisfied with the answers it will proceed
with the ordination service, which concludes with prayer and
the laying on of hands.

"Laying on of hands" is a Biblical term; it is a solemn act.
The one being ordained kneels and one by one the Council members lay their hands on his head, speaking words of encouragement and blessing. "Laying on of hands" is also mentioned in
the Bible regarding praying for the sick.

Deacons and others dedicated to serving God by specific responsibility, also are ordained.

Preaching Point
Gathering of people for worship or Bible study; usually at
regular times. It may be in a home or a rented room. Generally it is hoped that a church will develop from this.

Service
A time of worship, singing of hymns, prayer and Bible study
or preaching.

Soul Winning
The activity of sharing ones faith with others, with the objective of aiding them to come to a personal faith in Christ
as his/her Savior and a lasting commitment to follow His
teachings as a life style.

Spiritist
One who engages in the worship of spirits. In Brazil, the
higher forms of spiritism come from the teachings of Allan
Kardec, a French philosopher. The more primitive forms
come from Africa.

Training Union
A weekly program promoted by Southern Baptists for all ages.
Usually on Sunday night, the purpose was to train church
members in doctrine, and how to witness about their faith.

World Missions Conference
A gathering for interested people in a given area (state,
Association, city) for promoting world missions; thereby
inspiring and aiding the local churches to come to a fuller
understanding of the world missions program of Southern
Baptists.

BIBLIOGRAPHY

"All The Way My Saviour Leads Me"
  "New Baptist Hymnal" Page 360
  Broadman Press, Nashville, Tennessee
  Copyright 1926 by The American Baptist Publication Society
    and Sunday School Board, Southern Baptist Convention
  Published August, 1926

"Babes In The Woods" Anonymous
  Furnished by the Las Vegas, New Mexico, Public Library;
  source unknown

"Cuddle Doon"
  "One Hundred and One Famous Poems" Page 90
  The book was given to Wilma by her father; it is well worn,
    without cover, front and back. No publishing date.

"Give the Flowers to the Living"
  As sung by Wilma's mother

"I Am Thine, O Lord"
  "Treasury of Song" Round Note, No. 70
  Property of Carroll, Nebraska, Baptist Church
  Pages giving publisher and copyright are missing.

"I've Got A Pain In My Sawdust"
  Recalled by Jessie Martha Gemmell Back

"Sweeping Thru The Gate"
  "Favorite Songs and Hymns" Shape Notes, Page 84
  Stamps Baxter Music & Printing Co., Inc., Dallas, Texas
  Copyright 1939

"The Bastards of Burma," by Michael F. Gabbett, Page 21
  Desert Dreams, Albuquerque, N.M. 1991
  Used by Permission

"The Solid Rock"
  "Treasury of Song" Round Note, No. 337
  Property of Carroll, Nebraska, Baptist Church
  Pages giving publisher and copyright are missing

Scripture taken from the HOLY BIBLE, NEW INTERNATIONAL VERSION
(NIV). Copyright 1973, 1978, 1984 by International Bible
Society. Used by permission of Zondervan Publishing House.

Scripture taken from the New King James Version (NKJ). Copyright 1979, 1980, 1982 by Thomas Nelson, Inc. Used by permission. All rights reserved.

250.

INDEX TO SCRIPTURES

INDEX OF SUBHEADINGS

Subject   Page

NOTE: Names of Brazilians are listed by first name.

INDEX OF SUBHEADINGS (Continued)

Subject   Page

INDEX OF SUBHEADINGS (Continued)

Subject   Page

Subject   Page

INDEX OF SUBHEADINGS (Continued)

Subject   Page